Challenging the News

Challenging the News

The Journalism of Alternative and Community Media

Susan Forde

First published 2011 by
PALGRAVE MACMILLAN

Palgrave Macmillan in the UK is an imprint of Macmillan Publishers Limited,
registered in England, company number 785998, of Houndmills, Basingstoke,
Hampshire RG21 6XS.

Palgrave Macmillan in the US is a division of St Martin's Press LLC,
175 Fifth Avenue, New York, NY 10010.

Palgrave Macmillan is the global academic imprint of the above companies
and has companies and representatives throughout the world.

Palgrave® and Macmillan® are registered trademarks in the United States,
the United Kingdom, Europe and other countries.

ISBN: 978–0–230–24356–9 hardback
ISBN: 978–0–230–24357–6 paperback

This book is printed on paper suitable for recycling and made from fully
managed and sustained forest sources. Logging, pulping and manufacturing
processes are expected to conform to the environmental regulations of the
country of origin.

A catalogue record for this book is available from the British Library.

A catalog record for this book is available from the Library of Congress.

10 9 8 7 6 5 4 3 2 1
20 19 18 17 16 15 14 13 12 11

Printed in China

Contents

Acknowledgements

This work has emerged from a variety of projects and collaborations. I particularly want to thank my close colleagues and friends, Michael Meadows and Kerrie Foxwell, who have partnered with me in two national community broadcasting projects in Australia and whose ideas, advice, collegiality and friendship are central to most of the research work that I do. Our collaborations will continue for many years to come, provided we can convince Michael not to retire just yet. I also want to thank our colleague, Jacqui Ewart and our key senior research assistants, Derek Flucker and Heather Anderson who joined us in the community broadcasting audiences project which led to the report, *Community Media Matters*. I also thank my colleagues from the Griffith Centre for Cultural Research, and Griffith University's School of Humanities, for the support and mentoring you have provided in bringing this work to fruition. I wish to acknowledge the improvements made to this work through the various peer reviews of both the original proposal, and the manuscript and appreciate the time and attention given to the work by the people at Palgrave Macmillan, particularly Petra Jones, Paul Sng and Rebecca Barden. I also thank former Palgrave editor, Emily Salz, for supporting my original proposal and commissioning *Challenging the News*.

Funding support for this work has been provided primarily by various internal research grants from Griffith University, and also by the support for various projects from the Australian Research Council, the Australian community broadcasting sector, and the department formerly known as the Department of Communications, Information Technology and the Arts. The work on which this book is centrally based would have been impossible without the considered thoughts and time generously given by a range of alternative journalists, editors and managers who contributed to the most recent research project, *Rethinking Journalism*. They are detailed in Appendix A, and I thank them all sincerely. I thank all the journalists, producers and audience members who participated in our community broadcasting research. I am also regularly reminded of the important role that former journalism colleagues and sources from my years before scholarship play in my working life, and the memory of them and their work continues to inform the heart of my research.

I thank my family for the support they have offered in ensuring I can pursue this work, which I believe fits within a field – the study of alternative and community media – that is to play a heightened role in the future shape of our news media. I am indebted to my husband Derek and to our five children, particularly my oldest two daughters, Tani and Keara, who have shouldered some of the load when it was most needed. I also thank my parents for the support and encouragement they have always given.

Publication acknowledgements: I wish to note that sections of *Challenging the News* have been published in earlier versions/incarnations in other fora. In particular, parts of Chapter 1 were presented and published as a conference paper at the 2009 Journalism Education Association conference in Perth, Australia; sections of Chapter 2 examining the history of alternative journalism were published in *Media International Australia* in 1998; parts of Chapter 3 were presented at the 2008 Communications Policy & Research Forum in Canberra, Australia and published as part of their refereed proceedings; sections of Chapter 4 have been published as a research article in *Pacific Journalism Review* (2010) and in our *Community Media Matters* report; and short sections of Chapter 6 appeared as passages in our 2002 report on Australian community radio, *Culture, Commitment, Community*.

Susan Forde
Brisbane, Australia
May 2011.

Introduction

As someone who worked in the alternative and independent media sectors for a time before moving into academia, I have sometimes struggled with the 'disengaged' nature of research, with its limited (very literate, very intelligent) audience and the fact that it is inaccessible to many who could benefit from it. As an alternative journalist, I was committed to and driven by the social change that my words could make – the impact they could have on communities; on political movements; and on the broader public who might be able to see an issue for what it really was. Further, the publications I worked for were covering issues that received no coverage in the mainstream, or they were covering news *differently* to the mainstream, with different sources, different understandings of 'credibility', new perspectives that were not usually aired and a closeness to their sources and audience that a large mainstream publication could not achieve. I saw the intrinsic value of, and the undeniable connection between, what I and my fellow alternative journalists and editors were doing every day and broader political and democratic processes. The purpose of academic research is not as overtly 'political' although it certainly can be. Clemencia Rodriguez's recent words ring true and resonate with me – one of her fundamental assumptions is that 'academic research should be *at the service* of praxis; in other words, that the knowledge we produce within academia is most valuable if and only if it becomes useful for those in the field trying to make our societies better places to live' (2010: 133). In this vein, I want this book to be useable in a range of contexts: for alternative journalists who want to see how others are doing it, and perhaps succeeding where some are struggling; for journalism educators who are teaching the journalists of the future and may be able to integrate some of the knowledge contained herein into their courses; for mainstream journalists who want to integrate some alternative journalism practices into their own work, even if only to see if they can; for researchers who are grappling with and contributing to this growing and fertile field of thinking, understanding, and 'working out' what is happening in the burgeoning alternative/community/radical media sector; and to journalism students who, like many who have gone before them, are driven to make a difference.

The starting point for this work is a predictable but important one in providing a consideration of what is meant by the term, alternative journalism.[1] Throughout this work, I will interchange the concepts of community, radical, independent, citizens' and participatory journalism as they all form sub-sectors of what I agree can be broadly called 'alternative journalism' (Atton and Hamilton, 2008). Importantly though, not all community *media* produce alternative journalism; nor do all participatory *media;* nor all independently-run blogs, ezines, fanzines and so on. The key is the *journalism* which is distinct from the broader, organizational 'outlet' (i.e. the media).

Turning things around

When I conducted the first national study of Australian alternative press journalists 15 years ago, the basis of my analysis was comparative. I was overtly familiar with work examining the professional values, roles, self-perceptions and so on of mainstream journalists, and used this as a point of comparison for my own work. In essence, I was trying to answer the basic question of how alternative press journalists offered different practices to the mainstream. I was grappling with what the 'alternative press' was actually 'alternative' to (Downing, 2001: ix). The aim of this work is similar, although now much broader in scope as it encompasses all media, not just press, and is extended to the United Kingdom and the United States in terms of its original data and to much broader fields in examining the work of others. However, I want to make the practices of alternative journalists the focus here. And so, I will be presenting the views and processes of alternative

---

1 I usually use the term 'alternative and independent journalism' for reasons that will be discussed throughout the book, but essentially because a number of journalists reject the tag 'alternative' because of the marginalizing connotations it has. 'Independent' implies to these journalists, by convention, independence from both commercial and political influences. The longer term, however, is too cumbersome to be repeated over and over so I have simplified, in line with Atton and Hamilton (2008), to 'alternative journalism'.

journalists and analysing them, and to some extent considering how mainstream journalists deviate from that. In a sense, I'm trying to turn around the analysis. Not, how is alternative journalism different? But more, how is mainstream journalism different? I do this for a simple reason – the practices and *raison d'etre* for alternative journalism have been around much longer than the commercial mainstream practices which have dominated for the past 100 years. The growth of professional, objective, detached journalism is, as many have argued before, simply the result of the need for commercial media outlets to appeal to the broadest audience possible (see, for example, Seaton and Curran, 1991; Bagdikian, 1983; McChesney, 2008; Gitlin, 1980; Hamilton, 2004; Golding and Murdock, 1991; Schiller, 1989; and Herman and Chomsky, 1988 among others referenced variously throughout this work). In order to do this, they must refrain from presenting particular viewpoints, avoid controversial topics or at the very least avoid taking a stand on controversial topics lest they turn away potential readers and viewers. It is important for mainstream news organizations to connect with and engage their audience, but only in so far as it ensures that audience keeps coming back and enhancing their audience figures. This ensures regular advertising and well-paid advertising slots. I do not make these statements, which are not at all original, with any sense of distaste or criticism. Commercial media organizations attempt to maximize their audiences, and to do whatever they need to in order to achieve that – it's simple economics, and they are running a business. I think as media and journalism scholars we should be a lot less surprised about that than we are. Recognize and critique it by all means, but don't expect anything different. Our key role is to try to make the general public more aware of it, if they are not already. Media executives should relax and be a little more open about the fact that the news they cover, the people their journalists interview, the way they frame topics is dependent on what they perceive their audience will swallow, and not just swallow, but be happy with. They will always form a part of the broader media landscape. However, when we have concepts such as 'democracy' at play it is not good enough for this to be the primary format through which people receive their information. It simply cannot provide diverse, truthful, unbiased, empowering, *useful* information that people can move forward with. Non-profit media movements around the world are trying to reinforce this fact: Bob McChesney and Josh Silver's Free Press movement in the United States, and Corporate Watch and MediaLens in the UK provide essential information and critique about the commercialized nature of the media. Public broadcasting has a key role to play here, and in Australia and the UK, the Australian Broadcasting Corporation, the Special Broadcasting Service and the British Broadcasting Corporation fill an important gap. But they can't do it all on their own.

This is why alternative and community media forms have not just 'sprung up' all over the world in recent years, but why they have always been around and indeed, *were* the mainstream prior to the period around the 1850s. Some of the publications included in this study have been publishing, without interruption, since the early 1900s. And prior to that, partisan and often radical newspapers were the popular publications, with the highest readerships which often took a stance on political issues, similar to the 'alternative media', in all its forms, that we know today. Essentially, the practices of alternative journalism are older than the practices of professional commercial journalism, even though media and journalism scholarship has, overwhelmingly, focused on those mainstream practices and ideologies since the development of the media studies field. The reason why we now see alternative journalists as existing on the margin is because it is their practices which are now less familiar and less dominant both in the industry, and in journalism and media scholarship. I want to make a small contribution to rectify that. The way alternative journalists do journalism is the focus in most of the chapters contained in *Challenging the News,* and in only one chapter, Chapter 6, do I purposely juxtapose these practices against mainstream journalism. I am conscious of the dangers of this approach and generally, once again concur with Rodriguez that a binary approach to the myriad of activities that 'citizens' media undertake is undervalued by a straight alternative-mainstream dynamic (2001). Chapters in this book will certainly show that the driving force behind much 'alternative' journalism is not simply a resistance to the 'alienating power of mainstream media' (2001: 20) but in many ways takes little account of what the mainstream does – it is true to its roots of political, activist, truth-seeking journalism which engages its writers and its audiences and in doing so, carries out a democratic task and responsibility which is as old as the hills.

In fact if we consider that, apart from this period of the last hundred or more years[2] (perhaps even less) alternative journalism practices are more the norm than mainstream commercial practices, we might begin to see mainstream journalism more for what it is. It is a type of journalism, but it is just one type. I see it as Wal-Mart journalism, or Kmart journalism, or Harrods journalism. Wherever you are, whatever your all-purpose, one-size-fits-all, national-chain type department store is, that is what mainstream commercial journalism is. It may be in your face, and there may be one in every town, but the existence of Wal-Mart, Kmart, Harrods and so on does not mean the corner store, or the local boutique that carries gifts and knick-knacks that you can't find anywhere else, or the small community-based chain is illegitimate. In fact, the corner store and the niche boutique store has been around a lot longer than the huge national chain and there will always be demand for it. The notion that one form of journalism, in the supposed marketplace of ideas that constitutes healthy democracy, might do an all-encompassing job barely requires discussion.

Methodology

The data that provides the basis of much of this book comes from a variety of research projects conducted since 1996. It is grounded in four research projects: a two-year study running from 2008–2010 examining alternative journalism practices, as described by journalists operating in the United Kingdom, the United States and Australia; a large joint industry/Australian Research Council project on community radio and community television audiences completed in 2007, which was the first national audience study of community media; a joint Australian Research Council and community broadcasting industry-funded project on journalists and producers in the community radio sector completed in 2002; and a national survey of alternative and independent press journalists in 1996–97. The research methodology combines quantitative and qualitative research techniques – specifically wide-ranging

---

2 ...during which, incidentally, the credibility of journalists as a group has nose-dived to languish at the bottom of occupational rankings alongside used-car salesmen, real estate agents, sex workers, politicians and telemarketers (Readers Digest, 2010).

telephone surveys, community media audience focus groups, and qualitative semi-structured interviewing. The findings presented in this book are drawn from:

- Semi-structured qualitative interviews with 19 alternative journalists working in the United States, the United Kingdom and Australia
- A series of a 55 focus groups with community radio and community television audience members in a range of urban, regional and remote (isolated) geographical regions
- A quantitative survey of 150 community radio station managers, and more than 200 community radio journalists and other volunteers
- A series of 13 focus groups with community radio station managers
- A quantitative survey of 73 independent press journalists and editors, conducted in 1996–97 and again in 2008–2009 with a smaller, updated sample incorporating new media and broadcast formats
- In-depth one-on-one interviews with 73 journalists and editors in 1996–97
- A case study of online news activist campaigns produced by GetUp!

The scope

The difficulty with the approach I use in *Challenging the News* is that the norms of alternative journalism have not been discussed and analysed properly for quite some time, if they ever were (there are recent exceptions, of course – Atton and Hamilton, 2008; Harcup, 2003; Curran, 2003; and some literature from the counter-culture era, e.g. Johnson, 1971; Whittaker, 1981 although these two latter works are mostly descriptive). And so the first task is to establish what alternative journalism's norms are as, while there has been a great deal of important theorizing and explanation of the functions of alternative media in recent times, more can be done to hone in specifically on the journalistic practices of these outlets. Indeed, Atton helpfully notes in 2009 that it is the *practices* and the 'craft' of alternative journalists that is the one area currently lacking in our field and, particularly, the lack of a rigorous consideration of these practices means there are very few journalism schools and curricula mapping and teaching this unique set of practices (2009: 284). He notes that alternative journalists offer a 'critique in action' that can encourage those involved in the field to think epistemologically about journalism (2009: 284). Chapter 1 establishes the boundaries of this work as it is important to ensure that we are all on the same page. Due to the very welcome research attention on this field in recent years, there is a significant amount of research and literature which is examining, variously, the wide range of alternative, radical and citizens' community media initiatives happening around the world such as, for example, Indymedia (Platon and Deuze, 2003; Downing, 2003; Atton, 2003; Hodge, 2009; Atton, 2007a; Hyde, 2002), US public access television (Stein, 2001; McChesney, 2008; Linder, 1999; Halleck, 2002), online alternative media sites such as *Huffington Post, The Onion, OpenDemocracy.org, The Drudge Report, Salon.com, Slate.com, SchNEWS* and probably thousands more (Atton, 2002; Curran, 2003), bloggers and high-profile 'citizens' journalists (Pepe and Gennaro, 2007; Coyer, Dowmunt and Fountain, 2007), community media (Lewis, 2008; Meadows, Forde, Foxwell and Ewart, 2009 and Forde, Meadows and Foxwell, 2003; Gordon, 2009; Halleck, 2002; Howley, 2005; 2009); community radio and citizens' media projects in developing nations (Rodriguez, 2001; Tacchi and Kiran, 2008; Rodriguez, 2003; Pavarala and Malik, 2007; Seneviratne, 2007; Bathily, 2004), and the list continues. To see the amount of research currently being done, and the level of analysis given to this sector, is an indication of the importance that many now place on the work of alternative media. But there is a need for a great deal more work, and particularly original research, which examines *journalism* as it occurs in this range of non-mainstream media. This is the focus of *Challenging the News*, with an ever-present consideration that this journalism, this alternative journalism, is the enduring practice and form. Chapter 1 examines previous definitions and considerations of alternative journalism to set the boundaries for the ensuing discussions.

I wish to note an important point here. It is a limitation of this work, which I acknowledge, that the evidence presented is drawn primarily from journalists operating in developed nations. To a large extent, their comments, motivations and roles relate to that of an alternative journalist working in an established democracy although undoubtedly, there are a great deal of synergies between, for example, Indigenous community media in Australia and Canada and their counterparts in Mexico and parts of Asia. However community and alternative media initiatives in developing and Third World countries sometimes have an entirely different set of goals and principles to those in established democracies, as we might expect. The limitations of my data do not suggest that there are not significant community or alternative media initiatives occurring elsewhere, particularly in the Third World where such media is perhaps even more urgent. To this end I have attempted where possible to include consideration of community and alternative journalism occurring outside the developed world through the research of others. Rodriguez, for example, points to the importance of participation, organization and connection in Colombian communities which experience regular civil unrest, violence and disadvantage (2010); and in earlier work in Southern Chile (2003). Tomaselli similarly identified education, access and community organization as the key functions of the anti-apartheid alternative press in 1980s South Africa, when 80 per cent of the nation was denied access to proper housing, education and opportunity (1991: 9, 167). Castells Talens notes a worrying tension surrounding government funding for Indigenous community radio in Mexico, where the expression of audience dissent against government is often difficult and sometimes discouraged due to the nature of the funding arrangements (2010: 268). Tacchi and Kiran found participation, capacity-building, local solutions and recognizing the holistic nature of 'poverty' (the need for higher income and access to better food and education sits alongside the need to be empowered and listened to) to be key to the success and long-term sustainability of community media initiatives in Sri Lanka, Nepal, India and Indonesia (2008). Riggins' edited collection also offers a great breadth of information about the way ethnic minority media operate in a range of both developed and developing nations around the world (1992). I will draw on this and other work throughout the book to, albeit in a limited way, recognize the significant 'alternative' journalism occurring in communities outside the developed world.

Chapter 2 provides an examination of changing alternative journalism practices through the lens of history, picking out the practices of alternative journalism that have been present through time and that have also, as with all dynamic forms, adapted to their changing environment. While it is essentially an historical account of alternative and radical media and their journalists, it is written with a particular focus on identifying certain practices, processes and journalistic attitudes which were evident 150 years ago or more, and which are still at play today. Chapter 3 begins to build the foundations of contemporary alternative journalism and, drawing on original data from interviews with Australian, UK and USA alternative and independent journalists, looks at the role of alternative journalism in society and examines the journalists' own self-definitions of their work. This aids later understandings of the function of alternative journalism in democracy. Indeed, Chapter 4 expands on this further and looks specifically at the news decisions of alternative journalists, attempting to discover, simply, what makes something 'a good story' for an alternative journalist. What sorts of values and definitions of 'news' do they apply in their subjective daily processes? While classic studies of the mainstream journalism decision-making processes such as Breed (1955) and White (1951) were the beginnings of understanding how this occurred in professional *commercial* newsrooms, this chapter looks more specifically at how alternative journalists handle those daily decisions. It also discovers how alternative journalism is better able to engage its audiences, based on the processes it applies. It emerges with a broader understanding of the cultural process of alternative journalism and the notion, as I have reported elsewhere with colleagues (Meadows et al, 2009a), that the *process* of producing alternative journalism and the interactions and participation of audiences in this process (particularly evident in the community broadcasting context) is sometimes as important as the content it creates.

Chapter 5 draws on a case study of an internet-based democracy movement, GetUp!, as a demonstration of the ways that new forms of alternative media can connect with audiences. It presents the views of alternative journalists about the place of new media in the contemporary industry and sees internet-based media as a source of both hope for alternative journalism due to its reduced cost, global nature and immediacy; but reservation for some due to the plethora of alternative media being produced and published. While this chapter is specifically focused on internet-based initiatives, they are woven throughout discussions for the duration of *Challenging the News* as some of the journalists featured are from online-only alternative publications. Chapter 6 keeps the focus on the practices of alternative journalism, but this time it is examined through the 'professional' lens of objectivity. Specifically, this chapter examines alternative journalists' perspectives on objectivity and the role it plays in their work (if any), and this discussion gives rise to some consideration of the meaning of objectivity in different contexts – specifically the commercial media context versus the alternative media context. I also give some examples of exemplary journalism coming out of the under-resourced but motivated and driven news processes that epitomize alternative journalism. Chapter 7 takes a sharp turn and moves the discussion to the policy arena, examining policy initiatives and considerations that have occurred in the European Union and Australia. The overarching policy umbrella which drives United States media policy, the liberalist free market approach, is woven throughout. Of course, any discussion of contemporary policy (in any discipline) must take account of globalization, and so considerations of the development of a 'global media policy' are also evident but always with an anchor to the needs and context of alternative and independent journalism. To this end, then, the policy discussion in Chapter 7 is directly targeted at particular policy initiatives which have been shown to enhance the appearance and shape of community, alternative and radical media.

My thoughts are drawn together in Chapter 8, a conclusion but also an important opportunity to give all of this practical information its proper context. While I have attempted to weave analysis and reference to previous work throughout *Challenging the News*, there is a need to sit, and think for a moment or, as Downing so descriptively says, 'draw out a few recurring themes and chew on the succulent things gently for a moment more' (2001: 388). In this, I am looking for those issues that I alluded to earlier in this introduction – the enduring themes and practices, the underlying motivations and the meanings that can be drawn from it – for alternative journalists, journalism educators, researchers, mainstream journalists prepared to give it a go, and journalism students. To all, I hope you find the pages within enlightening, heartening, concerning, thought-provoking – and perhaps, above all, motivating.

Chapter 1

Understanding alternative and 'independent' journalism

The impetus for this book came from years of practising, thinking and writing about the unique characteristics and motivations of people who work in the non-mainstream media. These thoughts gained some context after a simple comment by the former editor of an independent political news magazine, *The Monthly* produced in Melbourne, Australia. Sally Warhaft left her position as editor of the increasingly successful progressive publication, featuring quality longer-form journalism, in controversial circumstances in mid 2009. In attempting to discover why *The Monthly* considered itself 'independent', I had asked Warhaft how she felt *The Monthly* did journalism differently. She answered that the publisher, Morry Schwartz of Black Inc, had made a deliberate decision *not* to employ a trained journalist as the editor in an effort to elicit a different way of thinking about the publication's content (Warhaft, 2006). While she indicated Schwartz had respect for 'good journalists', Warhaft's background as a lecturer in politics, and as an anthropologist working in the slums of Mumbai in India had placed her in the realm of someone involved in, and interested in, political and social issues but without the journalistic training which might provide more predictable editorial outcomes (Warhaft, 2006). She intimated that a trained journalist would consistently frame the

1

news, and discussions of current news events and social issues, in a fairly conventional way which was not the type of journalism and writing *The Monthly* was interested in. This suggested that perhaps what alternative – and I interchange the word 'independent' with alternative throughout this work – journalists do is not merely a reaction to the mainstream, but in some cases takes very little account of mainstream journalistic practices and values. It is not necessarily a product of its current context, but a considered and *instinctive* set of practices, carried on in various ways for around 150 years and which now, in the internet age, have come to the fore as genuine alternatives to the highly flawed professional norms of mainstream journalism.

I am more than aware that many in our broader journalism and media studies research disciplines are sceptical about the journalistic value of alternative and independent media outlets, primarily based on concerns about their marginal audiences; their sometime subjectivity and, apparently by implication, their lack of 'professionalism' (Schudson, 1978; Hampton, 2008). This book seeks to put that scepticism to rest, premised on an argument that alternative forms of journalism have been around as long as – nay, longer than – conventional journalistic practices. While the advent of the internet with all its empowering, democratic potential is a significant moment in the development of alternative journalism, it is primarily another outlet, another way for alternative journalists to organize and to impart their message. It does not change their motivations, their values, and their determination which is really what defines alternative journalism and journalists. These are all investigated in further detail throughout this work.

I have fallen back to the use of the term 'alternative journalism' in part due to its increasingly widespread use (Atton and Hamilton, 2008) but also because 'alternative' seems to be the only term which can encompass all the different media we refer to – community, grassroots, radical, citizens and independent. All these terms are a little too specific for what I want to consider in this book. 'Radical', for example, does not necessarily include localized, participatory 'community' media which are often quite moderate in their political viewpoints. 'Grassroots' and 'community' do not necessarily include the professional, independently-owned opinion publications which provide fresh and innovative perspectives on public sphere debates and which are free of any obvious political and commercial ties. So alternative, I feel, and occasionally 'independent or alternative', encompasses all. These terms also include far more than this book attempts to consider, though, so it is important to establish boundaries. I hope one of the contributions of this work will be to give a firmer, albeit still blurry, perimeter for the understandings and theorizing of alternative journalism as at the moment, our conceptions of 'anything that occurs outside the mainstream news media' (Hirst, 2009: 2) are simply too broad to be meaningful. Note the following discussion is limited to defining 'alternative and independent *journalism*' and not their *media* which, again, encompasses a far broader scope.

Considering alternatives

The increasing attention given to alternative media and journalism is, to a great extent, married to the rising chorus of voices critiquing mainstream media news practices, and which naturally extends to concerns about the future of robust democracy. Atton and Couldry argue the crises in Western democratic systems with decreasing voter turnouts, the growth in the global social justice movement and other worldwide trends are making the work of alternative media outlets more relevant than ever before to the agendas of media and communications research (2003: 579). Deuze finds that alternative news outlets produced specifically for ethnic community groups – particularly print outlets – are experiencing 'exponential growth' in the United States and in European countries such as The Netherlands (2006: 262–63). And Deuze does not accept that the development of this media is due to the growth of such ethnic populations in Western democracies such as the United States. Rather it is consistent with the 'worldwide emergence of all kinds of community, alternative, oppositional, participatory and collaborative media practices' (Deuze, 2006: 263). Scholars writing in this field consistently define what it is *they* mean by the range of terms used for all the non-mainstream media and forms of journalism that are emerging and receiving so much scholarly, and public, attention. The term 'community media', according to the international professional body for community radio AMARC, and also accepted by Carpentier et al, tends to refer to non-profit media outlets which, generally, encourage the participation of their community (whether that be a geographic community or community of interest) in developing content (Carpentier et al, 2003: 53; also AMARC, www.amarc. org). Clearly, different outlets that we might generally consider to be 'non-mainstream' come in many different forms – some are commercial organizations, for example, while others consider that their non-profit status defines them; some attempt to include their communities/audiences in production, while others do not; some are structured democratically or in a cooperative arrangement (Atton, 2002) while others work on fairly traditional media organizational structures (Forde, 1997a). A far more considered discussion of the nature of these organizations is provided in Carpentier et al (2003) and although they use the term 'community' rather than 'alternative and independent' as it is applied here, their recognition that the organizations under discussion stand outside the mainstream through their attempt to offer 'an alternative for a wide range of hegemonic discourses on communications, media, economics ...' (2003: 51) suggests their discussions are entirely relevant to definitions of alternative, independent and radical media outlets as well as community media outlets. Indeed, these terms very frequently overlap. In his later work with co-authors Bailey and Cammaerts, Carpentier helps identify that the existing framing of alternative media rests on an 'unsustainable set of distinctions, such as that between non-commercial and commercial or radical and non-radical alternative media' (Bailey et al, 2008: xii). In line with Rodriguez's approach to *processes* as a means to define or distinguish alternative media (2010), Bailey, Cammaerts and Carpentier suggest the identity of alternative media, and by extension its content, 'should be articulated as relational and contingent on the particularities of the contexts of production, distribution, and consumption' (2008: xii). In essence, there is no 'one-size-fits-all' definition and indeed, their work suggests a broadening of the definition of alternative media to include a wide spectrum or a range of media 'generally working to democratize information/ communication' (2008: xi). Rodriguez takes this further, stressing that Colombian community radio initiatives in conflict zones (2010: 150–51, original emphasis included):

> ... are not communication discourses *about* mediation and conflict resolution; rather, they are communication spaces to be used to mediate and interact (Rodriguez, 2004). The stations are not sending messages

to the community *about* how to solve conflict in nonviolent ways. Instead, the stations themselves are mediating conflicts ...

Stein's study conducted under the auspices of John Downing's work on radical media and social movements (2001) found public access television in the United States had facilitated a space for grassroots political communication, but 'a restructuring of access television resources would further strengthen the democratic potential of the medium' (2001: 300). We can only assume from Stein's conclusions that, in 2001 at least, public access television in the US was not providing the space for alternative journalists that was originally envisioned – i.e. 'a public space where, liberated from the economic and editorial constraints of commercial television production, citizens could air their views over the most powerful and pervasive communications media of the era' (2001: 299). Downing points out that it is unhelpful to simply provide a binary definition of radical media, i.e. mainstream and alternative media, as it fails to recognize the complexity of the spectrum of media that exists both within a 'mainstream commercial' context, and within the alternative context. Certainly, if there are two separate spheres of media that do not and cannot intersect, 'that position would discount any movement toward democratizing large-scale commercial media, which would let them off the hook much too easily ... It would downplay the uses that oppositional movements and groups may sometimes be able to make of mainstream media. It would also flatten out the very considerable variety of radical media' (Downing, 2001: ix). He offers ten defining points of the radical media (v–xi) as part of the introductory comments to his important 2001 study, but it is the concluding sections of his work which perhaps best encapsulate what radical media – and by implication, radical alternative journalists – offer. He brings his analysis into a 'hexagon' of recurring themes in radical media, notably artistic flair, memory levels, pragmatic realities, social movements, time frame and the power structure. Without examining each of these, we can summarize that Downing sees radical media as something much more than their content, or their processes: they create memories of past movements ('memory levels'); provide sparks ('artistic flair'); share organizational and financial struggles ('pragmatic realities'), are something much more than a group of 1960s counter-culture media initiatives ('time frame');

and share a common view of established power as an obstacle, and a target ('power structure') (2001: 389–91). Essentially, his view of radical media is rooted in social movements which are 'the life blood of these media, and they are the movements' oxygen' (2001: 390). Downing's work does not attempt to cover all alternative journalists but he also certainly sees much 'radical' journalism, as he calls it, being produced by political activists and political movements, with political and social change as the primary purpose of such journalism (Downing, 1984; 2001). A survey of Australian alternative journalists conducted more than ten years ago confirms the importance of the way alternative journalists identify themselves with a developing definition of 'alternative' or 'independent' journalism, and also found that journalists working for a range of alternative and independent print media in 1996–97 often identified their journalism as an extension of what they otherwise were: an activist; a community aid worker; an Aboriginal person representing their community; a freelance 'writer' and so on (Forde, 1997a; 1997b).

Social and political movement media form a part, but only a sub-section, of the group that Atton and Hamilton (2008) refer to as 'alternative journalists'. Atton and Hamilton not only attempt to define the key term but also offer important frameworks for thinking about alternative journalism. Among the many points that their work makes, a common theme is the conceptualization of alternative journalism as 'amateur' (Atton, 2002; Atton and Hamilton, 2008; Atton, 2009). '[Alternative journalism] is produced by those outside mainstream media organizations. Amateur media producers typically have little or no training or professional qualifications as journalists; they write and report from their position as citizens; as members of communities; as activists, as fans' (2009: 265). Much of the scholarship around 'community' media forms follows this (for many parts of the sector, quite accurate) identification of amateur production, of the non-professional nature of the medium and the journalism it produces (Jankowski, 2003; Lewis, 1976). Atton's definitions extend to what he terms 'cultural journalism', exhibited in fanzines and alternative journalism produced by individuals rather than collectives through blogging but the common theme is the 'ordinary people' involved in the production of this alternative journalism (2009: 268).

Hirst, in his critique of Atton and Hamilton's offering, suggests alternative journalism can perhaps simply be identified as occurring outside the boundaries of 'acceptable' topics:

> The news media revolves around what Daniel Hallin (1989) calls the spheres of consensus and limited controversy – debate is limited to acceptable topics and boundaries, beyond which lies deviance (and perhaps alternative journalism) (Hirst, 2009).

In order to take a step beyond how the journalists might be superficially labelled (i.e. as a journalist, an activist, an aid worker etc), we should consider their practices in more detail. The journalism of alternative media, Atton and Hamilton suggest, is primarily informed by a 'critique' of the dominant practices of journalism. That is:

> Its critique emphasizes alternatives to, *inter alia*, conventions of news sources and representation; the inverted pyramid of news texts; the hierarchical and capitalized economy of commercial journalism; the professional, elite basis of journalism as a practice; the professional norm of objectivity; and the subordinate role of audience as receiver (2008: 1).

Such a definition accounts for not only the work of scholars on community, participatory and citizens' media (Rodriguez, 2001; Howley, 2005; Meadows et al, 2007; Gordon, 2009; Deuze, 2006; Gillmor, 2006; Harcup, 2003) but also the political economy work of those examining the cooperative editorial structure of alternative media organizations (Atton, 2003; Collins and Rose, 2004) and the commercial imperatives of the mainstream (Hamilton, 2004; McChesney, 2003; 2008). Atton and Hamilton's words also point to the (to date, fairly limited) research so far about the breakdown of the audience-producer barrier in different forms of grassroots, community and alternative media (Forde, Foxwell and Meadows, 2009; Lewis, 2008; Howley, 2005; Tacchi and Kiran, 2008). So this understanding of alternative journalism as a form which proposes a range of anti-mainstream practices and structures is incredibly useful and sufficiently broad to capture much of the activity of alternative journalists. Significantly, Atton and Hamilton's work recognizes the development of alternative journalism over time and indeed its longevity as a form.

> The key insight of this overview is that alternative journalism is not an unchanging, universal type of journalism, but is an ever-changing effort to respond critically to dominant conceptions of journalism. Accordingly, alternative journalism is best seen as a kind of activity instead of as a specific, definitive kind of news story, publication or mode of organization. What alternative journalism is at any given moment depends entirely on what it is responding to (2008: 9).

His suggestion, however, that alternative journalism is an evolving 'type' or concept which is *reacting* to the times in which it exists – i.e. its form depends 'entirely' on what it is responding to – suggests something which Rodriguez specifically challenges. She argues, simply, that alternative media forms, what she calls 'citizens' media', need to be defined by what they *are*, not by what they *are not* (Rodriguez, 2001); and says that the terms 'community media, alternative media, autonomous media and radical media all fit within the broad definition of "citizens" media' (Rodriguez, 2010: 132). Rodriguez overwhelmingly focuses on the *processes* of participation, organization, and connection between people as the key defining characteristic of citizens' media, and does not really address 'what it is responding to'. Rather it is a consideration of the *mediations* that occur rather than the media itself (2003: 190). This disparity perhaps highlights more than anything the undeniable diversity in the field we are engaged with.

Scholarship in the field of alternative, independent and grassroots media then clearly recognizes, appropriately, that the field is broad and diverse, and difficult to accurately define. But the assessment that alternative journalism is constantly 'responding' to something else is somewhat unsatisfying. It suggests a lack of strength and conviction about the task at hand, and perhaps rejects the notion that alternative journalism, over time, and despite technological changes has always demonstrated a core set of features and practices. This issue is particularly examined in the next chapter, which looks at the history and development of alternative journalism, but is a constant theme throughout. If we are to evaluate the potential for independent and alternative journalism practices to be integrated into both mainstream practice and into the way budding journalists are trained, we must be able to identify key consistencies and traits. Practitioners are able to offer an important perspective here.

How do practitioners see 'alternative journalism'?

The preceding sections suggest that a number of 'ways of seeing' the sector have developed among different theorists of alternative media and alternative journalism, particularly when examining what it is the sector is really doing, and aiming to do. Practitioners from the sector have a fresher, and a somewhat more grounded idea of the work of independent journalists. Some of it, however, is critical of the shape and operations of the sector. Australian freelance journalist Margaret Simons, who has worked for both mainstream and alternative media outlets, certainly does not idealize the *modus operandi* of many alternative publications. She wrote in 2005 that *Crikey (crikey.com.au)*, the successful alternative online newspaper which provides daily e-newsletters to its subscribers and which had clear inside links to all major and progressive political parties, was influential but somewhat haphazard in its content and operation:

> Mayne [Stephen Mayne, the former conservative Liberal Party staffer who founded *Crikey*] is fond of referring to his 'Crikey army', to whom he often appeals for leads. But none of the independent internet outlets pay their contributors anything like industry standard rates, and most pay nothing... So far independent internet journalism mostly depends on a mixture of philanthropy and idealism or, as Graham Young, editor of the not-for-profit *Online Opinion* puts it, 'drudgery and despair' (Simons, 2005).

Simons, who is now the regular media commentator for *Crikey* and appears as a source later in this work, goes on to describe the publication more fully, writing at the time when original founder Stephen Mayne sold the independent online news site to Eric Beecher's left-of-centre media stable. She found that, like most alternative media, Crikey was 'asking questions nobody else was asking' and that at times the publication had been 'scrappy, inconsistent and often sneered at by the more polished journalistic professionals'. Nevertheless, she wrote, 'it has been more influential than most would admit' (Simons, 2005). Independent press colleagues in New Zealand who ran a successful alternative newspaper for eight years, the Wellington *City Voice*, drew on their own motivations as a way of defining their practices, and this is a useful tool. If we can understand what *motivates* independent and alternative journalists, it provides important pointers to what they might actually be doing, or aiming to do, in the field. It also has synergies with Rodriguez's focus on process over content, unlike Simons' considerations above which are wholly focused on the journalistic output. Collins and Rose reported that they aimed to produce a different kind of newspaper which 'tried with public journalism to empower people to understand issues and to actually do something about them'. Their journalistic processes were focused on accessing non-elite sources: 'if we were writing about schools, we aimed to interview the students; if the subject was prisons, we would interview the prisoners; if it was drugs, we would interview the drug addicts' (2004: 34).

Indeed, more independent press journalists reported in the 1990s that they undertook their duties for the higher ideals of autonomy, the chance to help people, and editorial freedom rather than the superficial concerns expressed by mainstream journalists such as the pay, fringe benefits, the chance to 'get ahead' and job security (Henningham, 1996: 211; Forde, 1997b). Furthermore, they are more committed to the active public and 'citizens' form of their craft, reflected in Collins and Rose's comments about public journalism, in that Australian independent news journalists nominate 'providing context to the news', 'motivating the public' and 'giving a voice to the voiceless' as their primary journalistic aims (Forde, 1997a: 118). Independent and alternative news publications practise a journalism that is based on strong notions of social responsibility (Atton, 2003: 267) and their journalists generally demonstrate stronger commitment to the idealistic norms of journalism than their mainstream counterparts (Forde, 1997b; 2010). Indeed, if we consider the aims of publications such as *The Monthly* (Warhaft, 2006) and the Australian-based but global online alternative publication *Eureka Street* (Cranitch, 2006), they describe their journalism in a way that is entirely consistent with Jankowski's definition of 'community' media, focusing on providing news and information relevant to the needs of the community members; 'to engage these members in public discussion, and to contribute to their social and political empowerment' (Jankowski, 2003: 4). Their practices and motivations also have much in common with the notion of 'public journalism' and I wish to consider this now in a further attempt to clarify the essential nature of alternative journalism.

Public journalism, the public sphere and alternative journalists

In my original study of the practices and motivations of Australian alternative press journalists in the 1990s, I found the then emerging concept of public journalism to be a particularly useful way to describe the activities of the journalists I surveyed and interviewed. Since the early 2000s, however, public journalism has been torn down as a preferred *modus operandi* for contemporary journalists as experience has shown that it cannot work as its proponents had hoped in the commercial context (Ewart, 2002; Haas, 2007). More likely, public journalism was perceived to be a fairly cynical attempt by commercial media to allow their audiences to 'feel' as though they were engaged and involved without providing any real opportunities for that. Additionally, mainstream practices of tapping into elite sources, ignoring 'ordinary' people and attempting to maintain neutrality and detachment destroyed any opportunity for public journalism to work in the mainstream context. It can, however, operate quite successfully in alternative media, and does (Forde, 1997a; 1998). The national study of community broadcasting audiences around Australia found community broadcasting journalists were regularly and successfully engaging their audiences; involving audiences; and more fully meeting audience needs to becoming part of the community they were working for (Meadows et al, 2007; 2009a; 2008), which is a key principle of public journalism. They were redefining 'news' as it related to their local community and often saw community announcements, talk shows and interviews with local people as 'local news content' which they considered a unique service of community radio (Meadows, 2008; Forde, 2010). Let's revisit the notion of public journalism for the moment, to evaluate where it began and where it has gone in the 15 years since its early proponents boasted of its culture-changing potential.

Jay Rosen and mainstream newspaper editor Davis 'Buzz' Merritt worked closely together throughout the 1990s to define public journalism and to encourage United States journalists to adopt the practice as an industry standard. In general terms, public journalism calls on the media to take an active role in strengthening citizenship, improving political debate and reviving public life (Merritt, 1995; Rosen, 1995). Indeed, public journalism saw the professional notion of objectivity as one of the primary reasons for the long-term malaise in public life (Rosen, 1995; Merritt, 1995; also Haas, 2007). Gunaratne further defines public journalism as a practice which questions the value of objectivity, standard news values, and accuses the mainstream media of failing to connect the public with participatory democracy (Gunaratne, 1996: 64). Merritt argued that journalism's tendency to 'merely provide information – simply telling news in a detached way' was not helpful to public life or to journalism (Merritt, 1995: 11). He argued that journalism had neglected its obligations to provide an effective public life (1995: 5) and that newspapers had to start seeing people not as readers, customers or an audience, but 'as a public, citizens capable of action' (Merritt, 1995: 11). Merritt, as editor of a Knight-Ridder daily mainstream, noticed a decline in public life and the efficacy of journalism, and assumed the two were related. At the height of the public journalism movement, he argued (1995: 11):

> The objective of our journalism must be to re-engage citizens in public life. To make that shift, we must take two steps; (1) Add to the definition of our job the *additional* objective of helping public life go well, and then (2) Develop the journalistic tools and reflexes necessary to reach that objective.

Public journalism was identified as a fundamental change to journalistic practice. Indeed, in the 1990s it was identified as a major (journalism) cultural change which would take at least ten years before its potential could be properly evaluated (Merritt, 1995: 13; Rosen, 1995: 17). That time has been and gone, and much of the current research suggests public journalism, in practice, has done little to revive public life and public debate. While my earlier studies found key aspects of public journalism were alive and well in the Australian alternative press industry, and presumably, in alternative media industries globally, it did not evolve as a practice that could be successfully transplanted to mainstream, commercial media organizations. Public journalism provides evidence, if any more was needed, that the institutional structures of the mainstream commercial media repel journalism which fosters a more (politically) active public. Despite this, it is a concept that helps us to understand what it is that alternative journalists might be doing; and what it is about their practices that make their contribution to public life and the public sphere unique. Certainly, views from community broadcasting audiences would suggest that a form of 'public journalism' is being successfully carried out by community broadcasters, at least in terms of public engagement and audience 'attachment' to, rather than detachment from, their media (Meadows, 2008). Public journalism, on paper, has a great deal in common with the processes of the public sphere (Habermas, 1989; Rosen, 1991). Dahlgren also notes that the contemporary understanding of the public sphere relates directly to strengthening citizenship and improving political participation (1991: 1), the cornerstones of public journalism:

> The public sphere is a concept which in the context of today's society points to the issues of how and to what extent the mass media, especially in their journalistic role, can help citizens learn about the world, debate their responses to it and reach informed decisions about what course of action to adopt.

So for public journalism to be effectively practised, the media must create a forum in which people can discuss, engage and interact, and where they are empowered. Audience studies of the community broadcasting sector in Australia found this was indeed occurring in the 'third sector' of community media (Meadows et al, 2007); but among other factors, the audience/producer barriers which continue to exist in mainstream commercial media do not facilitate the full integration of the concepts of public journalism. Certainly, the more recent focus on citizens' and community-oriented forms of media has usurped any significant discussion about the future of public journalism as a form (see Haas, 2007, replacing discussion of 'public journalism' with discussion of 'the public's journalism'). Dominant journalism's commitment to the 'neutral' aspect of their professional norms, particularly objectivity, further prevents journalists from encouraging people to take part in political action and from motivating their audiences which is a key requirement of public journalism. It is still the case that mainstream journalists see it is as their role to impart information, to give audiences as many viewpoints as they can, and to let audiences make up their own mind. The problem with this approach is that, sometimes, someone (perhaps a source) is wrong. Sometimes, a source or a political player's viewpoints are so ill-informed and damaging that they should not be covered. But they are, because the mainstream

journalist is required to cover 'all' or 'as many' sides of the story
as possible, without judgement. They increasingly fulfil the type of
'stenographer' role that McChesney alludes to (2003: 303). Their
professional processes require them to make no comment; and to
hope that the audience can read between the lines and see a faulty,
misinformed source for what they are.

Public journalism called on journalists to leave this professional
trait behind by engaging, attaching, participating and calling on
others to participate. Mainstream journalists could not and did not
do this. Alternative journalists did, and always have done. Indeed,
Atton and Hamilton suggest that much of the critique of public
journalism identified it as 'patrician efforts to legitimize professionalism' (2008: 64) which presumably, was never intended to root out
the true basis of mainstream journalism but instead, to reinforce it
by tinkering around the edges only. They suggest the concept fell 'by
the wayside due to historical and political-economic imperatives'
(2008: 152); and even proponents such as Haas (2007), and Haas
and Steiner (2006) recognize that public journalism has a large battle
on its hands in pushing against the power of economic imperatives
in commercial media. Indeed, they suggest that individual commitment from journalists is one of the key requirements that will
ensure public journalism's future as a 'journalistic reform movement' (2006: 238; Haas, 2007: 186), but this ignores the structural
forces at play which I argue render such individual commitment relatively futile. Further, research examining public journalism finds
that most journalists are in agreement with the general principles of
public journalism, but are more comfortable with using the public
journalism practices that closely resemble standard, professional
journalism (Haas, 2007: 189). This reinforces the suggestion that
public journalism, while reforming on paper, has barely discernible
results in practice and has had very little impact on the way journalism is done in the United States where most public journalism has
occurred (Haas, 2007: 188). In terms of defining alternative journalism, then, the principles of public journalism have something to
offer in terms of engagement with and involvement from community, and encouraging citizens to take motivated action on a range
of local and broader national issues if necessary. Importantly, political engagement is an underlying basis. However, it does not suggest
any practical solutions about the ways in which conventional, mainstream journalism might be radically reformed.

Alternative journalism and commercial motivations

Notions such as public journalism, Habermas' concept of the public sphere, the views of practitioners, and scholarly research into alternative media suggest much about the practices of alternative journalists. Importantly, professional associations for alternative media outlets provide further perspective on how we might begin to define alternative journalism and, subsequently, to properly evaluate it. One of the key discussions to be had about alternative journalism surrounds its status as a commercial or non-commercial entity. Some definitions suggest alternative journalism must be 'not-for-profit', carried out by grassroots, community organizations, but this definition is far too limiting and excludes some excellent independent journalism occurring around the world which must, surely, be considered alternative journalism. An appropriate place to begin this discussion about alternative journalism and commercialism is the United States.

Sections of the US alternative media industry are well-structured and organized, with a range of representative bodies and professional associations reflecting the interests of the varied alternative print, radio, television and online organizations that are operating. The Association of Alternative Newsweeklies (AAN) is one of the longest established professional bodies for alternative publications in the United States, and has fairly clear membership guidelines which provide, to some extent, a working definition of what 'alternative' means to a subset of practitioners in the United States. Interestingly, it leaves out *all* of the niche media that authors such as Atton, Downing and Rodriguez include in their definitions, and excludes also any of the radical political media. In essence, members of the Association of Alternative Newsweeklies offer an editorial 'alternative' to the mainstream media in their local area, but they must do this within certain constraints. For example, AAN members must publish at least 24 times a year, which immediately excludes most publications that we would term 'alternative' in Australia, many of which are monthlies. They must also be general interest publications, so outlets focusing on Indigenous issues, environmental issues, ethnic communities etc are also excluded. Again, this would exclude many of the community radio stations in both the UK and Australia if the AAN definition were to be followed and certainly excludes fanzines, ezines, blogs and so on. In addition, while advocacy journalism and journalism with opinions is encouraged in AAN members, their journalism must be 'professional, thorough and fair' (AAN, 2009a). They openly exclude 'community newspapers' although overtly encourage members to stay outside the mainstream:

> By definition, alternative papers exist on the outside, and they should make an effort to stay there. What the [membership] committee likes is informed, well-researched, and well-written original reporting and reviewing with a strong point of view. Rocking the boat is a good thing, as is a healthy disrespect for authority and public-relations whitewash. Investigative reporting is a major plus. Service to the readers is key, and the mission of the alternative press is to give readers what they can't find elsewhere (AAN, 2009a).

Somewhat ironically, however, some AAN members are part of quite significant media chains, not on the scale of major media ownership but large ownership groups. The Village Voice Media chain, for example, owns 13 alternative newsweeklies in New York, Phoenix, Denver, Dallas, Houston, Miami, San Francisco, Los Angeles, Orange County, Minneapolis, Seattle, St. Louis and Kansas City.[3] The Phoenix Media Communications Group owns seven AAN publications, and also publishes the official yearbooks of national basketball team the Boston Celtics, and the national ice hockey team the Boston Bruins.[4] AAN member *Metro Pulse* is owned by E.W. Scripps, who also owns 14 daily and community newspapers, ten television stations and two news services.[5] The Times Shamrock Alternative Newsweekly Group is comprised of five entertainment and dining-oriented weeklies and two radio stations[6] while the New Mass Media Group, established in the mid 1970s in Connecticut, comprises three newspapers,[7] which regularly run similar copy syndicated between the titles (in February 2011, for example, the *Hartford Advocate* and the *Fairfield County Weekly* were running the same front-page top story, about

---

3 www.villagevoicemedia.com, accessed 20 August 2009 and 11 February 2011.
4 www.thephoenix.com, accessed 20 August 2009 and 11 February 2011.
5 www.scripps.com/heritage/about-us, accessed 20 August 2009 and 11 February 2011.
6 www.citypaper.com/about, accessed 20 August 2009 and 11 February 2011.
7 www.newmassmedia.com/about-us/blog, accessed 20 August 2009 and 11 February 2011.

online dating and STDs). Additionally, the AAN publications are unashamedly commercial, with the websites of even the smaller, more independent publications boasting the audiences they can sell to potential advertisers. The *Easy Reader,* for example, from Hermosa Beach has a circulation of 57,000 to residents in the South Bay area of California. On the *Easy Reader* website, the publication trumpets its alternative credentials (www.EasyReaderNews.com), its beginnings as an alternative, counter-culture publication founded in 1970 with an editorial policy rooted in the notion of 'truth force' endorsed by King, and Gandhi (Easy Reader, 2009). However, the aspects of the publication which are highlighted on the AAN Membership website emphasize the importance of marketing and commercial imperatives:

> *Easy Reader* is a weekly, community newspaper serving the South Bay area of Los Angeles, one of the largest, most affluent retail markets in the country...*Easy Reader*'s monthly 'Peninsula People' edition reaches 25,000 homes in Palos Verdes, which has the highest per capita income of any zip code in the United States.
>
> The strength of the paper is its aggressive news reporting. Each issue also offers an in-depth cover story, local news, and extensive entertainment listings. *Easy Reader*'s home delivery offers three times the market penetration of the *Los Angeles Times* and more than twice that of the *Daily Breeze.*
>
> Easy Reader's stitch and trim format and 4-color, electrabright cover give it a magazine quality appearance (AAN, 2009b).

The primary concern in defining the alternative newsweeklies as 'alternative' is not only their occasionally overwhelming commercialism, but the apparent homogeneity of the AAN publications in the United States. This is not to suggest that AAN publications constitute the entirety of the US alternative media industry – far from it, as later chapters will show. Several radical US journalists and editors interviewed for this work had never even heard of the AAN. They are, however, one of the primary representative organizations for alternative print and online publications with significant membership and audiences. Several AAN editors and representatives have contributed to this study and their views on the commercial nature of their publications are examined further in Chapter 6 where we look at funding models for alternative journalism. For now, it is sufficient to say that there exists a significant group of publications in the United States, which call themselves alternative newsweeklies and are not associated with any of the major media ownership groups but which have, at their heart, a financial motive alongside their quite firm and overt commitment to 'alternative' journalism (see also Benson, 2003).

The issue of commercialism in alternative and radical journalism was raised by the editors of the Wellington (NZ) *City Voice,* with views in stark contrast to the principles of the AAN group. Collins and Rose noted that, unlike almost all other mass media in New Zealand at the time, '*City Voice* did not exist primarily to make money. It aimed to earn its workers a decent living, but primarily it existed for reasons that are summed up ... by the word democracy' (2004: 32). Atton and Hamilton clarify, though, that '... one of the strengths of alternative journalism – and perhaps its abiding ideology – is its resistance to homogenization. This resistance derives from critiques of the political economy and ideological practices of professional journalism' (2008: 138), suggesting a rejection of any form of commercialism within the sector. Certainly community broadcasting in Australia and the United Kingdom must be provided by non-profit organizations, which is a condition of their licensing. In some cases, they are undoubtedly producing strong alternative journalism but there can be no commercial motive tied to this, and any money that is made from sponsorships must be put straight back into the organization to better their service. Community and public broadcasters in the United States, and indeed, one of the AAN publications, the *Texas Observer,* also have not-for-profit status which enables them to draw income from foundations, granting bodies, and through donations from their readership. In contrast, independent and alternative online news sites such as *Crikey, Huffington Post, The Onion,* and *Salon.com* sell alternative journalism to their audiences, and make a profit from doing so. Commercial motives then, as they relate to alternative and independent journalism do not appear to be a defining characteristic although it can be argued that commercial imperatives probably have some impact upon the type of alternative journalism that is produced. We will return to this in Chapter 6.

Working towards a meaningful definition

From the mouths of practitioners and the alternative journalism sector, then, defining 'alternative' can be just as difficult and as broad as the offerings of theorists and researchers who have observed the field, often from the outside, for many years. If we consider overall the work of scholars and practitioners in the field of alternative journalism, and based on the literature and data assessed here, the main points defining alternative journalism suggest:

- It may be practised at a commercial or non-commercial publication, website or radio/TV station
- It may occur in an independently-owned *or* a chain-owned outlet, providing the chain-owned outlet does not belong to a 'mainstream' or 'major' media ownership group
- Coverage of *news* from an alternative perspective is important, but not essential as many definitions include music fanzines, blogs and niche publications which do not cover news at all
- Attachment to a political party/movement is accepted by Atton, Rodriguez, Downing, and others; but rejected by alternative media representative bodies such as the US Association of Alternative Newsweeklies; and by individual alternative media and journalists
- Those working for the alternative media outlet could be amateurs (e.g. working in small-scale community radio, or on fanzines, blogs or citizen's media projects); or professionally trained journalists
- The news they produce may be incredibly local in nature – in the form of community service announcements, 'what's on' information and so on; or it may be highly skilled investigative journalism
- It may range from a daily program or publication reaching a significant audience to an individually-produced blog or fanzine read by less than ten people.

In essence, what I am suggesting is that the definitions offered so far, across the range of theorists and practitioners, are simply too broad. If we take into account all that has been offered, 'alternative media' and 'alternative journalists' could include any type of communications which is not made by a recognized major media ownership group. Such a broad definition is not helpful and the ensuing chapters seek to offer data and perspectives which draw us closer to defining – and thereby better understanding, critiquing and theorizing – alternative journalism and its practices.

Summary

While the community, grassroots, and radical media field has experienced increasing attention from research scholars, established theories about the sector and a universally accepted way to 'frame' its activities are still in their early phases. This situation is exacerbated by the explosion of technology and electronic communications, much of which lays claim to being part of the 'alternative' forms of communication, user-generated content, citizens' journalism and so on that has become the focus of much discussion in both research and more public fora. Ultimately, though, the definitions currently applied to the field of alternative journalism in particular are far too broad to be meaningful, and it is important that they become meaningful because this sector of our media landscape has much to offer the future shape of journalism. Significantly, our understanding of precisely what alternative journalism is and how it is practised will have direct implications for the way journalism is taught into the future. If we are to accept, as so many do, that the mainstream media is in crisis and producing thinner and weaker journalism, with little investment in investigative or quality work (McChesney, 2003; Hamilton, 2004; Anderson and Ward, 2007; Trigoboff, 2002: 12; Walley, 2002: 1, 22; Westin, 2001: 35), then we must look to the practices of alternative, independent and community media journalists who are, research indicates, producing content relevant to their audiences and relevant to the role of journalism in democracy. The last 15 years has shown us that while the *concept* of public journalism appeared to have much to offer, in practice it has done little except to effect minor changes in local newspapers. But alternative journalists are practising journalism in ways that are engaging audiences, including ordinary people, and creating a more active public by moving outside the definitions of professional news that we have become accustomed to consuming, and teaching in journalism education.

Challenging the News is intended to provide some input into the developing discussion about the nature of independent and alternative journalism, working to identify what lies at the heart of it. It is only when we discover this, in a specific and practical way, that we will be able to integrate it into journalism education curricula and see its impact on the dominant practices of journalism and I believe on the machinations of democracy. These issues of definition are returned to in Chapter 3, when practising alternative journalists provide definitions of their work; and their perceptions of the role of their journalism in the broader social and political milieu. First though, we return to the roots of alternative journalism and seek, through the past, to understand contemporary motivations and practices.

Chapter 2

Defining moments in the history of alternative journalism

This chapter identifies and analyses the major developments in alternative and community-based journalism, particularly focusing on four key 'defining' periods: the nineteenth century radical and working class press; the pre- and post-World War I anti-capitalist era; the counter-culture movement of the late 1960s and early 1970s; and the advent of the plethora of new forms of citizens' journalism (Rodriguez, 2001) and alternative journalism facilitated by the internet from the late 1990s onwards. As this book primarily concerns itself with alternative journalistic practices in established democracies, the experiences provided in Britain, the USA and Australia illuminate much about the *raison d'être* of most radical, alternative, grassroots, and community media forms. While Atton and Hamilton note that alternative journalism 'is not an unchanging, universal type of journalism' but a consistent effort to respond to dominant conceptions of journalism (2008: 9), there is value in looking for the constants. What ideals and practices have endured through time? What have alternative journalists *always* done? How have they responded to changing social and historical contexts? To some extent, this book does not see alternative journalism as something that is forever changing because it is forever 'responding' to something even though the industry, as with all industries, adapts to changing times and technologies. There are enduring practices, enduring motivations, and this overview of the historical development of alternative journalism seeks to identify them.

If we are to move towards a clearer understanding of what it is alternative journalists do, and how that activity might be translated to a broader canvas, we need to return to the roots of alternative media. While there is much to suggest that the news and information industry has been revolutionized by the advent of the internet – and indeed it has facilitated the rise of citizens' journalism and many other forms of alternative journalism – the earliest forms of alternative media lie in the radical and working class press. The development of the alternative press itself, in its printed form, is reasonably well-documented, particularly the periods of the early working class press and later, the counter-culture publications of the 1960s and 1970s. The roots of many contemporary alternative newspapers, particularly the press of radical-left political movements, can be traced back to the popular presses of nineteenth century Britain, the big general strikes, the anti-conscription movement of World War I, the Great Depression, the 40 hour week campaign, and so on. Unfortunately, many of the publications which grew out of such political movements did not survive after the campaign was over. But the precedent they established paved the way for new papers to be launched, and for the alternative press to be continually revitalized. Indeed, the literature indicates that while the alternatives experienced a lull during the 1940s and 1950s,[8] by the early 1960s, new political movements had grown and gained popular support, and this meant rapid growth in the size and diversity of the alternative press. At the same time, alternative media forms such as community radio were formalized in legislation in Australia in 1972 with public access television beginning

---

8 This can probably be attributed to the conservatism of that era which followed World War II. Indeed this period represents the heyday for conservative governments in the United States, Australia and Britain. The conservative cause was assisted by growing anti-communism throughout the 1950s, and the development of the Cold War. The ultra-conservatism of this era was perhaps the very reason for the ultimate rebellion against accepted values throughout the 1960s and 1970s. Perry says the purpose of the alternative press of the 1960s and 1970s was to shock 'bourgeois sensibilities' (1977: 13). And in the United States, Johnson indicates that the growth of alternative publications was a direct response to the rapid social changes occurring, and a reaction against the high moral attitudes which existed in previous decades (1971: xii).

in the United States in the same era (Stein, 2001: 299), and the 'alternative press' truly became a multi-platform 'media' industry. The social changes highlighted in the 1960s and 1970s reflected a sustained and revitalized challenge to the established order and to the mainstream media's representation of society and culture although it is in no real way the 'cradle' of alternative media – it all began long before that.

Alternative journalism, indeed any journalism which operates outside the mainstream construct of 'professional journalism', has long been considered an illegitimate form in Western democracies. This has been primarily due to the failure of many alternative journalists to adhere to conventional journalistic norms of objectivity and a uniform set of professional news values (Gustafsson and Hadenius, 1976: 110; Garneau, 1993: 11; Glessing, 1970: 99; Johnson, 1991: 191) which, it would seem, many consider to be the cornerstone of credible journalism. In earlier times, though, the alternative media's audience was the source of its illegitimacy; many radical publications represented the working classes which marginalized them out of 'respectable' circles and cemented their place outside the existing power structures (Williams, 1978; Curran, 1978a; 1978; Turner, 1969; Kessler, 1984).

The radical working class press

There is a relatively long history of the radical press in democracies (among others, Curran, 1978; Hall, 1984; Williams, 1970; 1978; Turner, 1969; Kessler, 1984; Leamer, 1972; Weingarten, 2005). Other authors have provided comprehensive accounts of how and why the press developed at all, both in its radical, popular, and 'respectable' forms, and I do not seek to repeat that here in significant detail. An overview is necessary, but in providing this I am looking for the practices and values that we can detect in the earliest forms of alternative journalism that may have endured through time. Indeed it has been the case that alternative journalism has not always been 'alternative', and through periods of the nineteenth and early twentieth century many radical publications, and I interchange that term with 'alternative', enjoyed large and apparently quite mainstream readerships. In 1836 in Britain, for example, gross readership of the radical press exceeded that of the regular newspaper press, with more than four million people choosing an alternative publication (Curran, 1978: 200). Hopkin reports on a study conducted in Britain in 1977 which found more than 2,000 British working class radical papers existed between 1800 and 1914 'revealing a rich and varied tradition of local as well as national journalism' (Hopkin, 1978: 294). Curran believes the reason for the dominance of the radical press throughout the nineteenth century was the relatively small establishment costs – newspapers could be printed on hand presses and one of the largest radicals cost only six pounds to produce each week (Curran, 1978: 207). The radical press also did not carry any advertising, but survived on the sale price alone.

> This absence of dependence on advertising profoundly influenced the character and development of the radical press. Newspapers could attack industrial and commercial capitalism without the need to pander to the political prejudices of advertisers (Curran, 1978: 210).

These early alternative publications catered principally to working class readers who were unrepresented by the mainstream press which, in those days, reflected middle/upper class conservative values more overtly than the contemporary media (1978: 203). Publications such as *The Poor Man's Guardian*, the *Northern Star*, *Reynold's News* and *Clarion* attracted large readerships while relying on cover price, rather than advertising revenue, for survival. The publications varied in political colour – some, for example, were attached to socialist parties or movements, others represented the Chartist movement of the mid 1800s, or anarchist politics (Hopkin, 1978: 298).

In 1819, the British government infamously cracked down on people found in possession of 'unstamped' (radical/underground) newspapers, and much of the underground press was effectively put out of business in the first half of the nineteenth century due to both legal and financial impositions on the radical press (Sparks, 1985: 139; Curran, 1978: 201). Other attempts at direct control of the radical press, such as prosecutions for seditious libel and blasphemy, were also applied by the government (Curran, 1978a: 61). When enacting the Newspaper Stamp Duties Act of 1819, which pushed many radical papers out of business, the government clarified that the bill was 'not against the respectable press...but against the pauper press' (Williams, 1978: 46). Despite government attempts, the radical press continued to operate; indeed, some of the government's tactics even boosted the sales of radical newspapers (Curran, 1978a: 61). Titles such as the *Twopenny Trash, Poor Man's Guardian* and *Dispatch* continued to be distributed widely throughout the British Isles:

> [They]...carried news that none of the respectable papers carried; it focused attention on the common problems and identity of interest of working people as a social grouping (Curran, 1978: 203).

Direct methods of the attempted repression of the radical and working class press by the state largely failed (Curran, 1978a: 62); and a similar effect occurred in Australia in the early twentieth century when government attempts to thwart the radical anti-war press had the reverse effect, making heroes of radical editors and journalists who were jailed and boosted readership considerably (Turner, 1969). Importantly, while this oft-recognized form of alternative media, the radical working class press, was continuing its earlier nineteenth century traditions across the globe, the Aboriginal print media, a truly early form of what we now know as 'community media' was even further advanced with the emergence of the first Aboriginal newspaper, a weekly newsletter called the *Flinders Island Weekly Chronicle* as early as 1836 in Australia and Canada (Rose, 1996; Burrows, 2009; Molnar and Meadows, 2001). The United States saw the emergence of the first native American press even earlier still, in 1826 (Molnar and Meadows, 2001).

The British daily 'respectable' press Williams identifies, which gained a toehold on the market with the establishment of *The Times* newspaper in the early 1800s, had certainly caused the radical press to confront difficulties. Not only did they face competition from the tightly controlled ruling class press (which had strong links with government), but the emergence of *The Times* indicated the establishment of an independent, commercial 'middle class' press (Williams, 1978: 47; Atton and Hamilton (2008) refer to the work produced by this middle class press as part of the evolution of 'bourgeois journalism'). However, the radical press continued to run campaigns against the establishment perspective of new publications such as *The Times*, and agitated against the government's repressive 'taxes on knowledge' (Hall, 1984: 35). Eventually the radical press succeeded, and all stamp duties were abolished by 1855. This success demonstrated the large role the radical press played in establishing true freedom of opinion during the nineteenth century. Unfortunately, it was the new middle class press, rather than the radical press, which eventually benefited from these freedoms won by the radicals (Hall, 1984: 35). Williams (1978), and later Atton and Hamilton (2008) reinforce the role of this early 'bourgeois journalism' in the development of alternative journalism, in that the latter directly responded to the growing impact of commercial imperatives on journalism and the absorption of the bourgeois media into the form of the 'commercial popular' media that we know today (see Atton and Hamilton, 2008: 12ff for detailed discussion). Indeed, it was the adoption of the professional norms of objectivity as the only path to 'legitimate' journalism (Atton and Hamilton, 2008: 17) that fuelled a greater need for politically based and radical publications to subjectively represent those whom the commercial (formerly bourgeois) press had now forgotten.

In the late 1800s, growing commercialism had led to a new set of cultural values which redefined 'freedom' – it came to simply mean freedom from the state, with opinion regulated exclusively by the market, private ownership and commercial imperatives (Hall, 1984: 35). As with the contemporary press, the late nineteenth century commercial publications were 'formally' free in that ownership and opinion were not regulated, but they were limited to the classes that could afford to establish newspapers. Their journalism began to reflect the professional norms of objectivity, journalistic detachment, and reliance on official sources as 'credible' sources of information to ensure the broadest possible audience. It was a decided departure from the subjective, advocacy journalism of the radical press which had, overtly and quite popularly, represented the interests of 'paupers' over 'respectable' people (Williams, 1978). It was after this redefinition of 'freedom' that the radical press began to disappear in any significant form as they could not compete with the growing capital of the establishment newspapers which published, distributed and marketed more widely. In addition, the readership of the bourgeois press was far more attractive to potential advertisers because of its enhanced purchasing power (Curran, 1978: 69, among others; this forms the basis of much analysis of the growth of the commercial press, for example, Bagdikian, 1983; 2004; McChesney, 1999; 2003; 2008; Hamilton, 2004; Carey, 1989; and King, 1997). By the early 1900s in Britain, alternative publications were finding it increasingly difficult to survive. Even popular publications, widely read by the working class such as the *Daily Herald* which outsold most of the 'respectable' middle class press were not viable because they could not raise advertising revenue (Sparks, 1985: 140; Seaton and Curran, 1991; and more recently Nerone, 2009).

> In short, one of four things happened to national radical papers that failed to meet the requirements of advertisers. They either closed down; accommodated to advertising pressure by moving up market; stayed in a small audience ghetto with manageable losses; or accepted an alternative source of institutional patronage [e.g. political party, trade union] (Curran, 1978: 221).

But they were soon to receive a shot in the arm. The growing socialist movement in industrializing nations was to revitalize the radical press. Davenport indicates socialism in the United States 'came to be one of the most powerful political ideas by the last quarter of the 19th Century. The socialist reorganization of society was viewed in an almost millennial light, a simple and universal solution to poverty, inequity, and injustice of all sorts' (Davenport, 2004: 6). Indeed, in the 1890s in the United States J.A. Wayland's masthead *The Coming Nation* improved circulation from 14,000 in its first six months to more than 60,000 less than a year later, making it the largest circulation socialist newspaper at the time in the United States. These readership figures were to be surpassed by Wayland's later project, *The Appeal to Reason*, with circulation topping 140,000 by the end of 1900, with some special editions, such as the November 1900 issue selling 927,000 copies. In Australia and the United States radical groups such as the Industrial Workers of the World (IWW) were making their mark, primarily due to growing opposition to what they considered the 'capitalist war' in Europe. Efforts in Australia to force young men to enlist (conscription) led to a significant anti-conscription movement pushed along by radical and socialist groups. This era gave rise to the second key moment in the development of alternative journalism, again featuring the subjective and advocacy journalism practised by its nineteenth century counterparts and driven by anti-mainstream forces.

Pre- and post-World War I

Like the British radical press of an earlier era (Curran, 1978), the alternative press in the early 1900s mainly represented the anti-capitalist spirit which dominated the labour movement at the time. Along with the radical press, community forms of media such as the African-American press began to grow and consolidate, with Ida B. Wells' *Free Press*, and Josephine St Pierre Ruffin's *Women's Era* forming an integral part of what Squires has identified as 'the Black Public Sphere' in the United States (Squires, 1999). In Britain, the originally socialist weekly *The New Statesman* was established in 1913, taking over the leftist (but less so) *Nation* and *Athenaeum*, while across the Atlantic in the United States, various newspapers of socialist orientation and more 'respectable' alternative leftist publications such as *The Nation* and *The Spectator* were emerging. J.A. Wayland's socialist *The Appeal to Reason*, mentioned above, was regularly printing 500,000–750,000 copies per week, with special issues sometimes reaching print runs in the millions. From 1900–1915 circulation sometimes rose to 4.1 million copies for a single-issue press run, making it the largest-ever socialist newspaper in US history with a significant readership (Davenport, 2004). The World War I years ultimately saw the demise of *The Appeal to Reason*, partly due to Wayland's death a few years previously, in 1912, and the loss of many dedicated socialists to the war effort. Its impact lived on, though, in young radical journalists such as Upton Sinclair, who began his career at *The Appeal to Reason* and went on to form the 'muckraking' tradition of journalism in the United States which provided a significant challenge to mainstream society.

A movement which played an extremely important role in the workers' campaigns and which contributed greatly to the growth and popularity of the working class press of the time was the Industrial Workers of the World during World War I. Historian Ian Turner refers to the IWW, established in the United States in Chicago in 1905 and in Australia in 1907, as 'the strongest and most significant revolutionary movement the Australian working class had yet known' (1969: 12). It had much in common with the European syndicalist movement (Burgmann, 2009). Publications such as *Direct Action*, *Solidarity* and the Australian Workers' Union newspaper *The Worker* challenged the mainstream media's stereotypes of this anti-capitalist, anti-war group at the height of the IWW's popularity and influence (Turner, 1969: 3).

In the United States, organizations such as the IWW, trade unions, the Socialist Party and other left-wing organizations produced the bulk of the American radical press. The IWW's *Industrial Union Bulletin, Solidarity*, the *Voice of Labor*, and *International Socialist Review* gave voice to the organized labour movement's calls for radical industrial change, and indeed revolution (Kornbluh, 1964). Kessler refers to the journalists and editors of these publications as 'the forgotten men and women of journalism' (1984: 40):

> ... they are as vital to our appreciation of the richness of American jour-
> nalism as are Greeley, Hearst, Pulitzer, Ochs, Luce, and all the other
> giants. They are the men and women of America's dissident press –
> journalists who produced the alternative newspapers and magazines
> that are an essential part of this country's journalistic heritage.

In North America, left-wing groups published more than 600 news-papers and periodicals in the early 1900s (Kessler, 1984: 40). Kessler also found that alternative publications started by new European immigrants, which would today be identified as community media, reached a peak from the 1880s to the 1920s, with almost 3,500 foreign language publications established to assist the new migrants. While Australia's first ethnic community newspaper appeared in 1848 (a German publication, see Griffen-Foley, 2003: 47), the proper development of such a strong ethnic press did not occur in Australia until the post-World War II immigration boom. The development of a strong ethnic press in the United States and later Australia is certainly evidence of mainstream journalism's failure to accurately represent the interests of minority communities (Forde, Foxwell and Meadows, 2009; Deuze, 2006; Peissl and Tremetzberger, 2008: 7; Lewis, 2008). So while the alternative media industry in the early twentieth century was dominated by the working class/socialist/labour political press, it also featured a developing Indigenous or native press (Burrows, 2009); and an ethnic press designed specifi-cally to serve unrepresented migrant groups in the larger democra-cies, particularly the United States (Kessler, 1984).

Although the radical press experienced its peak during the time around World War I and the years immediately following, publica-tions such as the *Industrial Worker* continued through the 1930s. Indeed, *Industrial Worker* was still in publication in 1964 when Joyce Kornbluh produced an anthology of the United States radical (mainly the IWW) press. At its peak in the United States, the IWW had a membership of around 100,000 and produced a weekly newspaper, first the *Industrial Union Bulletin*, then *Solidarity* from 1909, and finally the *Industrial Worker* through to the 1960s. As in Australia and Britain, radical political groups in the United States felt continually misrepresented in the mainstream press and looked to their own publications for a more favourable view of direct action, strikes and industrial sabotage. During World War I, mainstream newspapers such as the *New York Tribune*, the *Cleveland News* and the *Chicago Tribune,* declared that IWW members were German agents (Kornbluh, 1964: 317) (similar claims were made in Australia: see Turner, 1969).

> Newspaper columns carried stories of IWW plots of destruction and sabotage which were never proved in court. News stories accused Wobblies [IWW members] of planning to arm themselves and take possession of industries, poisoning the nation's supply of beef, and plotting to burn crops and cities (1964: 317).

Kessler clarifies that many radical journalists claimed they would have preferred to work for mainstream publications to reach a larger audience, but were unable to properly present their ideas in a mainstream forum:

> They founded and maintained their own alternative journals not just because they believed in a cause, but because the mainstream press of the day ignored or ridiculed that cause (Kessler, 1984: 40–41).

Burgmann claims the US Industrial Workers of the World did not directly interfere with the US war effort, although anti-war action formed the basis of much radical politics in Australia at the time of the outbreak of the Great War (Burgmann, 2009). At its peak in 1917, The IWW's Australian newspaper *Direct Action's* circulation stood at about 15,000 copies per week[9] (Armstrong, 1990: 67; Burgmann

---

9 The current circulation for comparable socialist and communist papers in Australia is 6,000–8,000 per week for *Green Left Weekly*, and 1,500 fortnightly for the *Socialist Worker*. And while the 15,000 circulation for *Direct Action* in the pre-war period was strong, it was significantly less than that enjoyed by mainstream newspapers: as an example, Melbourne's daily *The Age* newspaper was circulating 150,000 copies in 1908, although that had reduced to 96,000 by the time WWII began (Nolan, 2001: 3) but around the same era circulation was somewhere between 100,000–150,000.

[2009, and see also 1985] indicates some sources claim circulation of around 26,000 at its peak, with a total readership of at least 50,000). Through his work at *Direct Action*, Tom Barker, editor and one of the most well-known names of the World War I era, produced the famous 'To Arms' poster of World War I, which directly attacked the mainstream press, among others and enunciated the radical press's identification of mainstream journalists and editors as part of the establishment to which they were so passionately opposed:

TO ARMS!!
Capitalists, Parsons, Politicians,
Landlords, Newspaper Editors, and
Other Stay-at-Home Patriots.
YOUR COUNTRY NEEDS YOU IN THE TRENCHES!
WORKERS,
FOLLOW YOUR MASTERS!!

Tom Barker in *Direct Action* (reproduced in Toscano, 2008: 11)[10].

Barker was charged with publishing a poster prejudicial to recruiting for the war effort and argued in court that he was seriously trying to recruit for the armed forces, but the courts 'got the joke' and Barker was found guilty. The radical journalists continually labelled mainstream press as the servants of the ruling and middle classes. Henry Boote, editor of the *Worker*, and an IWW supporter, criticized the stance of the *Sydney Morning Herald* and *Sun* newspapers when twelve IWW prisoners were released from jail:

> The rage of the prostitute press is the measure of the triumph won for justice by the release of the IWW prisoners. The ink is foaming at the lips of Sydney's dailies, morning and evening... They rave about the contamination of the fountain of justice, but when that fountain does not flow the way they desire they are ready at once to befoul it (in Turner, 1969: 241).

While the mainstream media of the time voiced other societal interests, usually of the 'respectable' sections of society, they declared journalistic objectivity in line with their reputation as the 'professional' commercial press. Compare, however, the following two paragraphs (prose, rather than journalism) written after war

---

10 To view a copy of the poster, go to http://links.org.au/node/1104.

was declared by Britain. The first was printed in the mainstream *Bulletin* magazine, a weekly news periodical representing an established, professional news outlet, and the other in the IWW's *Direct Action*, which had opposed working class involvement in the war:

> For Britain! Good old Britain!
> Where our fathers first drew breath,
> We'll fight like true Australians,
> Facing danger, wounds or death.
> With Britain's other gallant sons
> We're going hand in hand;
> Our War-cry 'Good old Britain', boys,
> Our own dear motherland.

Frank Johnstone, 'Sons of Australia',
Bulletin magazine (in Turner, 1969: 3).

> Let those who own Australia do the fighting. Put the wealthiest in the front ranks; the middle class next; follow these with politicians, lawyers, sky pilots and judges. Answer the declaration of war with the call for a GENERAL STRIKE.

Tom Barker in *Direct Action* (in Turner, 1969: 3).

The content suggests the commercial, professional press was just as partisan in its stance as the radical and openly advocatory *Direct Action* but shielded behind its protection of the established order and the war effort, the mainstream media is able to claim a heightened status. Miraldi reports that a somewhat radical US journalist of the time, Charles Edward Russell, who worked for both the mainstream press and socialist press through the early 1900s had been forced to seek an outlet for his views in socialist newspapers because the mainstream press of the day was completely closed to any notion of a socialist system (Miraldi, 1995: 2). While his socialist beliefs were well-known, it was his experience as a mainstream journalist in the midwest and New York that had radicalized him and caused him to look to socialist newspapers for an outlet (Miraldi, 1995: 1). Although Russell eventually ended his official ties to the US Socialist Party when he supported the US entry into World War I, his journalism, consistent with the work of other alternative journalists across time, was comprised of 'Attacks on the wealthy and on political corruption, alliance with the poor and downtrodden...' (Miraldi, 1995: 2; also Davenport, 2004). His journalistic methods have much in common with some of the more moderate alternative journalists but still provide some indicators of practices that have endured. It is worth repeating them here in detail:

> The press, buffeted by the demands of readers, advertisers, and profit allows for little radical commentary and discourages serious expose of corporate misdeeds. The work of Charles Edward Russell came, of course, in a different era, but those same demands existed at the turn of the century and had, in fact, first emerged in the years he worked for Pulitzer and Hearst and had only heightened with the growth of mass circulation magazines...he established separate reporting identities: in the establishment magazines he was an angry but moderate muckraker while in the socialist press he was a sarcastic advocate who offered radical solutions (Miraldi, 1995: 9).

Russell's advocacy of political causes (he was one of the founding members of the National Association for the Advancement of Colored People) separated him from mainstream contemporaries. Similarly, socialist publications in both the United States and Australia were openly advocatory and the overtness of their political stance is a characteristic that continually distinguishes the radical press from other forms of alternative media; and particularly from mainstream commercial journalism.

In 1917, the Australian Federal Government mirrored the actions of the nineteeth century British government, and attempted to shut down the increasingly popular radical press with legislation. On this occasion, they ordered the withdrawal of *Direct Action* from the postal service because it had acted against the national interest by opposing the war effort. The paper, which had become a weekly publication with the growing popularity of the movement, continued to be distributed on street corners and aboard ships and trains (Turner, 1969: 85). With its anti-conscription campaign, the IWW had become a strong and popular political force. Turner claims the May Day 1917 edition of *Direct Action*, which distributed 12,000 copies advocating the release of IWW prisoners, was one of the most widely read and distributed Australian radical papers (1969: 85). In late 1917, the presses of *Direct Action* were seized by police, and the newspaper banned from publication, after the IWW (which had changed its name to the Workers' Defence and Release Committee) was declared an illegal organization. Throughout 1917, and with a Labour government in power, Burgmann reports that 103 IWW members were imprisoned, usually for terms of six months with hard labour and there was considerable official and unofficial movement of IWW members between Australia and the United States at the time (Burgmann, 2009).

The Australian Workers' Union publication *Worker,* was achieving similar success to *Direct Action,* principally on the back of its strong anti-conscription campaign. During this campaign, the *Worker's* circulation increased by 35,000 up to 50,000 for one anti-conscription special issue (Walker, 1976: 252). It experienced similar problems with the government – editor Henry Boote was convicted for failing to submit articles on the war to the censor (Walker, 1976: 253). It seems that such publications also had a greater impact on the politicians of the time than contemporary socialist publications. Boote was invited to sit on a three-member board of editors to advise the censor on war issues in 1918, but declined the offer (Walker, 1976: 254). The heightened influence of these publications is most likely due to the strength of the workers' movement at the time, reflected in the strong circulations enjoyed by the radical newspapers. The Australian Workers' Union membership, for example, increased from 19,000 in 1905 to 61,500 in 1914 (Walker, 1976: 138). There were clearly growing socialist sentiments existing in Australia and other Western nations around the time of World War I (Kornbluh, 1964; Davenport, 2004; Miraldi, 1995).

In 1923 the newly formed Communist Party of Australia launched its own newspaper, the *Workers' Weekly,* which experienced a particularly strong period during the 1930s due to popular dissatisfaction with the economic downturn and massive unemployment of the depression (O'Lincoln, 1985). The labour newspapers also experienced some success during the 1920s and 1930s as circulation for the labour *Daily News* reached more than 62,000 in 1938 but this gradually dropped throughout the war until the paper was finally sold to major proprietorial group Consolidated Press in 1940. By the end of World War II, the heyday of the labour papers was well and truly over. Edgar Ross, an editor of many socialist, communist and labour publications since the 1920s, summarizes the function of the early socialist press:

> The party press has the job of exposing the lies of the so-called 'free' press of the capitalist monopolies... The Party press is indispensable as

an educator, agitator and organiser and building its circulation is one of the most important tasks confronting the Party (Ross, 1982: 142).

Following these early twentieth century heights, alternative media entered something of a lull throughout the post-World War II era with the rising challenges to established socialism and communism. It was not until the 1960s and 1970s that the industry re-emerged, revitalized, and took on a new face. Resurrected during and immediately following the conservative political eras of the 1940s and 1950s, the 'underground' or 'counter-culture' press represented an important stage in the development of an alternative media industry. Rather than present a unified socialist or working class view of politics, the underground publications set out to present the new counter-culture movement. Their aim, uniformly and in line with their early twentieth century radical counterparts, was to challenge and shock conservative moral and social values.

The underground emerges

Downing implies that too many studies bind radical media to the 1960s counter-culture and its aftermath (2001: 391). Indeed, his 2001 work and the case studies it contains, primarily drawn from the period of the 1980s onwards, are an attempt to realize the ongoing and dynamic nature of radical media (2001: 391). It is clear, though, that the rise of forms such as New Journalism and the plethora of non-mainstream alternative newspapers which emerged during the mid 1960s to mid 1970s constituted a significant period of growth and change for alternative journalists. At the same time that the underground press was popularizing the counter-culture movement, public access television began in North America, 'as a radical experiment in democratic communication' (Stein, 2001: 299) and community radio began in Australia firstly as a trial of university-based stations, and later as a formal third-tier (behind public and commercial radio) to the Australian broadcasting system. Community radio was born primarily due to the efforts of university students, left-wing political groups, ethnic minorities and, somewhat ironically, quite mainstream classical music enthusiasts who could not hear their favoured music on any mainstream stations (Bear, 1983). The alternative journalism of this era, practised across the different media of television, radio and press, was dominated by what became known as the underground or 'counter-culture' movement. Nelson explains:

> The underground press was to the counter-culture what Fleet Street journalism is to 'straight' society. The underground even created its own version of Reuters ... which ensured international dissemination of news ... (1989: 46).

Underground publications such as OZ magazine clashed with the authorities, with their editors sent to jail with hard labour on two occasions (Neville, 1995). In this, they had something in common with the radical publications of almost a century before who were often prosecuted for sedition and libel. By the 1960s, the authorities began using charges of blasphemy as a principal way of containing (or attempting to contain) the alternative press. Richard Neville and his fellow OZ editors Felix Dennis and Jim Anderson were arrested, charged and convicted in 1971 on obscenity charges in London. The convictions were quashed on appeal in the midst of a high-profile and ground-breaking court case (Neville, 1995: 357). Other British alternative publications such as *International Times (IT)* and *Black Dwarf* were also constantly monitored by authorities, and in 1969 Scotland Yard raided the offices of two alternative publications and confiscated more than 2,000 copies on the grounds of obscenity (Neville, 1995: 153; see also Fountain, 1988).

Elizabeth Nelson argues that OZ magazine was one of the true underground publications that reflected the social change and politics of the time:

> OZ managed to sustain a committed, if often verbose, journalism ... its articles [dealt] with politics, which generally conveyed a more historical, philosophic and universal view than did those of other underground publications (1989: 50).

OZ magazine had its roots in the early 1960s in Sydney, established when Neville and two university friends decided to set up their own psychedelic, counter-culture magazine which would satirize the news of the day and shock the moral sensibilities of the ultra-conservatives. The Sydney OZ magazine, which had a peak circulation of 40,000 in the mid 1960s, was most well-known for the trial and conviction of its three editors on obscenity charges. A front-page photograph depicted the three editors pretending to urinate on a new Sydney landmark, the P&O Shipping Line headquarters. The three were sentenced to six months' hard labour, but had the sentence reduced to a fine on appeal.

It is important to note, however, that while high-profile publications such as *OZ* – which really became famous due to the two court cases mentioned and the constant controversy over its use of nudity – are iconic representations of the underground media movement, the groundwork for their success had already been laid a decade earlier. In Sydney in 1958, for example, Tom Fitzgerald the financial editor of the mainstream and reasonably conservative broadsheet *The Sydney Morning Herald* established *Fitzgerald's Nation,* a fortnightly opinion publication dealing with issues of major national and international significance. From 1958 until its closure in 1972 (when it merged with *Sunday Review* to become the widely-read *Nation Review*), *Nation* gave voice to a number of writers who later became major players on the Australian political and journalistic scene: Mungo MacCallum (snr), Geoffrey Sawer, Bob Ellis, Manning Clark, Max Harris, Robert Hughes, Brian Johns, Sylvia Lawson, and Max Suich among others. Historian and one-time contributor to *Nation* Ken Inglis says Fitzgerald was spurred to establish *Nation* after the closure of two independent publications in the 1950s, Allan Fraser's *Observer,* and Harold Levien's *Voice.* Fitzgerald's personal opposition to the White Australia policy, and his belief that Australia needed to position itself more in the Asian region, rather than continually aligning with Britain, formed the editorial basis of the early editions. In the final edition of *Nation,* Fitzgerald wrote:

> The liberal and radical strains in Australian intellectual life, though substantial in numbers, are always struggling to have a vehicle of communication...liberals and radicals, without sinking their differences, must love one another or die as an articulate force in this country. There are occasions when the means of intercommunication are apt to snuff out altogether. Such was nearly the case in 1958 when 'Nation' came into existence...[at that time] each of several new periodicals coming on the scene were of right-wing orientation. They were precisely what was not required when the weight of the Press was already so conservative; the imbalance meant that the forces of reaction could have a long succession of field days of opportunity ahead of them (Fitzgerald, 1972: 3)

Throughout the time *Nation* was published, Fitzgerald was offered financial support by both the Fairfax and Packer publishing houses (two of Australia's major media proprietors), but Fitzgerald refused offers in the interests of maintaining his publication's independence. While he was not a true radical in the sense of the socialist journalists working for the early radical press; or one of the counter-culture journalists who were to succeed him, he did establish *Nation* because only the most conservative views were being heard through the mainstream press and media of the time; and he was convinced that something needed to be done to ensure broader information was available in the public sphere. To finance *Nation*, he retained his position as Financial Editor on the *Sydney Morning Herald* throughout most of his time at *Nation*. In the final days of *Nation*, Fitzgerald was unhappily working as editorial director at Murdoch's *The Australian*. He finally accepted an offer from millionaire Gordon Barton to buy out *Nation's* masthead and list of subscribers. *Nation* had actually made way for new publications to flourish, and despite its staid manner and layout, had opened doors for a new type of alternative publication to the Australian media landscape.

The story of Fitzgerald's *Nation* illuminates a historical consistency in the alternative press, in that it is common to see publications and community radio news programs run by current or former journalists who feel disgruntled with their main occupation and want to find alternative outlets to cover news they cannot get through mainstream news filters (Fitzgerald, 1972; Miraldi, 1995; Whitaker, 1981; Weingarten, 2005). Britain's *Liverpool Free Press,* for example, was established by a group of former mainstream journalists in the early 1970s. Although established at the same time as *OZ* magazine and other counter-culture publications, *Free Press* offered more political analysis and less 60s lifestyle content than other alternatives of the day. A pamphlet from the *Free Press* described the importance of non-commercial, independent presses to the free flow of information. The *Free Press* claimed that as long as newspapers were run by businessmen for profit, there would be news that was not reported and, '(t)he Free Press aims to report this news' (Whitaker, 1981: 103). The turn-of-the-century muckraking journalists in the United States (Miraldi, 1995) also reflected this trend of holding down traditional journalism jobs to help fund their radical journalism that could not be aired through mainstream avenues.

The United States' major contribution to the development of a strong alternative press took root in the 1960s with the development of New Journalism (Johnson, 1971: xi), a style of writing which, in many ways, defines the alternative journalism of the period (Atton and Hamilton, 2008: 20). Journalists such as Tom Wolfe, Hunter S. Thompson and Norman Mailer broke away from 'traditional journalistic practice to exercise the freedom of a new subjective, creative and candid style of reportage and commentary' (Johnson, 1971: xi).

> New journalism ... differs in many important ways from established journalism; but it also involves a realization of many of the neglected possibilities of its established, traditional counterpart, and at its best it involves a renewed commitment to principles of honesty and thoroughness that should be part of any good journalism (Johnson, 1971: xii).

Weingarten suggests Wolfe and his contemporaries had discovered, through their own attempts to work within the confines of mainstream journalism, that traditional journalistic practices were, simply, 'inadequate to chronicle the tremendous cultural and social changes of the era ... how could a traditional "just the facts" reporter dare to impose a neat and symmetrical order on such chaos?' Johnson similarly sees the development of New Journalism as a response to the rapid social changes of the 1960s and an attempt by journalism to explain the 'fast and profound' changes in moral attitudes and understanding to the public (1971: xii): '... in one way or another it has proven more thorough, more honest, and more intelligently critical than traditional journalism' (1971: xiii). But he also highlights some of the shortcomings of the New Journalists and their publishers:

> ... it has exercised a freedom of informative expression not to be found at any other time or place in the world. That is not to say that it is without faults, because it has its own; and its expression is not totally free or wholly informed, because its freedom has been constrained in some ways and its information distorted by virtue of its humanity and its own kinds of bias. But it has succeeded far better than its traditional counterpart, if as yet only on a limited basis, in trying to present to the American public a full picture of its world (Johnson, 1971: xv).

New Journalism represented an important stage in the development of the industry and perhaps paved the way for major newspapers to 'loosen up' their 'objective' hard news style, if only a little.
But it was not only the 'New Journalists' who were making an
impact in the social and political changes of the 1960s. More traditional forms of alternative journalism rose again, along the lines
of the early twentieth century investigative journalists ('muckrakers'); and some very much in tune with the early Socialist press.
I.F. Stone, who established *I.F. Stone's Weekly* in the 1950s, was
recognized as a journalist who, like the New Journalists, was also
'outside journalism, and a founding father of the underground
ethos' (Johnson, 1971: 4). Stone wrote in 1969 that 'I tried in every
issue to provide fact and opinion not available elsewhere in the
press' (in Johnson, 1971: 5). The full range of alternative print
media of the 1960s sought to create an 'alternative consciousness' in
their readers and was a reflection of the alternative culture present
at the time (Stein, 2001: 301). There were several underground
press networks which operated in the United States throughout
the 1960s–70s: the Liberation News Service and the Underground
Press Syndicate (Johnson, 1971: 5). The Alternate Media Centre
in New York also served as an organizing point and centre for the
campaign for public access television, but it was the alternative
press, popularized by the mostly psychedelic counter-culture publications, that were really in their element during this period. The
number of counter-culture publications operating in the United
States grew from one 'truly underground' newspaper in the 1950s
– the Greenwich *Village Voice* – to 300 in 1971 (Johnson, 1971:
7). The *Village Voice*, established in 1953 and probably the most
financially successful alternative publication in the United States,
was eventually merged with the mainstream *New York* magazine
in 1974 and is now part of the large, but apparently still alternative, media chain Village Voice Media which owns 13 alternative
newsweeklies across the States. It was the first successful newspaper to be started in New York since the *Daily News* in 1918,
and at the time of the merger, produced sales of 4.6 million US
dollars with $452,000 in profits (McAuliffe, 1978: iii). McAuliffe
described the *Village Voice* as '*the* alternative weekly, the one that
had made all the others possible, the one that had shown the way to
a new kind of journalism in America' (original emphasis, 1978: ii).
It was quickly followed up by Jim Haines' *International Times* in

the UK, and later, *Black Dwarf* which built on huge street protests in Europe. Another of the most successful alternative newspapers in the United States in the 1960s was the Los Angeles *Free Press*, which by 1970, had achieved a circulation of almost 100,000, a staff of 32, and a gross annual income of US$450,000 (Johnson, 1971: 13). Despite their popularity, the US underground newspapers predictably attracted criticism from those who preferred a more subtle approach to news (Gray, 1970: xiv). John Sim also has some reservations about the benefits of the American alternative press of the 1960s, and comments:

> Some carry a tag of 'underground' although nothing in this land of the free forces them underground or into any kind of clandestine existence. The term seems to be loosely used to cover newspapers with an irregular schedule and a precarious financial footing, some having to flee unpaid printing bills (1969: 140).

Sim's claim that 'nothing in this land of the free forces them underground' ignores the impact that commercial pressures and structures have on news content (Hamilton, 2004), and also denies the real legal threats that these newspapers faced in publishing what they did. Indeed, many public access stations in the United States were shut down about seven years after their establishment due to changes in the legislation which favoured the commercial imperatives of cable operators, who had previously been required by legislation to provide public access channels in their service, over the public's right to access and produce their own material (Stein, 2001: 302–03). The very nature of much of the information contained in alternative media outlets, information which may alienate some readers and challenge the political stance of some potential advertisers, means it is not commercial-friendly. To this extent, the alternative media ekes out an anti-establishment, anti-status quo existence which often marginalizes them, and minimizes audiences.

Glessing conducted a study of 30 alternative publications from the United States in 1970 in an attempt to analyse the attitudes of editors, journalists and audiences. He concluded the underground press would continue to 'question a society whose major media seems unwilling or unable to ask the necessary embarrassing questions about American values and American lifestyles...[it]

has provided the only consistent radical critique of fundamental American institutions. It has been a watchdog press. And it will not go to sleep' (1970: 60). Many of these publications, as is the way with so many in the alternative press (Curran, 2003), had short lives. Some survived more than 12 months, others lasted only a few issues. However, Cock notes that many editors and journalists involved in the alternative scene did not usually disappear with their newspapers. New publications were started up by working collectives, creating a steady stream of new and different alternative press (1977: 4). The Australian Aboriginal publications of the 1960s and 1970s, which also included the more 'militant' *Koorier* and *Black Action* (Rose, 1996: 68) were tied to a specific political cause, but their emergence was clearly due in part to the increasing profile of new political movements such as land rights, environmentalism and feminism during this counter-culture era (Burrows, 2010 provides a comprehensive analysis of the Indigenous print media in Australia throughout this era). In the United States, the anti-segregationist and civil rights movement was served by publications such as the *Pittsburgh Courier,* the *Chicago Defender,* the NAACP's publication *North Action Jackson* and other 'freedom' papers such as *Citizens' Appeal* and *Freedom Journal (*Squires, 2009: 62ff).

Despite the persistence of many of the political alternative publications which continued to publish through the counter-culture era and indeed saw a (not unexpected) growth in their readerships, since early this century they have not achieved the large readerships or the commercial success of other alternative publications. By the time the successful Australian alternative weekly *Nation Review* folded in 1981, most of the Australian counter-culture publications which had emerged from the socially radical days of the 1960s and 1970s had also died. O'Lincoln identified a general dissipation of political activity towards the end of the 1970s across the democratized world, which in part explains the disappearance of many titles. He describes protesters from the Vietnam War era as 'showing signs of fatigue...many had been intensely active for a decade or so, only to find they were achieving less and less as time went on' (1993: 182). Indeed, while the alternative newsweeklies from the United States experienced their heyday during the counter-culture era, and many did not survive the late 1970s and 1980s, many original founders still work in the industry today, albeit with a different, more commercial face.

Cock summarizes the role of the alternative press and its journalists in the 1960s and 1970s:

> Irrespective of particular successes or failures, the alternative media and centres helped to generate a sense of movement. They provided vehicles for communication within the movement, and between it and the corporate state. They were as much a part of the movement as a vehicle for it (Cock, 1977: 9).

The political nature of alternative and independent journalism

So far, this chapter has examined three key periods in the development of alternative journalism: the radical-popular press of the mid–late nineteenth century; the working class press of the early twentieth century closely aligned to the socialist movement and the Great Depression era; and the counter-culture period of the 1960s–1970s which saw the rise of a significant number of new alternative press mastheads and community broadcasting and the New Journalism form. We might also consider the current internet era, with all its *potential* as a site of democratic and socially empowering journalism, as a key moment in the development of alternative journalism.

It is a truism to say that alternative journalism, and the alternative media, is to some extent a product of its immediate social and political environment (as perhaps all media are). The counter-culture publications of the 1960s and 1970s, for example, were a direct response to the ultra-conservatism of the post-war 1950s and emerged along with a diverse range of socially conscious music, fiction, and political activity. In the same vein, the working class socialist publications of the early twentieth century arose as the trade union movement was in its early development, when workers' consciousness and identity was building, and at moments when capitalism was in crisis (such as the Great Depression era, the World War I era, the increasing appearance of socialism and communism across the world, etc). It is consistent across time that alternative media respond to their environment and their contemporary context. What is important though is to consider *how* they respond, and *why* they respond. If we examine the reasons why those media arose and the motivations of the people involved, we begin to see some essential and very important consistencies. Atton and Hamilton, clarify, for example, that alternative journalism 'is a response most generally to capitalism as a social, cultural and economic means of organizing societies, and to imperialism as a global dynamic of domination and consolidation' (2008: 4). This suggests the political basis of alternative journalism – and this is the key. Alternative journalism is political. It is not always radical; it is not always 'progressive'; it is not always empowering; but it is always political because it is always a reminder of what the dominant forces in society *are not providing, or are not able to provide*. It is therefore always, and across time, a statement against dominant media practices, content and context. Historical accounts show us a consistent message from alternative journalists; namely, to give a voice to the voiceless, to fill the gaps left by the mainstream, to empower ordinary people to participate in democracy, and in many instances, to educate people with information they cannot access elsewhere. In this sense, we might begin to see that the role of alternative journalism through time is consistent with Couldry and Curran's idea that the (presumably mainstream) media is not just there to 'guard us against the overweening influence of other forms of power' (i.e. act as The Fourth Estate) but that 'media power itself is part of what power watchers need to watch' (2003: 3). Alternative media and its journalists have fulfilled this role of *watching* and warning against mainstream media power. This role, to be the 'watcher' of mainstream media power, is a key characteristic of alternative journalism and emerges as a key theme in historical accounts.

Apart from its political basis, alternative journalism is often considered a site for the dissolution of the audience-producer barrier. However, despite the significant role that community broadcasting has played in empowering audiences and breaking down the audience-producer barrier since the early 1970s (Lewis, 2008; Forde, Foxwell and Meadows, 2009; Rennie, 2006; Howley, 2005; Rodriguez, 2001), the strength of alternative media and the role of alternative journalism has not, overtly, been to facilitate the extensive involvement of 'ordinary people', outside the circle of those already producing the publication/programme. Certainly, many alternative journalists are non-professionals and activists presenting their information and opinions, but historically the alternative media have not had the facility to provide a broad canvas for numerous voices and views. Community radio is one form of alternative media that, since the early 1970s, has had the potential to deliver in this area. Most recently, the internet has provided this potential to empower audiences and to reinforce the suspension of the audience-producer barrier that community broadcasting initiated. For this reason, the final section of this chapter examining key moments in the history of alternative journalism will consider the growth of the internet and its role in the development of alternative journalism.

The internet era

The opportunities offered to alternative media by internet technology has been well-covered by scholars and practitioners. The wealth of work completed on the value and empowering possibilities of the electronic media, including its creation of communities; participatory potential; its potential to diversify homogenous mainstream news; and its 'mass to mass' communication, is considerable (Waltz, 2005; Atton, 2004; Nightingale and Dwyer, 2007; Lister et al, 2003; Platon and Deuze, 2003; Castells, 1996; various contributions to Coyer, Dowmunt and Fountain, 2007; and so on). Note I use the term 'potential' here, and the 'possibilities' of the internet to democratize media, and provide an outlet for alternative voices etc, as it is precisely that – its potential – which makes it unique and perhaps, transforming. It is salient to remember, however, that the most visited news websites remain those published by the largest news media corporations in the world; and that many radicalized internet-based initiatives, such as Indymedia, have been compromised by their very openness and lack of filtering which can threaten the credibility of their content (Atton, 2003; Platon and Deuze, 2003). This section seeks to provide an overview of the development of the internet as a site for alternative journalism, and frames the work occurring through internet-based alternative media sites in terms already discussed – what are the consistent elements of alternative journalism that continue to arise?

Atton identifies PeaceNet in the United States and Green Net in the United Kingdom as two of the earliest internet-based media projects. Both were founded in 1985 and preceded the later media sites which emerged after the development of the World Wide Web (www). Native Net, a site providing information on and for Indigenous peoples around the world, and EnviroWeb were some of the earliest forms of downloadable alternative media on the

internet (Atton, 2007b: 59) and perhaps highlight the most important characteristic of alternative journalism on the web: the diversity of forms it offers. Blogging, electronic clips services, email
newsletters, pdf newspapers and magazines, interactive websites,
protest mass emails, and web-based political movements such as
MoveOn.org in the United States and GetUp! in Australia are just
some of the formats that alternative journalism may use in the
internet era. Platon and Deuze suggest that the 'inherent democratic, chaotic, decentralized nature and freedom from official
control has made the internet a strong medium for civil society'
(2003: 337; also citing Dahlgren, 1996). Despite its potential, even
in the early 2000s internet-based publications, both alternative
and mainstream, were struggling to survive commercially and
this impacted on the ability of alternative publications to properly
take advantage of the low cost alternative of the internet. There
was still more advertising revenue to be found in hard-copy print
(Curran, 2003). Curran reported that the *Financial Times's* failed
attempt to charge customers for selected online features confirmed that there were only two categories of web content at the
time that were profitable: financial information and pornography
(2003: 234) although in more recent times the *Financial Times*
has successfully charged for some online content.

Throughout the 1990s then, and into the early 2000s, the same
forms of radical alternative media which were crossing geographical boundaries and attracting broader readerships were still not
providing a financially sustainable form of alternative journalism. The Independent Media Centres, or Indymedia, for example,
represented a significant moment in the development of the internet as a site for alternative journalism and yet, they did not offer
any new models for financial viability. The Indymedia network
emerged during the Seattle demonstrations against the World Trade
Organization summit in 1999. The concept of giving amateur
journalists, protesters, activists and anyone who cared enough the
opportunity to write and be heard seemed incredibly powerful and
soon, Indymedia sites began appearing all over the world. While
the original Seattle Indymedia site was complemented by a hard-
copy activist publication called *The Blind Spot*, it soon developed
its own exclusive following and the democratizing and participatory potential of the concept caused a surge of Indymedia sites
(Platon et al, 2003: 337). By 2002, three years after the Seattle

demonstrations, there were 80 Indymedia sites around the world with millions of pages uploaded every day. The web technology enabled immediate updates, streaming audio and video files, and seemingly unlimited photographs and text which a hard-copy publication could never provide. There was no editing of the written copy, and audio and video footage was uploaded often unedited although the editorial collective for each Indymedia site did have the power to remove any contributions considered 'unsuitable' (Atton, 2007a: 74). Platon and Deuze theorized that Indymedia journalism had roots both in forms of traditional journalism and in alternative media in that it operated in opposition to mainstream news media (2003: 341). They suggested it also contained elements of innovative types of journalism such as public or civic journalism (championed by Rosen, 1992 and 1995 and Merritt, 1995 and 1995a, among others), and open-source journalism which had been made possible by online media (2003: 341). Hyde's analysis reflects a great proportion of contemporary scholarship which trumpeted the success and democratizing power of Indymedia which, he says, provided an 'unabashedly liberal counterpoint to the mainstream press', and further:

> From grassroots beginnings in Seattle, this online alternative to corporate media has spread like wildfire. That's not bad for a loose collection of non-profit, volunteer-staffed journalists and activists...the rapidly growing number of Independent Media Centers are providing an outlet for scores of disaffected and disenfranchised groups by reporting differing versions of the news than the mainstream press (Hyde, 2002).

Hyde was not alone in his praise for the Indymedia concept. Despite his concerns about analysts being 'overenthused' about new media developments, Downing also compliments the Indymedia movement as providing new empowering potential 'entirely consonant with the best in the socialist anarchist tradition' (2003: 254). However some scepticism has since developed about Indymedia, as its open-publishing format enabled just as many homophobes, racists, and conservatives to blog to the Indymedia sites as it did the progressive activists it was intended for (Atton, 2003: 269) compromising its place as an 'alternative' news site. Atton questions whether Indymedia truly does represent 'socially responsible journalism in action' or whether the unfettered access provided to the Indymedia sites, where the reader can immediately become a contributor by clicking the 'Publish' button, is actually harming its attempts at progressive social change[11] (2003: 270). The great majority of blogs – although by no means all – providing comment on current political and social issues suffer a similar lack of credibility unless, it seems, they are attached to an 'official' and established news website with some level of editorial filtering and quality control, or alternatively a hard-copy newspaper with similar editorial processes in place.

Bennett appropriately reminds us that it is the context of the technology, and not the technology itself, that needs to be evaluated if we are to understand the true power of the internet as an empowering tool. He clarifies:

> The Internet is just another communication medium. Admittedly, it has a number of distinctive design features and capabilities, but these differences do not inherently or necessarily change who we are or what we do together...In short, the question of whether we go shopping or make revolution on the Internet...is more the result of the human contexts in which the communication occurs than the result of the communication media themselves (Bennett, 2003: 19; and citing Agre, 2002).

Curran further sees the internet as just the latest in a long line of new technologies touted to democratize the media, but hope around these technologies was inevitably and always short-lived: 'New technology has not fundamentally changed the underlying economic factors that enable large media organizations to maintain their market dominance' (Curran, 2003: 227). Curran's cynicism about the true impact of the internet on actually empowering and democratizing the media is well-founded. His life-long analysis of media has seen many new innovations heralded to be placing media power in the hands of the people to change the world. He elaborates:

> If Darwinism dominates evolutionary theory, Dawnism presides over the study of alternative media. The literature on alternative media regularly proclaims breakthroughs in which a glad confident morning has dawned...(2003: 227).

---

11 These issues are canvassed further from the perspective of contemporary alternative journalists in Chapter 5.

Curran's cynicism is checked, though, through his study of the *OpenDemocracy.org* site which he says is helping to redefine journalism primarily due to the technology it uses (the internet). Curran's study supports the identification of the internet age as a significant moment in the development of alternative and independent journalism. He sees its relevance in three major areas: firstly, the capacity of internet enabled *OpenDemocracy.org* to become a truly global magazine with an international range of contributions, and an international cultural frame of reference which forced it to move away from its original incarnation of something like a virtual *New Statesman,* or *Spectator.* Secondly, low production costs enabled the older print journalism style to evolve into a 'new hybrid cultural form' of journalism which often carried long essays of 6,000 words or more, accompanied by innovative and artistic visual material which, he claims, more closely resembled documentary film-making than any form of print political journalism. Thirdly, the interactive nature of the internet, which also enabled the publication to offer space to reader/contributors along with established and very 'literary' official contributors moved the publication further away from its initial incarnation as a thoughtful literary/political publication, to one which enabled the regular involvement of its audience (Curran, 2003: 235–37).

This analysis leads to a couple of conclusions: firstly, some of the characteristics attributed uniquely to the internet have been appearing in other community and alternative journalism forms for some time. While Bennett notes, for example, that the internet has delivered a forum for more people who have traditionally been 'receivers' to increasingly become producers and transmitters (2003: 34), this is not a quality unique to the internet. Community broadcasting globally has provided an opportunity for 'ordinary' community members to produce their own programs and put them to air for almost 30 years in Australia (Forde, Meadows and Foxwell, 2009), with other forms of public, community and pirate radio fulfilling similar functions in other parts of the world (Howley, 2005; Rodriguez, 2001; Downing, 2001; Pavarala and Malik, 2010). Forde, Foxwell and Meadows found the audience-producer boundary had 'collapsed' in Indigenous and ethnic broadcasting, supported by data from a wide range of focus groups with Indigenous and ethnic community broadcasting audiences, and interviews with personnel from community radio over a ten-year period. So while the internet has perhaps *enhanced* opportunities for the audience-producer boundary to come down, and for it to also occur in areas where there is *not* community radio, this is not a trend or a development that can be credited to the recent internet era.

A second point is that the internet has, particularly since the early 2000s, provided a more stable opportunity for alternative publications to actually survive. While advertising levels are still quite low for most radical publications, many alternative news sites such as *OpenDemocracy.org* are attracting strong readerships and advertising; and in other cases, publications that could simply not afford to continue publishing anymore have been able to at least stay alive by going entirely online (for example, *Eureka Street* in Australia; *People's World* and *Wind Chill Factor* in the United States; *SchNEWS* in Britain). So the internet age is significant because it offers new, low cost opportunities for alternative and independent journalism forms to, at the very least, continue to service their sometimes small but dedicated readerships and to continue to have an impact on broader public sphere discussions.

Thirdly, and Bennett reinforces this point, historical studies of alternative media on the internet indicate that the simple globalizing impact of publishing on the internet has made a considerable difference to the way alternative journalism is done, and presented. This is because the potential *audience* is no longer limited to the community radio station's transmission area; or the immediate circle of activists or campaigners; or the distribution footprint for the give-away alternative weekly (Bennett, 2003: 25). He clarifies:

> ...it is the interaction between the Internet and its users – and their interactions, in turn, in material social contexts – that constitute the matrix within which we can locate the power of the new media to create new spaces for discourse and coordinated action (Bennett, 2003: 26).

However Bennett notes the recognized rise in global activism, demonstrated by a range of events involving mass protest organized primarily through the capabilities of new technologies, cannot be wholly attributed to the reduced costs of the internet and its potential to coordinate campaigns and actions across geographic borders with the click of a mouse (see Pepe and Gennaro, 2007). More, he suggests it is the 'social and political dynamics of protest' that have changed, 'due to the ways in which economic globalization has refigured politics, social institutions, and identity formation within societies' (2003: 25). Simply, it is the globalization of economic forces that has caused different aspects of our societies to change, and not the technology itself, and this has triggered changes in the way people demonstrate and protest (and, by extension, the way those activities are organized, reported and presented; see also Atton, 2007b: 63).

This work pinpoints the key changes that global communication infrastructures have undergone and it is for these reasons that the internet age can be seen as a significant moment in the development of alternative and independent journalism. Essentially, the internet has facilitated the production of (on some occasions) high quality content by ordinary people, the creation of large-scale interactive networks which are engaged by that very content, the transmission of the content outside its original geographical boundaries, and the convergence of media systems so that micromedia content has greater potential to enter mass media channels (Bennett, 2003: 25). It is the potential audience for this content also, which now extends across national and continental boundaries, which distinguishes activism and alternative journalism on the internet.

Summary

Media historian Lauren Kessler identifies a key difference between the motivations of alternative journalists and the dominant main-stream form. It is an obvious difference, but the essence of what it is to be alternative is not reinforced enough. Kessler found that throughout American history, groups had published alternative publications not because of a dedication to journalism, but as a means to reach people with ideas, to organize their movement and promote their beliefs: 'Publishing a newspaper or magazine was not the path to wealth; it was the path to a better world' (1984: 42). Whether writing for the radical working class (popular) press of the nineteenth century; or the socialist and Industrial Workers of the World newspapers of the war and inter-war years; or the coun-ter-culture 'New Journalism' publications or community radio stations of the 1960s and 1970s; or indeed an Indymedia site, an online alternative publication, or an emailed political newsletter, alternative journalists have continued to write from 'a position of engagement with the event or process that is their subject' (Atton, 2007a: 75). Essentially, this historical overview shows us that alternative media journalists are distinguished by their belonging to the campaign or movement for which they write or broadcast. Further, their overriding commitment is to their public sphere, whether they perceive that sphere to be the Aboriginal community, an ethnic grouping, the socialist political movement, the environmental lobby, the anti-war campaign and so on. And always, their public sphere is quite simply that which is not being served, or served properly, by the mainstream media which exists, whether that be commercial media, or publicly-owned media which generally follows mainstream journalistic processes and mores. So, to return to the questions posed at the start of this chapter: what does the history of alternative journalism suggest are the consistent characteristics of alternative journalism through time? That is, what have alternative journalists *always done* that they continue to do today through the increasing range of alternative and independent media?

I believe alternative and independent journalists can be thought of in the following way, based on the evidence from these four key developmental periods of alternative journalism. I see these defining and enduring characteristics as, firstly, resonating with the unrepresented; secondly, working outside established societal power structures; thirdly, being overwhelmingly dedicated to the role of journalism in democracy; and finally, perpetually fulfilling a place in the mediascape as an endangered species. Let's consider these one by one. Firstly, they are more closely aligned than any other journalists with the unrepresented, the 'poor and downtrodden' (Downing, 2003). This returns to the notion that alternative journalism has an overwhelmingly political basis. Kunda Dixit perhaps best summarizes this characteristic:

> Journalists are expected to show super-human aloofness and not be moved by injustice and greed. And even if they are moved, the anger is not supposed to be reflected in copy. Thus, most Western status-quo journalism is biased by virtue of being blind to wrongs (1994: 22).

So, the alternative journalist's ability to identify wrongs when they see them, and to present them to their public as a wrong, has consistently been a strength from the mid eighteenth century to the present day. Secondly, they identify what they do in terms of what they *do not* do: they are not servants of the ruling classes, members of the social elite, conservative establishment figures, or part of the existing power structure, and they work outside these frameworks which, on the whole, they consider to have greatly failed democracy. Thirdly, and importantly, while some alternative and independent journalists are amateurs or audience members/ readers who become producers (and this lack of boundary between audiences and producers is an important defining characteristic for some sub-sectors), there is also evidence that many alternative journalists are *professionals* who are committed to the role of alternative journalism, often in the form of advocacy journalism, in democracy. Numerous periods in history, and in modern times, feature mainstream, working journalists writing for alternative publications who find the agendas of the mainstream far too limited but who must work within it to survive. This suggests not all alternative journalists are activists, or amateurs, but that in fact some of them are ordinary 'professional' journalists who move in between mainstream and alternative journalism (Atton and Hamilton discuss this also, 2008: 46), unwilling to suppress their convictions in order to be considered 'credible' and unwilling to forego their dedication to journalism's central role in public debate.

Fourthly, and finally (and unfortunately), an enduring characteristic of the alternative journalist across time is their status as an endangered species. Multitudes of publications, community radio programs, magazines, and now online outlets have come and gone and the alternative media is undoubtedly distinguished by its often limited life. Curran (2003) recounts the 'seemingly typical, rags-to-failure saga of alternative media production', and lack of resources and funds is a defining characteristic of the job for many alternative journalists and one which, we will see, continues to dominate their considerations and processes today. In 1984 Wolmar encouraged alternative journalists to 'get out of [their] ghetto' in the interests of attracting more readers and a stronger financial base, and indeed, lack of commercialism is part of the very nature of alternative journalism and its producers, but there are contemporary examples defying this trend. All four of these enduring characteristics have, at their heart, a political basis and it is this which I believe needs to be embraced in any attempts to define alternative and independent journalism.

The ensuing chapters move on to consider these characteristics in the contemporary context, through an analysis of the processes and routines of alternative and independent journalists.

Chapter 3

Finding the basis for alternative and independent journalism

Journalists working outside mainstream media structures do so for a reason. Sometimes, people working in alternative media organizations are students, or budding journalists, looking to get publication or broadcast experience before they move into mainstream work. This is particularly the case in community radio, which has provided a fertile training ground for journalists and broadcasters wherever it appears (Forde et al, 2002: 63ff; Australian Government House of Representatives, 2001). Most often though, journalists working in alternative and independent media are there because of the freedom and autonomy it brings; and the journalism such media allow them to do. This chapter begins with views from contemporary alternative journalists about how they define themselves. This is inextricably tied to the journalists' perceived role of alternative journalism in society. This assists with establishing the parameters of the discussions which will occur in the next four chapters. In this chapter I also investigate exactly what it is that makes an alternative media newsroom different for a journalist. It looks at organizational and structural issues – cooperative editorial arrangements; participatory journalism training; and journalistic autonomy, among other things. The discussion contained here provides a basis for the following chapter, which tries to get closer to the heart of the matter by investigating the news values of alternative journalists and how these news values work to bring audiences to alternative and community journalism. For now, though, let's look to alternative journalists to discover how they see their own work; and simply, why they do what they do.

How alternative journalists define themselves

A telling way to begin an analysis of any occupation or perhaps, indeed, anyone, is through self-definition. How do alternative journalists define what they do? A decade ago, Australian alternative press journalists were most likely to define themselves as 'journalists' rather than as activists, writers, subeditors, or even their main full-time occupation of a historian, a doctor and so on. The more recent qualitative study of alternative media journalists found most still identified as 'journalists' above anything else, although several saw themselves as both a 'journalist and an activist' (Rai, 2010 – see Appendix A), or a journalist and an 'educator' (Bouknight, 2009). Another saw herself as a journalist and a writer 'depending whether I'm talking to the bank manager or a publisher' (Simons, 2010). But for the most part, alternative journalists from a range of radical, community, grassroots, and independent media organizations considered themselves journalists, even some who had not carried out formal journalism degrees. Ten years ago, alternative press journalists in Australia were wary about calling themselves journalists and often qualified their self-definition ('I consider myself a journalist, but I've never done a degree or studied it formally'); while today, in the era of citizens' journalism and blogging, people feel freer to identify as a 'journalist' if they are working in the public forum, providing general news and information. Two of the interviewees were now and had been working in management for quite some time in the sector, so did not identify as anything but a 'manager' as they were not writing regular copy; but of those remaining, most identified as journalists, while just over one-third identified as either an activist, a campaigner, or an educator. Some, such as Bob Parry from the investigative *ConsortiumNews.com* in the United States, Carlton Carl from the similarly investigative *Texas Observer,* or Jeff Clarke from Northern California Public Broadcasting are long-term journalists who have moved from mainstream journalism careers to alternative journalism. Most of the others who identify as journalists, however, see a keen connection between the journalism they do, as an alternative journalist, and activism. Jessica Lee from New York's *The Indypendent* explains:

> I consider myself a journalist and I guess from certain perspectives you could consider what we do as social justice journalism or activist journalism. Just because we give regular people, people in the grassroots movements more of a voice in our articles than you might see in a different publication.

Milan Rai from the UK's *Peace News* which has published consistently since 1936 as the publication of the peace and non-violent action movement sees a similar, dual role for himself:

> I think that the role that I play is a hybrid between activism and journalism and that brings tensions and it brings dilemmas but fundamentally for me, the two things overlap and converge…politically committed activism and politically committed journalism…should still mean objective and honest activism and objective and honest journalism.

These comments were fairly typical and were reiterated by people such as Peter Barr, a talks producer and journalist at RTRfm community radio in Australia; Terrie Albano, editor of the *People's World* newspaper in the United States (loosely affiliated with the Communist Party); and others. Journalists with a background in mainstream media, then, were most likely to deny the tag of 'activist' as it carried connotations of being wedded to a political movement which they rejected. But on the whole, most of those who identified as journalists also drew connections between their journalism and activism. Those who rejected the self-definition as a journalist preferred to simply be referred to as an activist who saw it as part of their activism to work in alternative journalism or as an educator; or an 'investigative researcher'. Darryl Bullock from the UK's *The Spark* magazine, an ethical quarterly which distributes 34,000 copies and operates at a small profit, rejects the term journalist but does not go on to define how he sees his work:

> I've always hated the word journalist. I think it conjures up a really ugly image of people in hats chasing after ambulances. I don't like the word journalist. I don't think it adequately describes what people like

us do. I don't really see myself as an educator either...I think that's too specialist.

John Hodge from the UK's *SchNEWS* was more definite about his role as a 'media activist':

> I would call myself a media activist. I'm not trained as a journalist. I really don't have the trappings of a journalist, my networks are within social and environmental movements rather than journalism. I feel that the best way that I can help these political movements – with the skill set I have – is to be involved in the media side of them.

Another identifiable theme was to self-describe as an 'educator', although this was suggested by only three of the respondents. Still, their perspectives were consistent with one another, and did indicate something of an emerging theme about the role of the alternative journalist in 'educating' the public about issues or little-known political movements. This was certainly a theme that emerged as a key role for community broadcasters in Australia, particularly those working in remote Indigenous communities (see Meadows et al, 2007: 52ff for more on this). Tristan Miller from the UK's *Socialist Standard* said his journalism was an extension of the organization's political campaigns, which were to link local issues and local struggles and connect them to national issues. He saw this as an educational and activist role as it informed people, and connected people:

> I suppose I could be described as an activist when I am writing. But if I were to choose the term myself, I would probably say I'm an educator, because overwhelmingly, most of our audience or most of our intended audience who hasn't heard of us before, doesn't necessarily understand our point of view, what we mean when we say socialism...our job is to tell people what it is, educate people and show them how we see the world and how we view current events...

The way alternative journalists view themselves is inherently connected to how they consider their role in society. So, while many mainstream journalists when asked this question answer along fairly established lines – their role is to impart information; inform the public; get information to the public as quickly as possible, and so on (Henningham, 1996; Schultz, 1992a; Weaver et al, 2003) – alternative journalists are more likely to see their role in the broader context of social change. I asked the respondents a series of questions around 'why they do what they do' to establish the basis of their work. The detailed application of these broader concepts, such as the use of particular news values, will be looked at in the next chapter but for now I wish to move on from broad self-definitions to see how these translate to the perceived role of alternative journalism in society.

Alternative journalism and social change

In the mid–late 1990s, mainstream and alternative journalists' attitudes to their role in society were compared. The two groups shared several broad perceptions of their role, notably that their job was to 'uncover and investigate problems' and to 'impart information to others'. However, a range of more proactive roles which were presented to both sets of journalists began to highlight the differences between the two cohorts. The aspects of 'influencing the public', 'influencing public policy decisions' and 'championing particular values and ideas' were rated as much more important by alternative journalists. More than three-quarters of the independent press sample felt it was either very or quite important to influence the public, where only 49 per cent of the mainstream sample considered this important. Overall, ten years ago alternative press journalists nominated that 'providing an alternative view', 'contextualizing the news', 'motivating audiences and providing access for audiences' and 'balancing the mainstream' were key themes of their work. In 2010, those themes still resonate although the general description to 'provide an alternative view' is now, through the qualitative data, a little more complete in its form as 'covering stories others won't cover'. Importantly, a new theme has emerged which was previously not nominated by either mainstream or alternative journalists, which is to provide local news to a local audience. This was also identified by both community broadcasting volunteers and journalists; and community broadcasting audiences as a key function of, particularly, community radio news (Forde et al, 2002; and Meadows et al, 2007). This theme also re-occurred in discussions about news values, which will be covered in the next chapter.

Overall, alternative journalists feel they have two key roles in society: to provide in-depth coverage and context to issues already in the public sphere; and to educate the public about issues and campaigns. As an extension to this theme of education, part of that role was to educate/train audience members in how to take part in alternative journalism ventures. Other issues also emerged, although to a lesser extent, such as the role of journalism in 'activating' the public (activism); and the watchdog role of alternative journalism which, in this context, is consistent with Downing's notion of challenging and targeting existing 'power structures' (2001: 391). It also resonates with Couldry and Curran's description of alternative media as the 'watcher' on media power (2003: 4). The most commonly occurring themes were to provide in-depth coverage and context; and to educate so we will consider those first.

It was expected that those publications primarily run to provide investigative journalism, and publications such as the UK's *The Spark* ethical quarterly would identify their overarching role to provide longer-form journalism. However, alternative journalists nominated this as their role even when they were providing daily journalism, such as at Australia's *Crikey*. Proprietor and journalist Eric Beecher refers to the publication's role as looking 'under the bonnet'[12] of Australian politics to get the story behind the story. Similarly, Jeff Clarke at Northern California Public Broadcasting in the USA, which runs daily news and current affairs programming, identifies a key difference between what his organization does, and what the mainstream journalists do that he worked with more than 30 years ago as a broadcaster for commercial radio and television, and prior to that with the American Forces Radio and Television service:

> I think the real essence and the real difference between independent journalists, public broadcasting journalists and the mainstream media is there are different levels of depth and quality in the arena that independent journalists are handling, versus what I would call the 'mile-wide and inch-deep' coverage that we get in the normal mainstream media. Both have a purpose but I think where we have excelled in the public broadcasting landscape has been to really provide a level of intelligent information that really covers the ground of a specific story or issue, or conflict in a way that allows people to make up their own minds... people want to get behind the headline and really see the depth of story.

While Clarke's comments suggest NCPB is not concerned with 'motivating' their viewers or taking on an activist role, he does believe that a number of the 'in-depth' journalism projects that

---

12 In this context, Beecher means the bonnet, or 'hood' of a car.

public broadcasting has undertaken have had broad-reaching effects on communities (see Chapter 6). Tony Ortega, now editor-in-chief of the somewhat commercial 'alternative newsweekly' in the United States, *Village Voice,* reminisces about his time as a journalist on the street for some of the US alternative newsweeklies, and identifies the relaxed timeframes of a weekly publication and the benefits this brings to its journalists:

> Even though when you gather all the material, it can be very tedious...you know going through government documents or conducting long interviews with people can be really difficult work...We weren't rushed like the people at the dailies. We weren't forced to just write just a small part of what we do. We were really encouraged to write the full story...you weren't asked just to do a 'he said, she said', surface story but get to the bottom of a mystery...So you start out as kind of a detective. You're trying to figure out, how do I get enough information that I can feel that I now have something valuable to say to solve this mystery?

Terrie Albano from the weekly *People's World,* which at the time of writing was morphing into an online-only daily emailed newsletter and pdf after 86 years of continuous hard-copy publishing as a daily and then as a weekly newspaper,[13] recognized that as a weekly publication editor she could not compete with the daily media, but nor did she want to. Audiences did not go to her outlet for 'breaking news', but for analysis and interpretation of news. While Carol Pierson, from the US National Federation of Community Broadcasters notes that individual stations' abilities to carry out good, in-depth alternative journalism depends entirely on their resources, it was an over-arching goal of most of the stations to provide contextualized news and deeper analysis as much as they could:

> ...we were definitely looking at more [substantial] stories than what a lot of the commercial stations were covering, which tends to be a lot of accidents and crime and those kinds of stories. So we were looking

13 *People's World* began as the *Daily Worker* in 1924; and was renamed the *Daily World* which merged with the Communist Party's *People's World* in 1968 to form the *People's Daily World.* It published daily until 1991, when it became weekly and was renamed the *People's Weekly World.* In its most recent incarnation as an online publication, it has dropped the 'weekly' and is now simply (again) the *People's World* (from http://www.peoplesworld.org/about-us; and Encyclopaedia Britannica online, http://www.britannica.com/EBchecked/topic/149887/Daily-Worker).

at stories that were about issues that made a big difference in people's lives ... we also wanted to do longer pieces and more in-depth reporting so we gave people more time to work on stories.

The 'more time' factor is an issue, and is one that is perhaps an advantage of alternative journalism that needs to be recognized. Many mainstream journalists, given similar circumstances, might also be able to write long-form, investigative journalism. The reality is, however, that the chances of mainstream media organizations investing time in journalists producing one strong story a week; or perhaps taking several weeks or even months to work on a significant investigative piece is dwindling. Newsrooms are being downsized all over the world and there is irrefutable evidence that mainstream organizations, particularly commercial ones, no longer see the economic benefit in investigative journalists delving 'behind the story'. In fact, the opposite is the case with demand increasing, every day, for more news, more quickly, due to the insatiable appetite and unlimited news hole of news websites (Paterson, 2006; Barker, 2009; Johnston and Forde, 2009; Gawenda and Muller, 2009; Australian Press Council, 2008). So while it may not be the 'fault' of mainstream journalists that they are not doing more in-depth journalism, which alternative journalists strongly identify as one of their key roles in society, it is certainly the case that this content that alternative journalists are producing is becoming more important as mainstream newsrooms scale down even further and journalists become 'disseminators' rather than 'gatherers' of original news (Barker, 2009).

While only a small number of alternative journalists self-defined themselves as 'educators', they did see an educative role for their publications as one its key functions. Tony Ortega from the *Village Voice* saw this in fairly straightforward terms: enabling readers to 'absorb all the things that [I] had learned' by understanding complex issues and communicating those complexities in an accessible way to his audience. Many of the other journalists, consistent with their own self-definitions, saw the educational role of their publications as inextricably entwined with the importance of activism. John Hodge from *SchNEWS* in the UK described himself as a 'media activist' and said his role in that sense was to educate people through the media. Billy Wharton, editor of the USA's *The Socialist* said that his journalism was primarily an extension of political campaigns, and it naturally played an educational role.

He couples the educational function with political activism. Terrie Albano from *People's World* clarifies:

> But I am still an activist and I think journalism as a whole plays an educational role. So, I don't necessarily see myself as an educator but I see that through the writing, through the reporting, through the struggles, education happens.

Jess Lee saw a more participatory, educational role for her publication, *The Indypendent,* which provided journalistic training for anyone who wanted to be involved to ensure copy presented was well-researched, thorough and newsworthy. Within this framework, however, training journalists (usually ordinary community members) were given gentle guidance in story ideas and had autonomy to follow their own interests. The trajectory of the story's development was checked a couple of times with guidance from the Editorial Committee. *The Indypendent* provided regular half-day workshops for anyone who wanted to become involved in the newspaper in basic research, writing and journalistic training. Lee explains:

> I think this year we're only going to manage to do three [workshops] but we call them Journalism 101 and we start with media criticism, how to read a news article and think about it while you are reading it. Then we go over the basics of research and interviewing and what a lead is and what a paragraph is, like the sources are in quotes and so the idea is at the end of the workshop that everyone knows how to write just a very basic news story, and at the minimum be able to be a more critical reader when they read the news...we think that's more valuable teaching people to be just more engaged in society and definitely a more educated person when it comes to participating in democracy.

Darryl Bullock from *The Spark* picks up on the importance of participating in democracy and his words have strong resonance with themes identified a decade ago to 'motivate people to take political action' (Forde, 1997a). Bullock says:

> I think my job and our job as a publication is to pass information on to people and to give them the tools to take that further if they want to. It's always been our aim in *The Spark*, kind of to tell people about what's going on, to introduce them to people who are making changes in the world, both at local, national and possibly international level and then give them the opportunity, the understanding, the information that

they might need, if that subject interests them, to take it further, to get involved at whatever level they can.

Peter Barr from youth community radio station RTRfm in Perth, Australia echoes a number of other alternative journalists when he highlights the importance of providing contact details and information about 'when and where' things are happening to give audiences the immediate tools to do something. There is a sense that if audiences are left to chase things up themselves they might not, even though they might feel strongly about an issue, so the immediate availability of the information might be the difference between whether a listener/reader acts, or not:

> ...certainly in letting people know that these kind of actions are on, giving them details of where and when and most importantly why and letting people decide for themselves. But often times they're quite small protests or rallies over various matters and I don't think they get much coverage in the mainstream. I don't know if the mainstream really likes reporting on large crowds gathering in one place. If they do, I think they are hoping for some sort of friction to erupt. But we don't think along those lines.

Darryl Bullock again reiterates the importance of providing, essentially, 'how to participate' information for audiences in his publications' pages and this I believe is one of the key identifiers of alternative journalism that can be integrated into existing mainstream practices easily. I have reproduced Bullock's advice at length because it is representative of the sorts of things many other journalists have said:

> For example, you might read a story in a local newspaper about, say, the airport expansion thing. You'd probably read a thing in the local paper which would be pretty much exactly the same as you would read in the press release, telling you that something's going on, there's been a demonstration at the airport and that's it. We wouldn't do that, we would expand on that... We would also give you a whole set of contact details at the end of that so if you for example, felt really strongly about it, you would know where to go, who to complain to, who to get in touch with, who to find out more information from. If you wanted to, if you felt so strongly that you wanted to go on the demonstration, you would have those details there. We know from our own experiences because we've all been involved in the industry for so long that giving people information is vital. Expecting them to just do all the work for

themselves, they might not do anything. People can be reasonably lazy. I know I am at times and putting that information in front of them makes them much more likely to get involved in something.

This is perhaps a theme that has resonated across time and through a range of methodologies and questions. When alternative journalists are asked varied questions about their perception of their 'role' as a journalist in society; how they make their news decisions (Chapter 4); what makes something a 'good story' for them; why they find their job so satisfying, and so on, it is very common for alternative journalists to allude to their ability and what they see as their *responsibility* to get people up, and out. Not necessarily in protests and demonstrations, although this is a common goal also, but often, in community media organizations, to simply encourage people to take part in community activities, to volunteer at their local school, to help elderly people in the community, to organize public meetings about health, education or whatever might be on the public agenda at the time. The previous chapter demonstrated that this motivation, this drive to 'activate' the public, has been evident for many years in radical political organizations and their media, and in independent media initiatives. Even publications such as the more moderate *Crikey,* or the US alternative newsweeklies still allude to a desire to better inform people so they are able to make knowledgeable decisions about government, policy, the activities of local businesses, public officials and so on. So this identification of the role of journalism to encourage 'activism' or perhaps *participation* in public life is evident across diverse alternative journalism initiatives. This helps to describe a range of activities undertaken by very diverse parts of what is broadly 'alternative media' and there is some debate in our field about the importance of extending definitions of 'alternative' beyond the 'radical political, social or cultural agenda' (Couldry, 2010: 25; Atton and Hamilton, 2008; Atton, 2004). This overarching frame – to think about alternative journalism as a process which encourages audience participation and action in public affairs – enables us to include in our understanding of *how* and *why* these media operate the well-known radical, independent, progressive and community initiatives as well as the radical right-wing and some religious media which also exist outside mainstream avenues.

In particular, when speaking about their 'motivations' for what they do the large majority of alternative journalists put their work in the context of what I have termed 'enhancing journalism and democracy'. Indeed, many of the journalists identified that they were not, and could never be, in the business for the money or the dependable wage. Most people working in the alternative journalism industry were doing so out of a sense of the potential for social change. Carlton Carl from the *Texas Observer*, Carol Pierson from US community broadcasting's representative body the National Federation of Community Broadcasters, and Jon Bouknight from community radio KPOV in the United States, illustrate:

> ...everyone draws a salary, they're not huge salaries. One certainly wouldn't go to work for the *Texas Observer* to get rich and it's unlikely that anybody would ever go to work for the *Texas Observer* if they didn't share our mission for enhancing equality and justice and so forth [Carl].

> Well I would say that it's not so much the good pay; that it's much more a real dedication to getting information that's important to people so they can act responsibly in a democracy and have an insight into what's going on [Pierson].

> ...at KPOV, all our journalists have to have a day job to pay the rent...because there is no money in this. At least if you feel like part of a group doing something and having a bigger impact on a community than say what an individual could, my hope is that...it still allows for sort of an additional motivation, 'I'm doing this for the group, I'm doing this for the team'. You can't quite get the motivation that we get from people that want to play soccer but maybe some day! [Bouknight].

Peter Barr from Australian community station RTRfm just wants to 'pay my rent and buy some fruit' and if he can do that, he will continue to work in his position at RTRfm because he would rather be just getting by, financially, than doing well and feel 'stifled and bored'. Terrie Albano from *People's World* saw her position as 'a gift' and that through the newspaper, she was able to make some level of social change which many people did not have the opportunity to 'feel' in their lives – that potential to make a difference. Along with Margaret Simons from *Crikey* in Australia, Albano was also motivated by a love of writing and a belief in the power of words. Indeed Simons says giving people information 'is one of the most radical things you can do and so in that sense, I might be an activist...'. Darryl Bullock says his greatest motivator is having readers approach him and indicate they enjoyed something he had written, or that a story he had published had made them 'go out and do something [political]'. So the motivations that alternative journalists nominate in answering, simply, 'why they do what they do' are strongly wedded to their perceptions of their own occupation (i.e. as an activist, a journalist and an activist, a journalist and an educator and so on); and to the way they define alternative journalism.

Structures in the alternative newsroom

Along with the journalists'/editors' own motivations, the superficial structures that exist within alternative journalism outlets can also help to define this sector. In a study conducted throughout 1996–97, I discovered that journalists working in alternative press newsrooms in Australia reported an informal structure, often run by editorial collectives rather than by one editor (Forde, 1999). In addition, even when the structure was more formal, many editors commented that they consulted extensively with journalists about angles to take on a story, with the tack taken more of a cooperative decision between the editor and journalist rather than a solely editorial one. Johnstone et al found in 1976 that the organizational structure of alternative papers was a feature which distinguished them from the mainstream, again principally because of the collective or cooperative management arrangements (1976: 165). They similarly found that most people working in the alternative press were multi-skilled and responsible for a range of tasks within their organization:

> ...it is not atypical for them to be involved in the full range of tasks required in production and management...keeping books and managing budgets, correspondence, handling subscriptions and advertising, preparing copy and editing it when necessary, designing layout....In the alternative media 'clean' and 'dirty' work tends to be shared by all (1976: 168).

The *Media and Democracy* project carried out during the early 1990s found that European journalists were also more likely to be involved in several levels of the production process of the newspaper – they would write, edit, and sometimes construct comment pieces about a news event, and had more control over the final representation of the news story (Schultz, 1992b: 6). My earlier investigation detected a similar pattern among Australian alternative press workers who were involved in multiple aspects of the newspaper's production. This is partly due to the size of most alternative publications. Their finances do not allow for a large staff and the general scale of production does not justify specializations. It is also characteristic of small publications (alternative and mainstream), which provide journalists with the opportunity to gain experience at all levels of newspaper production and enable greater control over the final presentation of copy. In 2009–10, similar patterns are evident although now, we can draw on data from the United States and the United Kingdom as well as Australia. In addition, our knowledge extends beyond just the alternative 'press' to all forms of alternative media – journalism produced in a community radio setting, a radical newspaper, an online news site, a free street newspaper with an established web presence, and so on.

In 2009–10, alternative journalists were less likely to talk about the organizational structures of their newsrooms. In my earlier study, a quantitative survey, journalists were asked specific questions about a range of topics, including newsroom structures, which were then quantified and coded. In time, though, I have come to adopt more qualitative methods to my research which gives the data and the views of the journalists' interviews more depth and context – indeed, something alternative journalists themselves endeavour to do. As was the case in the mid 1990s, and for many years before that, all of the *radical political* publications and news websites I canvassed for this new qualitative study followed a fairly structured, editorial committee organizational structure which variously, saw people elected to certain positions on the board of the organization (say, the Socialist Party of Great Britain), with sub-committees elected to run the newspaper and other parts of the organization. Journalists and editors from such political groups generally referred to the fact that the organization was 'democratically run', but ultimately decisions rested with the various Committees. Tristan Miller, from the UK's *Socialist Standard* newspaper, describes a fairly classic socialist newspaper structure:

> The party in general is run democratically. All the members have a say and therefore what the members do is every year, they elect a 10-member executive committee which is charged with the day-to-day running of the party. Now that includes running *The Socialist Standard*. However in practice, the Executive Committee will appoint

an Editorial Committee for *The Socialist Standard*, a sub-committee which is drawn from nominations made from the membership at large. So I think currently we have three members on the Editorial Committee of *The Socialist Standard*.

Others report a looser political affiliation and way of operating, such as the UK's *SchNEWS* which is a flexible cooperation of anarchists and left-wing writers who bring out a widely read, weekly two-page pdf document, which is emailed free to anyone who subscribes and is also distributed in hard-copy by post, and on the street. There is no official editorial structure there although there is an understanding that most contributors and volunteers are drawn from the ranks of left and anarchist organizations (see Atton, 2002: 93–95 for a case study on *SchNEWS*). Jessica Lee, one of the editorial coordinators at New York's *The Indypendent* reports a more structured cooperative decision-making process which has attempted to strike a happy medium between the 'difficult' consensus model which occurs at most Indymedia collectives, and a traditional hierarchical editorial structure. *The Indypendent* is run by journalists from some US Indymedia initiatives who considered the Indymedia open-publishing format sometimes too open to poorly written and poorly researched work. At the time it was established in 2000, Lee says the group was responding to a sense that not all New Yorkers had access to the internet, and so a newspaper was one way of getting their message across to 'walking-class' New Yorkers through street drops and subway distribution (Lee, 2009 – see Appendix A). She describes the process which moves away from the consensus model – requiring editors to consult on every decision about every story – to a working democratic structure:

> ...It's very hard, as you can imagine to try to make all decisions with consensus decision-making. You can't possibly edit an article that way so...Everybody can come together and participate in a facilitated discussion about stories that are in the works, how to report something and how to research something. But the actual selection of the content and the editing is done by what we call our editorial committee...at the same time we do have standards and we do have a hierarchy of experience and people are charged with certain tasks, but ultimately we are accountable to each other.

There were many alternative journalists who also reported a fairly traditional editorial structure, across a range of both commercial and non-commercial, radical and more moderately 'progressive' outlets. *Crikey*, in Australia, for example, is sent as a daily emailed newsletter to paying subscribers and is edited by Sophie Black, with proprietor and journalist Eric Beecher also taking a strong role in the running of the publication. It follows a relatively traditional, although more relaxed, editorial flow and it appears many of *Crikey's* contributors have an enhanced level of control over their content. All the US Association of Alternative Newsweeklies we interviewed also operated with fairly traditional editorial structures (*Texas Observer*, and *Village Voice*); as did independent investigative journalism US news websites like *ConsortiumNews. com;* National Public Broadcasting outlets in the United States; and news-oriented community radio stations in Australia such as RTRfm in Perth and *The Wire* current affairs program which is nationally syndicated through COMRADSAT, the community radio satellite network. Essentially, the organizational structures at work in most contemporary alternative journalism newsrooms are diverse and depend on the history, context and content of the outlet. Undoubtedly though, cooperative and consensus-based editorial structures exist far more frequently in alternative newsrooms than they do elsewhere, and cooperative editorial newsrooms are more likely to occur in leftish publications tied to a particular political organization.

Summary

When Professor John Henningham conducted the first national survey of Australian journalists in the early 1990s, he applied a long-tested quantitative survey to his sample of more than 1,000 journalists which replicated work by David Weaver and Cleve Wilhoit in the United States (1986; 1991; 1994a; 1994b; 1996; and Weaver et al, 2003). One of the questions he asked was designed to test journalists' commitment to the public service ideals of journalism, with a series of questions which asked respondents why they chose journalism as a career. Most nominated their ability at writing as the primary reason for becoming journalists, while issues related to the glamour and excitement of journalism were second most important. Less than four per cent of journalists nominated the desire to serve the public (tested by categories such as 'finding the truth', 'putting things right' etc) as an important reason for entering journalism (1996: 210). Henningham concluded: 'Hence, a strongly service-oriented notion of journalism was not found among Australian journalists...' (1996: 210).[14] The responses of alternative journalists lay in direct contrast, as alternative press journalists were found to be significantly more committed to the public role of journalism, to serving the public interest, influencing public policy through information and providing background and context to information in the public arena. In 2009 and 2010, those values hold true and perhaps appear stronger through these qualitative interviews across three continents than they did through the original Australian-based quantitative survey. Anderson found similarly in her study of information-based programming on 4ZZZ community radio in Brisbane, Australia that agitating for action, educating audiences, and organizing communities of like-minded people were key values of some parts of the community radio sector (2005). This study reinforces that alternative journalists see their primary role as providing context and depth to information already (perhaps cursorily) available in the public sphere; and to both educate *audiences* about issues and campaigns, and potential *contributors* on the practices of alternative journalism. Most importantly, these functions are underpinned by a driving desire to motivate audiences to participate, whether in demonstrations, community life, or other forms of political action. It represents an 'imagining' of journalism as a key player in facilitating the public's involvement in democracy, in a variety of ways.

The next chapter carries on this discussion to examine in more detail how alternative journalists' definitions of their work are demonstrated in the news values they nominate. I will pick up on comments made in Chapter 1 which particularly grappled with issues of definition; and will also be looking for themes in journalistic practice which can be identified across media, across political boundaries, and across time.

---

14 More detail on Henningham's findings can be found in Henningham, 1996 and Henningham, 1995; and for detailed direct comparisons between my 1995–96 alternative press sample, and Henningham's 1991 mainstream sample on issues of public service, the public role of journalism and so on, see Forde, 1999 and 1997b.

Chapter 4

Looking for answers: How alternative media journalists engage their audiences

This chapter is designed to illuminate the daily news decisions that alternative journalists make in deciding what news to cover, how to cover it, and sources to use. As always, their decisions are informed by their own self-definition as journalists and activists, or independent journalists, or journalists and educators and are also informed by their understandings of their publication and particularly their audience. So for this next little while we're attempting to draw connections between the news that alternative journalists produce and the way that news, somehow, engages its audiences so much more than mainstream journalism can do. The basis for those outcomes is complex, and will be teased out as much as possible but essentially, we might be able to categorize the effective decisions as:

1. Alternative journalists prioritize local news or news immediately relevant to their (often) narrow audience.
2. Alternative journalists choose stories that encourage their audiences to participate either in the publication/program or in broader social and political activity.

3. Alternative journalists cover news that their audience may have already read about in the mainstream media, but which was covered inadequately, or cursorily, and they set about pointing that out, and addressing it.
4. Alternative journalists cover stories that their audience will not have seen or read about anywhere else and it is this original content that keeps their audiences coming back and that encourages interactions between the audience and the outlet.

These four principles are demonstrated when alternative journalists (and remember, this includes community, radical, and independent journalists) are asked about the news values they apply and their specific journalistic processes. We will focus on issues of definition first, not self-definition, but a broader description of alternative journalism in order to pick up on themes established in Chapter 1 which we are now able to put in the context of the views from contemporary, practising alternative journalists; and then we will move on to their specific news decisions and the pointers these might contain for engaging audiences.

Descriptions of alternative journalism

Ironically, the key descriptors that alternative journalists use for the work they do is, either, journalism that is *independent of* corporate interests, political interests and government; *or* journalism that is specifically non-corporate and not-for-profit. Some alternative journalists see their role as a partisan political one, representing particular political views and ideals; others see the importance of distance from perceived biases and political parties. The issue of alternative journalism being 'not-for-profit' is an important one, and one which will arise throughout this work. Certainly, as I've identified earlier there is some disagreement within the sector itself about the extent to which alternative journalism can be intertwined with commercial aims (see also Benson, 2003; Schoonmaker, 1987; Atton and Hamilton, 2008). We will continue the discussion here, and undoubtedly, the perception of alternative journalism as 'independent', and/or 'non-corporate and not-for-profit' contains a great deal of overlap and commonality.

Alternative and independent journalists who had a background as some point in time as either a mainstream journalist, or who completed formal journalism training were more likely to define the phrase 'alternative and independent journalism' in terms of the independence of their craft from outside forces. Bob Parry from *ConsortiumNews.com*, Eric Beecher from *Crikey*, Jon Bouknight from KPOV Bend FM (US community radio, Jon also teaches radio at a local community college) and Jessica Lee from *The Indypendent* all defined the work they do in terms of its independence. Still, others such as peace activist Milan Rai, and environmentalist and writer Darryl Bullock also defined 'alternative journalism' as something which was, at heart and quite simply, independent when other forms of journalism were not. Investigative journalist Bob Parry from *ConsortiumNews.com* explained:

> Independent journalism is that we're not really owned by anybody and we proceed, following more the ideals of journalism rather than sort of corporate structure or through a kind of ideological or partisan political structure. We try to approach stories as we see them having merit, it basically means we're not beholden to anybody in particular.

Darryl Bullock defined the work of *The Spark* in terms of his own independence from editorial direction, and the publication's refusal to run any type of advertorial material despite the fact that it did rely on advertising ('business listings') for most of its operating funds. This, for Bullock, meant the publication was free from any ties to advertisers and other commercial interests and their readers were aware of that. *Crikey's* Eric Beecher, and his writer Margaret Simons, were concerned to point out the difference between alternative and independent journalism. Beecher is not the first journalist working in some form of alternative or independent media who has rejected the term 'alternative' as it tends to imply a perpetual status on the margins. Jess Lee from *The Indypendent* expressed similar sentiments in that she felt to be constantly referred to as 'alternative' meant the practices and motivations of alternative journalists would never have the opportunity to become mainstream and this was a semi-regular theme in interviews I conducted in the late 1990s with alternative press journalists. Similarly, some community radio station managers and journalists were concerned about being tagged 'alternative' because of the danger of reducing the whole sector's operations to a simplistic dichotomy of mainstream vs alternative. One participant from an Adelaide, South Australia community radio station explained:

> ...for some people the word alternative is a dirty word because they focus on people with multiple piercings and dreadlocks and all that sort of thing, that's the image, and that's what alternative can mean.

Beecher, on the other hand, is concerned for the partisan and radical connotations that the term 'alternative' carries and always defines himself and his publications as 'independent':

> I think they're [alternative and independent] different. Alternative journalism I think is, as it implies, is something that is different to the mainstream or conventional journalism. It's consciously alternative. It comes from often a different political or ideological perspective. It often has, not always but often has a sort of undertone of being activist, sometimes partisan, that kind of thing...and then independent journalism, I think is quite different. Independent journalism relates to both the ownership and the mindset that stems from that ownership, which is to say, it's largely not the result or the product of large media organizations, but smaller organizations that often are structured or certainly positioned to be aggressively independent in the way they approach journalism.

He pitches his publication as 'vigorously independent' because its approach is less corporate and more informal than the mainstream newspapers that *Crikey* is, conceivably, competing with on some level. This mindset, for Beecher, meant his journalists carried out their work differently, but implies the chasm between a *Crikey* journalist and a mainstream political journalist is evident, but not huge. Milan Rai, UK peace activist and co-editor of *Peace News,* in contrast, also prefers the term 'independent' to 'alternative', but for different reasons:

> To me the term 'independent journalism' which I prefer means a journalism which is not compromised or trying not to be compromised by powerful interests in societies, dominant interests...journalism which is seeking generally to uphold the values of decency and honesty which mainstream media avow.

In the mid 1990s, alternative press journalists reported similar thoughts. Those press journalists writing for more moderate alternative publications were more likely to prefer the term 'independent' to 'alternative', and one indicated that his publication was completely independent from all interests: 'the libel laws are the only things that limit us...if I go to a movie and don't like it I can say so. We're truly independent'. So there is a strong sense that alternative journalism *is* independent journalism, but the independence refers to independence from established power, business and media groups. It has some resonance with Couldry's (2002: 25) definition of 'alternative media':

> By 'alternative media', I mean instead practices of symbolic production which contest (in some way) media power itself – that is, the concentration of symbolic power in media institutions.

This does not encompass all forms of alternative journalism, although based on the evidence it is a key *descriptor,* or trait, of alternative journalism.

Another is the general commitment within the industry to 'noncorporate, not-for-profit' journalism. Carlton Carl from the *Texas Observer,* an investigative publication which has won a number of awards for its political journalism and in 2005 won the Utne Reader's Independent Press Award for Best Political Coverage, says his publication is not partisan but carries a progressive agenda. This publication adopted a 'not-for-profit' status in 1995 to enable it to attract grants from community bodies and foundations and donations from readers. While journalists working at the publication primarily identify as journalists rather than political activists or politically partisan journalists, and are paid for their work, they all have a commitment to social justice and to improving the environment, writing about justice, corporate abuses and corporate control of public officials. This, to Carl, defined the journalism they did and placed it squarely as journalism with a progressive non-corporate agenda.

> I think it [alternative journalism] often means non-profit journalism but not always. Basically journalism that has grown up to provide alternatives, if you will, to corporate-owned media which has become the standard, I guess, in the United States and around the world.

While Carl's publication is officially an AAN newspaper, there is a general recognition within the organization that if the *Texas*

Observer were to apply for membership today, as a non-profit news-paper, it probably would not gain entry to the organization which focuses on alternative *commercial* newsweeklies. Tony Ortega, for example, Editor-in-Chief of AAN's largest circulation newspaper, New York's *Village Voice,* rejected the notion that alternative jour-nalists had to work for free or very little in order to be legitimate: 'you don't have to be a starving journalist to be an alternative jour-nalist'. We will investigate this issue of commercialism in alterna-tive journalism a little more in Chapter 6.

Tristan Miller, from the UK's *Socialist Standard* which has pub-lished since 1904, believes alternative journalism should be free of any corporate backing or sponsorship; and produced either by independent individuals or political groups which have no corpo-rate ties or interests. John Hodge from *SchNEWS* sees his work as something entirely independent not just from advertising inter-ests, but from editorial control as well. Terrie Albano, editor of the *People's World* which is closely aligned to the Communist Party and which had, until 2010, published consistently in hard-copy since 1924 comments that the anti-corporate nature of alternative journalism is paramount.

> I see it in very stark class terms. I see it [as] alternative from corporate journalism and especially in our country, right-wing journalism where many times those two things merge. Since we've had a very strong ultra-right political movement in this country for, I'd say since Reagan was elected that we're still dealing with, so I would say independent from and alternative from those forces and they are quite powerful, especially in the media. I would also add independent from monopoly media because I believe in our country at least, it may be six corpora-tions, [control] something like 80 or 90 per cent of things that people see, read and hear...

Others defined alternative journalism as simply journalism that covered issues the mainstream would not cover; two rejected both alternative and independent as descriptive terms of what they did; and one suggested alternative journalism was for the most part, voluntary. This latter suggestion would describe many citi-zens' journalists, bloggers, fanzines, democratic net-based initia-tives and so on, and it forms an important part of the sector. It does not, however, encompass all that alternative journalism is. From this, we can learn a few more things about alternative journalists and their work, primarily: alternative journalism is almost always *independent of* corporate interests and advertising pressures; it sits *in opposition to* existing power structures whether they be corporate or government; is *sometimes* not-for-profit; and is *sometimes* voluntary and/or amateur. These issues can be tested a little further through an examination of the news values of alternative journalists, so let us turn to that fairly significant task.

Making alternative news decisions

Three key factors drive alternative journalists' news decisions – localism, activism, and 'the scoop'. These findings reinforce the discussion in Chapter 3 as alternative journalists nominated similar factors when questioned about their role in society. Their conceptualization of their work, and their understanding of their purpose, is consistent regardless of the context it is placed within. Localism was found to be a key reason why Australian community broadcasting audiences tuned in, in strong numbers, to their community radio station and alternative journalists rightly identify it as one of the key functions they fulfil. It drives much of their news decision-making. The fact that they also consider activism to be one of the key considerations when deciding whether or not to cover an issue is entirely consistent with their self-definition and with their understanding of the role of alternative journalism in democracy. And the thrill of the chase, the desire to get 'the scoop', is something common to journalists around the world and certainly indicates to me that the people we are dealing with – these activists, educators, citizens' journalists, audiences-come-producers, whatever we wish to call them – are truly journalists who are out there, trying to shine a light wherever and whenever they can.

Localism

Even though many of the outlets covered here did not have specific 'local' audiences they still identified the importance of relating their news to their local audience even if only to show how local issues can be extrapolated out with national and international ramifications. This was particularly the case in newspapers such as *The Socialist* (USA) and *The Spark* (UK) which consistently attempted to draw connections between local activities and protests, and broader international actions. Billy Wharton from *The Socialist* explains:

> In general we look for the kind of story that is connected to an ongoing political campaign. We're also looking for stories that have national ramifications although they are locally based.

Darryl Bullock's publication was more likely to focus on entirely local issues, although his ethical quarterly did cover national issues particularly if it was felt they could affect his audience. His local issues were, as often as possible, connected to activist issues and events so he was regularly combining two of the key news values identified, localism and activism, in his work and editorial decisions. This 'localism' news value shares much in common with the mainstream value of 'impact' and 'proximity' which is taught in journalism schools. It suggests journalists should look for stories which are geographically close to their readers and which, by implication, will have some sort of impact on their lives. Alternative journalists' stated aim to allow the news value of 'localism' to drive their copy resonates with this, but in many cases, and particularly in community radio, it is more ultra-local and focused than much mainstream journalism. The value-added component of alternative journalism in this field of local content is that it often *involves* the locals, either as sources or producers. So the notion of localism does not just relate to the content, but the process – the participation of the local audience as well (see also Meadows, Forde and Foxwell, 2009 for how this works specifically in Indigenous and ethnic minority communities). Carol Pierson from community broadcasting in the United States reinforces the findings of our national audience study of Australian community broadcasting audiences, and also our previous work looking at community broadcasting journalism, particularly, as she identifies that local news and information is one significantly unmet audience need that US community broadcasters have identified. In fact, she notes that specialized music programming which our study found was still an important service of community radio was slightly less important now than five years ago due to the easy availability of specialist music formats through internet radio stations, iTunes, iPods and so on. But local news and information was still something that the internet could not always deliver:

> ...because of satellite radio and the internet a lot of the stations that [had] more emphasis on the music programming are finding that there's more competition. [In some] areas they couldn't get any jazz, they couldn't get any blues, any classical music, but now those are more available so that's not the most unique thing and the local news and public affairs tends to be the more unique thing that they are offering.

In complete synchronicity with the Australian experience, the buy-up of regional commercial radio by two or three major radio players, to the extent in the United States that some organizations now own literally thousands of radio stations, has meant a significant loss of local content. Community radio has stepped into the void, both in Australia and the US. Pierson also reinforces that it is not just local news that has been cut, but access to the station for local musicians, local cultural groups, local political groups and so on which she says have been 'pretty much wiped off the commercial radio stations'. So the takeover of so much local commercial radio by large conglomerates has not just affected local information, but an entire range of local content and culture which Pierson says has been 'abandoned' and again, community radio stations are now trying to fill the gap. Jeff Clarke from public broadcasting, which has a slightly different remit to community broadcasting in the US but also shares a great deal of common ground in the 'bottom 20 per cent of the spectrum', further echoes the findings from the broad Australian studies on community broadcasting in highlighting the ultra-local role that public broadcasting plays in emergency situations. While our Australian study has elsewhere reported on examples of medical emergencies, and the role of community radio during flood and cyclone (Meadows et al, 2010: 177), Clarke further explains:

> Public broadcasting in general is a place [for people] during disaster, people come for news and information about how to evacuate an area or what's going on...So it's really this whole idea of looking at providing content to people that really has an impact on their thinking, their lives, and in some cases, their survival. It's given certainly our enterprise, as well as many others across the US in public broadcasting, a level of capacity that isn't seen and it's also done without any real governmental control or influence on the editorial process.

Richard Karpel from the Association of Alternative Newsweeklies in the US draws the distinction between his member publications, and other independent media projects such as *The Nation* and *The New Republic* which he says are elevated as credible and trustworthy 'progressive' and independently-owned news sources. However, as nationally focused publications they cannot provide the local angle that the alternative newsweeklies can, even though Karpel, in line with the general tenor of the AAN organization, imagines his audience as a 'market' rather than a local community:

> These are not national newspapers, these are newspapers that exist in their cities, in their markets and that's where they're important. Some cover national news, some cover no national news, some are just completely locally focused but all understand that they have their city and their market is what they are focused on.

Scott Spear, Chief Executive for Village Voice Media, notes that 'each city has its own temperature and its own tune that it dances to'. While the AAN publications are run and written primarily by paid staff journalists, the local content seen on community radio and in many of the radical publications is provided by volunteers, usually audience members who have crossed the boundary and, now, are happily both. This connects to approaches which see community media as a process of cultural empowerment, so that content production is not necessarily the prime purpose (Forde et al, 2003; Tomaselli and Prinsloo, 1990: 156) as much as a facilitator of community organization and involvement.

Activism

The connection between local news and local activity, and/or activism, is a common theme for alternative journalists. *The Spark* sees no point in covering local news if it is not for the purpose of encouraging local people to take part in whatever that 'news' might be and surely, this is the absolute purpose of open-source publishing initiatives such as Indymedia (Platon and Deuze, 2003; Atton, 2007a: 74; Hyde, 2002; Downing, 2003: 254). Darryl Bullock explains that while there is an understood line between writers for *The Spark* and readers, the boundary is clearly often crossed with many sections in the magazine dedicated to social issues and activist issues written by freelancers who are, for the most part, actors in the events they are reporting on. Furthermore:

> We do a lot of stuff on local activism, so desperately trying to publicise
> how our readers can get themselves involved in issues, rather then just
> reading about them, reading about somebody else doing something.
> We see it as our job, kind of to help you as a reader to get involved in
> something locally, be it grassroots activism, be it in local food issues,
> be it in stuff that is going on in your local school, whatever else it
> might be.

Jess Lee from *The Indypendent* confirms that a journalist/writer's
involvement in a particular issue does not and should not exclude
them from writing about it, and in some cases they will often be the
best person to do so. This is another area where mainstream journalism deviates, whereby it has developed a 'norm' that the journalist
must be a detached 'observer' of the event rather than a participant.
It makes for dry, disinterested copy which may not offend anyone,
but also does not excite anyone. Lee says *The Indypendent's* coverage of tenancy issues, which is a key social problem in New York
City, is written by a renters' advocate and that the newspaper puts
his copy through the same fact checking and editorial processes
before publication as other contributors, Furthermore, the writer's
position as a tenancy advocate is stated at the bottom of his articles.
It does not affect the credibility of the copy, or the newspaper, to
do so. In fact if anything, readers at least know where he is coming
from and appreciate the publication's honesty. John Hodge says
SchNEWS staff are affiliated with either anarchist activist groups,
or with a range of loosely affiliated organizations such as ecological
groups, activists working on behalf of asylum seekers and refugees,
and this helps drive their news decisions. Atton reported in 2002
that many *SchNEWS* contributors were drawn from the 'Justice?'
collective (2002: 95). Any stories which arise related to protest
action, environmental issues, asylum seekers, student actions and
so on are immediately good copy for *SchNEWS*. Hodge explains:

> 'Information for action' is the main parameter for *SchNEWS*. We
> aren't simply an alternative social-justice/environmental news feed,
> we emphasise those stories which the reader can get involved in. We
> promote upcoming events, cover them as they happen (often counter-
> ing mainstream spin about them) and always include contact details
> for the group or campaign involved, encouraging the reader to become

proactive. Although we often find ourselves doing it, we are aware of the limited use of burdening readers with problems on the other side of the world which they can't do anything about.

Peace News has similar goals, and co-editor Milan Rai, who achieved his own mainstream news coverage a number of times when he was arrested in peace protests associated with the Iraq War, says his news decisions are driven by the power of a story to provide opportunities for readers and their friends, flatmates, work associates and so on to 'do something' about an issue. This function therefore feeds directly into the way he as an editor and writer makes news decisions. Rai analyses these news decisions in a considered way and sees the decisions occurring on two levels:

> ...the primary function of *Peace News* is to assist and encourage and enable people who are seeking to make positive social changes through non-violent means...So our news values are governed by that purpose which means to say that we've got two basic functions. One is to relay to people in a useful and useable form, information about the policies that they are contesting which they can use in their discussions and campaign work and so on...There's another function which is about reporting what it is that people like themselves are doing, to try to bring about positive social change.

Albano picks up on Rai's purpose to provide news which enables readers to draw connections with what they might be doing locally, and what is occurring more broadly. It is almost a way to show politically active people that they are not alone, that initiatives are occurring around their nation and internationally, run by people similar to themselves who are attempting to subvert existing power structures and force change. Albano's *People's World* has an 'editorial vision' to build unity and alliances and to demonstrate 'the power of what can happen when people get together and struggle to make the world a better place'. It harks back to the enduring process in alternative and radical journalism to create solidarity:

> ...we may come across an interesting story about some action and we are always looking for things...that show certain trends in our working class that are in motion that we think are important, including, or especially, for example, international solidarity. So we may show that.

We definitely look for fighting, struggle-oriented stories or stories that show people in motion on national issues that are gripping the country at a certain moment.

This notion of encouraging public discussion, and subsequently encouraging political participation or activity, is central to Habermas' description of the public sphere (1989). He described the public sphere as a neutral zone where members of society have open access to information affecting the public good; where they engage in discussion and make collective decisions free of state domination, and free of assumptions of 'status' (1989: 36). Habermas identifies the media as the manifestation of the contemporary public sphere (1989: 51) and argues the media should provide the arena for public debate 'by reconstituting private citizens as a public body in the form of public opinion' (Curran, 1991: 83). Curran points out that Habermas enables us to extrapolate a model of the public sphere 'where access to relevant information affecting the public good is widely available', and where 'people collectively determine … the way in which they want to see society develop … the media facilitates this process by providing an arena of public debate' (Curran, 1991: 83).

Alternative journalists can be said to be fulfilling this purer 'public sphere' role through their attempts to drive *participation in,* rather than simple *consumption of* debate. Along these lines, Weaver and Wilhoit (1996) identified a new function of US journalists in the late 1990s which they felt had arisen since 1982. They termed it the 'populist-mobilizer' function which partly relied on journalists mobilizing readers to participate (1996: 140). They considered that the arrival of this 'populist-mobilizer' function may indicate that a number of US journalists were, at that time, beginning to practise public journalism (1996: 140; Merritt, 1995; Rosen, 1995). However discussion since the late 1990s has tackled the concept of public journalism as little more than reform within the commercial media environment which has (fairly predictably, given the structure it was working within) mostly failed (Atton, 2003; Compton, 2000; also Glasser et al, 1998).

Getting the scoop

Based on the evidence so far, we can say that alternative journalism is guided by two primary news values – localism, and activism.

There is a third, which emanates from the alternative journalists' will to, among other things, give a voice to the voiceless, make up for the shortcomings of the mainstream commercial media, and probably out of an age-old journalistic instinct to 'get the scoop'. This news value was more evident in some of the more moderate alternative media outlets and/or among those who were run primarily by professionally trained journalists. There was still an alternative motive, but it was based in a journalistic tradition to scoop a competitive outlet. The *reason* for the scoop might be different for an alternative journalist, and we will investigate that, but still, it is based on looking for a new story that no other outlet has covered. Investigative publications such as the *Texas Observer, ConsortiumNews.com* and even the daily *Crikey* (which promotes on its website the ten major stories it has broken in the past ten years) emphasize the importance of covering original news, not merely providing a different perspective on something that is already on the agenda. Bob Parry from *ConsortiumNews.com* says he is not interested in 'value-adding' to a story already covered by the mainstream, but in providing new information that has not yet been exposed. He alludes to what he considers the sometimes unpleasant experience of reading on the internet, he feels it is more of an effort for many readers than picking up a magazine or watching the evening news, so it is important that the news they produce is of the highest quality and originality:

> ... we're not interested in trying to fill up the internet. We're not just trying to write about everything and without anything new to add ... I'm not really eager to spend the time and any resources on that kind of story ... The internet is not an easy medium ... So I want to make it so that people who go to that trouble for us, to go and see our stories come away with something that they haven't had before. They have an understanding of a topic that they may not have otherwise had or we have, we've loaded the story with interesting facts that we would hope inform them in various ways. So that is what I'm looking for, something where we can really give our readers something distinctive and special.

The *Texas Observer's* Carlton Carl says his publication has broken many big investigative stories over the past ten years which have been picked up by local and even national newspapers, one of which was a drug bust in Tulia, Texas, which former

Observer editor Nate Blakeslee exposed as a set-up. The Tulia story involved an undercover drug operation run by local law enforcement officials who had hired an undercover agent to help with the bust. The undercover agent, *Observer* reporters discovered, had planted evidence on and then arrested a 'huge number of citizens of Tulia, and most of them were African American' (Carl). In fact, the bust arrested ten per cent of the town's black population as drug dealers (Manne, 2004). Most of those arrested were sent to prison and the *Observer* gathered the evidence to show that the drug busts were a set-up; those in prison were released and the charges dropped and the undercover drug agent was indicted and convicted. Victims of the drug sting were granted around five million dollars in damages in 2004 (*Texas Observer*, 2004). While a mainstream Dallas newspaper picked up the story and ran with it the day after the *Observer's* Blakeslee broke it, the story was undoubtedly an example of original newsgathering by alternative journalists looking for stories the mainstream did not have the resources or the will to cover. There are more examples of this type of work in Chapter 6, including another story by the *Texas Observer* exposing sexual abuse in the Texas Youth Commission. While Carl puts such stories in the context of the *Observer's* goal to represent racial minorities and to expose the powerlessness of such groups in the face of the established order, Lee's brief at *The Indypendent* is more generally to cover stories that are not covered elsewhere in an effort to 'report the silences' and to give a voice to people 'who maybe aren't getting a voice in the traditional media'. Larry O'Hara from the UK's *Notes from the Borderland* is also looking for stories about the national security services, and the activities of extreme political groups that are not receiving coverage elsewhere. US community radio's Jon Bouknight says even though his radio station, which runs a regular news program, often runs 'soft' community stories, 'the media landscape in the United States is so bleak that even covering a variety of the soft news, a lot of our listeners get stuff from KPOV that they're just not getting anywhere else'. An alternative press journalist in the mid 1990s referred to his desire to scoop the mainstream as the 'Fuck Wow Factor':

> If an article comes into our office and makes the staff go, 'Fuck, Wow!' then we use it. We call it the Fuck Wow Factor. I like to shock.

Indeed, many alternative press journalists from 15 years ago indicated that exclusivity and running original stories is one of their main news criteria. *Crikey's* Margaret Simons said she is, still, after 29 years of practice driven by the thrill of 'getting the story', and her proprietor and fellow journalist, Eric Beecher, explains:

> [Our news decisions] really go to *Crikey's* sort of mission I suppose, or mandate for itself...Often it is information in terms of politics and media that mainstream organizations cannot or do not write about, partly because they're participants, or they have, if you like, a more corporate view of the way they run their journalism.

Many of the comments related to running original material were intertwined with suggestions that, if the story sometimes was not entirely new, the outlet was at least running a new *perspective* on it. So while more respondents indicated that their news values were driven by uncovering original stories, a significant group also said that in most stories they were either aiming for an entirely new story, or failing that a 'behind the scenes', in-depth angle on a story that the mainstream had already covered, in their mind, inadequately. Beecher refers to the importance of running stories the mainstream will not, but also talks about getting 'the story behind the story'. Tony Ortega from Village Voice media, who during his time at the alternative newsweekly *Phoenix New Times* was involved in covering the story of controversial Arizona Sheriff Joe Arpaio (see Chapter 6), enunciates the news values his alternative newsweeklies apply in addition to the standard mainstream values of timeliness, proximity, impact and conflict:

> The additional values would be completeness, would be sympathy, would be some wisdom and some context. Those are the things that tend to be missing from daily paper stories. Don't give me a surface, good guy, bad guy story, I want to know the details, I want to know the grey areas.

Scott Spear, a *Village Voice* executive, similarly argues that while many of the news values applicable in the alternative newsweeklies might also appear in the mainstream, some are certainly unique to the alternative sector. He says standard reporting and journalistic skills are critical, but 'we want them with an attitude. There's plenty of mainstream journalists who have an attitude, they probably just get stories spiked more often than they would if they worked for us'. The more radical *SchNEWS* uses the asylum seeker issue as an example, and says where mainstream newspapers are generally running the line to 'send them [migrants] all back', *SchNEWS* has the license, 'in the face of that type of naked propaganda' to go hard for the alternative viewpoint and argue that refugees and asylum-seekers should be welcomed and supported where possible. Jessica Lee details a concerted and deliberate approach to news values which expands beyond the 'who, what, when, where, why' of commercial practices which, as discussed in the opening sections, have *become* the norm but were not always the norm. Reporters for *The Indypendent*, often drawn from the ranks of ordinary New Yorkers who have attended the newspaper's half-day workshop in basic journalistic training, are asked to draw on their knowledge (also taught in the workshop) about 'how the world works and understand the broad and local systems of power, whether that be social, economic or political systems of power'. They are also asked to make their stories relevant to a global audience, in line with the international flavour of the Indymedia initiatives. Peter Barr from community radio in Australia says much of what his morning news and talk programs cover has already been covered in the mainstream media – issues such as climate change, Aboriginal deaths in custody, even natural disasters which may be linked into broader environmental issues. His news values come back to thoughts about issues that are 'under-reported' and issues that deserve 'good weighty time' in order to be properly understood.

> We're not afraid to talk to people at length and we think our audience appreciates that. Issues are given the full thorough analysis that they deserve.

I found similarly in the mid 1990s when looking at just the alternative press, and there is no doubt that much of the ability of alternative journalists to provide more depth and context to issues is due to the time available to them. At the extreme, publications like *The Spark* are quarterly publications and the deadlines and pressure to 'get the story' that their journalists face is almost incomparable to the pressure of a daily deadline. Indeed, it is certainly the role of such periodical publications to get behind the news, to cover angles and perspectives that the mainstream is unable to due to time and space constraints. Really, though, whether it is a time and space issue, or a political/corporate issue, the fact remains that commercial mainstream media are not equipped to cover many issues in depth. This is not openly recognized by the sector itself and it should be. Their own weekly news magazines, as readable and interesting as they often are, are still operating within the same context and institutional structure. The overarching premise of alternative journalism is what makes it different, what drives its news values and its roles, and particularly what makes its relationship with its audience quite different. It is this issue that we now turn to as a way to conclude this chapter.

Engaging the audience

Along with colleagues from Griffith University, I have reported elsewhere that community media outlets in Australia appear to be engaging their audiences far more successfully than many other media outlets. This is due to two factors: firstly, community broadcasters are intimately located in their communities of interest and cover news and information immediately relevant to this group; and secondly, community broadcasters *involve* their community of interest in their programming, including their news programming, which is appreciated not just by those involved, but also by other audience members. So, in our national study of community broadcasting audiences we found audiences, whether from an ethnic minority, Indigenous, or more mainstream 'generalist' community, consistently identified the non-professional nature of the community radio broadcasters as one of the key reasons why they listened. They perceived that the announcers and the journalists (where they appeared) were 'one of us', part of the community and importantly, that they were approachable. In essence, the audience-producer barrier which is so important to the professional image and reputation of mainstream media organizations does not exist in community broadcasting in Australia. And rather than this meaning that audiences see these stations as amateur, it endears them to their audiences and is one of the key reasons why they tune in (Forde, Foxwell and Meadows, 2009; Meadows, Forde, Ewart and Foxwell, 2009). This study referred broadly to community broadcasting per se, not specifically the journalism it carries out. What this study also showed us, however, was that audience definitions of news and journalism were not necessarily the same definitions that we as media scholars, educators or practitioners might apply. Community broadcasting audiences consider local talk, community announcements, events, information about travelling bands, cultural shows, and local perspectives on broader political issues to be local news. It does not, for the audience, have to come in the form of a news or current affairs program and may be sprinkled quite randomly throughout the day's programming. So when we visited some stations that we understood to run no news or current affairs program, and which had no journalists either employed or volunteering, we were surprised to discover that audience focus groups nominated 'providing local news and information' as a key role of the station. Clearly, the formal definition of 'news' and 'journalism' had no meaning for many audiences, and it was in fact the simple, local, community-connectedness of an outlet that engaged its audiences and indeed, made its audiences members feel like they, too, could become part of the station's programming.

The Council of Europe has overtly recognized the potential role of community media not just in promoting 'social cohesion' (Lewis, 2008), but in facilitating a wide range of audience engagement initiatives. In its 'Declaration of the Committee of Ministers on the Role of Community Media in Promoting Social Cohesion and Intercultural Dialogue' the Council specifically points out the role that community media can and does play in training local community people as producers. The Declaration indicates the Council is 'convinced' of the close relationship that community media have with their audiences, and 'serve many societal needs and perform functions that neither commercial nor public service media can meet or undertake fully and adequately' (Council of Europe, 2009). The Declaration also recognized the 'crucial contribution of community media' in developing media literacy through the direct involvement of citizens in creating and distributing media content, along with the well-established training programs and informal training ground that community media, not just in Europe but around the world, offers to students and ordinary citizens (Council of Europe, 2009; also Forde et al, 2003; Lewis, 2008: 24ff). The special relationship that alternative and community media share with their audiences is documented in a range of studies about citizens' media and movements such as Indymedia, where the audiences *are* the producers. This is also true in some sectors of community broadcasting, and particularly in the Indigenous and ethnic sectors of Australian community broadcasting.

In this study, the connections between alternative journalists and their audiences were particularly pronounced in the citizens' media projects such as *The Indypendent,* and in publications where on-the-ground activists often had a contribution to make to reporting from the frontline such as in *Peace News.* Unlike many forms of citizens' journalism, however, contributions from activist groups and protesters were always fact checked and sometimes rejected on the basis of not fulfilling *Peace News'* standards of accuracy and quality. Jon Bouknight from KPOV radio in Oregon has produced a citizens' journalism handbook which provides a comprehensive introduction for 'citizen journalists' joining KPOV to newsgathering, recording interviews, writing stories, encouraging sources and so on. He emphasizes that 'Community radio works because we contributors *are* members of our community' (original emphasis, 2008: 28). Amy Goodman (in Truglia, 2009) from the respected *Democracy Now!* program explains the importance of the 'ordinary voice':

> When you hear someone speaking from their own experience, whether it's a Palestinian child or an Israeli grandmother, a Venezuelan aunt or a Lebanese uncle, people hear the humanity and they identify... That's the power of community media.

This is also the case in citizens' media projects and internet-based projects such as Indymedia. Arianna Huffington, founder of one of the most successful online news sites of the past ten years, *The Huffington Post,*[15] told a US Senate Sub-committee that the future of journalism lay with digital media platforms and that citizen journalism would not replace 'traditional journalism' but would certainly augment their coverage (Huffington, 2009). She rightly identifies citizen journalists, which *The Huffington Post* uses extensively, as 'engaged readers' who can 'recommend stories, produce raw data for original reported stories, write original stories themselves... By tapping this resource, online news sites can extend their reach and help redefine newsgathering in the digital age'.

---

15 In a surprise move, *The Huffington Post* was sold to media giant AOL for $US 315 million in February, 2011. There has been a wealth of commentary about the pros and cons of the deal which sees Arianna Huffington named as Editor-in-Chief of all news content at AOL (see Pappas, 2011 among many).

Chapter summary

There seems to still be a line in the sand between audience and producer in some sectors of alternative journalism, and again, those publications which include trained, professional journalists among their ranks tend to be those which are less likely to involve audience members in their content production. This also applies to many of the radical newspapers, particularly those which have enough funding and readership to employ full-time staff writers. Community, citizens' and participatory media outlets, on the other hand, strongly involve their audiences in content but, many alternative journalists feel that there is a need for a level of quality control that citizen-generated content does not provide. Importantly, those publications which do not directly involve their audiences in production are still *engaging audiences,* because they are, through their news values of localism and activism, encouraging audiences to engage either in their local communities or in broader civil action. This might involve, as discussed, political activity such as demonstrations and protests, or it might be more moderate civil action such as writing to politicians, attending community hall meetings, or even just taking the time to find out more information about a particular issue. Their added commitment to 'scoop' the mainstream and to identify original stories is further rooted in their desire to empower and activate with new information. Alternative journalists seem to be, in the words of one, 'loath' to run stories which do not give their audiences, at some level, the opportunity to engage. This is the case particularly in those outlets which overtly identify as 'alternative'; and undoubtedly those in the sector which reject that term and prefer the more moderate tag of 'independent' journalism and which still reiterate an abiding commitment to the key news values identified in this chapter. 'Public journalism' tried, but the overarching structure that it operated within could not allow it to occur successfully. The structures that alternative journalists operate within enable them to engage their audiences on one (or both) of two levels: as involved audiences-come-producers; or as citizens engaged in broader action, possibly *as a direct result of* the information imparted by alternative journalism.

The next chapter provides some case studies of the ways in which alternative journalism can work. It looks at the Australian internet-based movement, GetUp!, based on the US *MoveOn.org;* and also explores two examples of alternative and independent journalism which, despite poor resources and a different set of journalistic tools and values, produce news of the highest quality. The key is the motivation of the alternative journalists themselves, as evidenced in some of their words above, combined with the mission of the outlet to produce journalism that makes a difference.

Chapter 5

Connecting with democracy: The 'new' alternative media

There is a significant volume of research and theorizing about the internet, and how it has democratized or revolutionized news and communications. The final section of Chapter 2 presented some discussion about these issues, and laid the foundations for the practical discussions that occur in this chapter. It presented previous research in this field, from Curran, Cammaerts, Atton, Couldry, Downing and many others who offer both theoretical and practical perspectives on new media and their contributions. These new media tools include Web 2.0 (specifically referring to interactive, user-driven content), news aggregators, blogs, email discussion lists, interactive online news sites, open-source publishing, online independent news and commentary, and so on. In this chapter, I will be referring to all of these initiatives as phenomena that have emerged out of the advent of the internet. In this chapter, I want to consider what the internet has actually achieved for alternative journalism. Alternative journalists themselves have views on this, and these will be presented here. Furthermore, I include a case study of a new media example – the GetUp! movement in Australia, an internet-based political group modelled on the US *MoveOn.org* – as a way of coupling the words of our alternative journalists with a contemporary example of an internet-based alternative media initiative. The question that this chapter seeks to answer, based on data from alternative journalists and a case study, is: how has internet technology changed alternative journalism?

If we were to summarize the views of current theorists and researchers about the ability of the internet to democratize communications, it would be this: the internet is a low cost production option that provides opportunities for groups of people to connect, across state, national and international boundaries, on issues of concern to them. Further, it enables alternative news publications which may be struggling financially to fund hard-copy print runs to continue publishing through either a website, emailed pdf document, daily newsletters and so on. Importantly, we could also say research shows the internet has enabled a huge rise in the number of citizen journalists, ordinary people with a view on issues who write blogs, and run online citizens' media projects to have their voices heard. This flippant summary is reinforced properly in Chapter 2, but I need to revisit and repeat it for our purposes here as I wish to test some of its assumptions.

Tempering the discussion – the internet, open-source publishing and democracy

Initially, writers such as Atton (2003), Hodge (2009, see Appendix A), Cammaerts (2008) and others who critique Indymedia and other forms of 'participatory' new media, have concerns about the ability of generic open-source publishing to properly service the type of progressive politics for which they are designed. Cammaerts adds a further dimension in his assessment that the participatory nature of blogging needs to be critically analysed, and identifies five key structural flaws in the blogging model. In particular, he argues, the blogosphere is increasingly 'colonized' by the capitalist marketplace,[16] political and social elites have appropriated it; and states and employers have attempted to control it. On the

---

16 Two of the most popular blogging host sites, *blogger.com* and *blogspot.com*, have been taken over by *Google*. *Google* has also bought out *YouTube*; and the popular social network *MySpace* which also has blogging options was sold to Rupert Murdoch's News Corp (Cammaerts, 2008: 5).

individual level, bloggers are themselves subject to attack, vilification and hate discourse from other bloggers, further emphasizing its limitations. In short:

> The purpose of this overview was to tone down the often-celebratory enthusiasm displayed by many authors about the democratic potential of the internet and the blogosphere. However, this does not imply that the potential for this does not exist, just that there are also actors and phenomena at work that attempt to stifle or limit these potentialities. At the same time, it remains important to reiterate that the internet cannot be treated as being a separate entity from the economic, political and cultural realities of the offline world; it increasingly forms an integral part thereof (2008: 19).

This concern, along with other reservations about the emancipatory and democratic potential of Indymedia and countless other internet-based alternative media forms arises out of the fact that, if the website is open to anyone to contribute, without immediate pre-publishing editorial control, sometimes inappropriate information is going to make its way into the publication. This has certainly been the case with Indymedia in some instances, again as discussed in Chapter 2. Despite the efforts of local editorial collectives to take a stronger editorial role in what goes on their sites, they can only monitor it once it has been published. They have created separate sections of their websites for content that they do not believe is in the broad interest of its readers, but which they do not wish to censor due to an overarching commitment to freedom of expression and the principles of open-source publishing. I want to examine this issue in light of the perspectives of alternative journalists and editors, as their views vary quite considerably. Indeed, comments about the 'power and potential of the internet for alternative journalism' was the theme commented on from the majority of people, and while quantity is not important in qualitative work, it does suggest that this is something (as you might expect) that is taking up a considerable amount of thought time for most in the industry. Many see the internet as a place of astonishing potential. Indeed, at least three of the contemporary publications included in this study would not exist at all without the internet, and the audience and footprint of many others is greatly enhanced by it. However, some are also mirroring somewhat mainstream concerns that the glut of bloggers and citizens'/ordinary/amateur journalists is making it difficult for the public to discern what is good journalism and what is just more 'shooting from the hip', badly researched and poorly written attempts at news commentary. Eric Beecher, from *Crikey,* has a great deal more faith in the ability of audiences to discern quality from 'the rest' and cites political news sites such as *Salon.com*, *Slate* and *Politico* as examples of well-respected and independently-owned online news services. Milan Rai, from *Peace News,* agreed that while he saw the limitations of some news sites like Indymedia, the hard-copy alternative press certainly did not have a monopoly on quality or credibility and cites the US online publication *New Standard News* as a leading example. Beecher felt it was 'absolute nonsense' that publications, as other interviewees had suggested, needed a hard-copy version to add credibility to the website's offerings:

> ... particularly in this field of quality, serious journalism covering the sort of subjects that we are talking about, the audience is not stupid. The audience is quite discerning and the fact that the internet happens to be a medium that is very broad and very diverse and therefore that contains some bad eggs as well as good eggs doesn't mean that people can't tell the difference.

Beecher has to have a great deal of faith in the internet, as his previous ventures in quality, independent journalism through hard-copy forms have commercially failed, primarily due to the incredibly high costs of printing. His purchase of *Crikey* was his attempt to bypass the high printing costs, but still produce quality journalism, with a paid editor, journalist and freelancers. So far, the model is working (see Chapter 6 for more). *Crikey's* writer, Margaret Simons, identified social networking sites, particularly Twitter, as 'the gamechanger', a communication avenue that was going to revolutionize the way news was done and create more and more niche audiences who were targeted with specific information entirely through the internet. Bob Parry is an investigative journalist who left his job with Bloomberg in 2004 to work full-time on *ConsortiumNews.com*, a website he had founded almost ten years earlier. He said the original idea of *ConsortiumNews. com* was to 'take old-fashioned journalism and bring it into the new medium [the internet]' after he perceived the dominance of frivolous news coverage such as the OJ Simpson trial and the Bill Clinton sex scandal. However, apart from these four exceptions, and admittedly, others in the sample recognized the importance of the internet to alternative journalism, a number also expressed reservations about the volume of content labelled as 'alternative journalism' coming through the internet. Some of the interviewees specifically referred to Indymedia and the fact that its open-source publishing format had led to much of it being discredited; others seemed to have quite a traditional mindset, perhaps due to the generation they belong to, that there is nothing like hard-copy. Arianna Huffington, in her address to the US Senate Sub-committee (2009), puts these sorts of comments into context when she suggests that until people who came of age *before* the internet are all gone, hard-copy papers will continue to have a market and an audience:

> There is something in our collective DNA that makes us want to sip our coffee, turn a page, look up from a story, say, 'Can you believe this?' and pass the paper to the person across the table. Sure, you could hand them your Blackberry or laptop … but the instinct is different (and, really, who wants to get butter or marmalade on your new MacBook Pro?)

There is certainly something in what Huffington says, and there is research which suggests the death of hard-copy newspapers and magazines is a long way off yet. And perhaps the reason for this is the mindset which is reflected in some of our alternative journalists, in that the quantity of news available on the internet does not mean quality; and people need to know the difference. For some, the 'quality' is demonstrated if the publication has a hard-copy version because readers then understand there has been some screening or editorial process that the reporting has gone through. Jess Lee, for example, is a committed New York City Indymedia collective member who began her journalistic career as an Indymedia journalist with the Arizona collective from 2004–2006, which she said as a budding writer she found incredibly empowering and inspirational. Her newspaper, *The Indypendent,* is an initiative of the NYC Indymedia collective which also publishes a children's newspaper called *IndyKids* and supports an IndyVideo news team. She says the newspaper came out of what seems to be a sense of frustration from some in the collective with the random nature of open-publishing on Indymedia and the fact that some of the collective members' own well-researched copy which contained interviews, background research and strong writing skills, was published alongside some quite ill-considered commentary. Of course, the Indymedia sites run in a completely different manner to an edited publication such as *Crikey* or *ConsortiumNews.com*, so the analogy to be drawn is not between open-source publishing and *all* internet publishing. However, the thoughts of Lee and others about open-source websites and indeed many unedited forms of journalism such as blogging are an interesting indication of how alternative journalists themselves value good journalism. Lee says new writers wanting to become involved in *The Indypendent* are first pointed to the Indymedia website to work on their style and to practise what they have been taught in the half-day 'Basic Journalism' workshops that Lee runs, but that on the whole she sees limitations with the IndyMedia model. Indeed, Lee seems a little 'over' the whole 'potential of the internet' issue and is calling for a return to more thoughtful journalism:

> ...this is [just] from my point of view is that, there was never a strong enough emphasis on education [in Indymedia]. So it's like, we're going to create all these websites for communities around the world so they can have access, like you can publish, but we're not encouraging people to learn the skills of journalism which aren't necessarily difficult but you do need to be taught them and you do need to practise them. Things like critical thinking, research, interviewing, note taking, organizing your thoughts, learning how to write a concise news story or feature and I think Indymedia should have attacked the *institution* of journalism but not the *craft* of journalism [my emphasis].

John Hodge from *SchNEWS* also identifies a general sense within alternative media that Indymedia has its limitations as a source of good content, and that while it has achieved an enormous amount in the past decade it is 'vulnerable to obsessive nutcases – as well as agents of the state and corporations, as we saw in the UK in 2010'.[17] He suggested that the open-publishing model was now 'at a juncture point', particularly with the rise of social networking sites. He feels Indymedia is '...falling between the poles of – on one

---

17 Hodge refers readers to a *SchNEWS* piece, http://www.schnews.org.uk/archive/news755.php.

hand – established publications who produce edited material, and on the other, sites who allow unedited self-publishing... and there's been an explosion of them since the birth of Indymedia in 1999'.

Milan Rai from *Peace News* refers to the 'age of Indymedia' and the impact this has had on people's perceptions of some open-source publishing and online citizens' media intiatives:

> I think that in the age of Indymedia for a newspaper like *Peace News*, there is still a role which I can't pretend that we fulfill to the extent that we'd like to, but there's a role for the considered, perhaps expert overview of what is going on. Indymedia news is fantastic at telling you that someone just occupied a factory in Nottingham, or a facility in Nottingham that's connected to the arms trade and you can see photographs of it straight away. Indymedia is not so good, necessarily at following through on that story to tell you exactly what happens to those people because it just depends on what people are most interested in doing on Indymedia....

Rai notes that in more recent times there have been some attempts by editorial collectives to distinguish between copy that has been vetted and edited by the collective to some extent, and copy which follows the original open-source publishing model and is 'self-posted', but that the sites still have their limitations. Jess Lee from *The Indypendent*, Tony Ortega from *Village Voice* and Darryl Bullock from *The Spark* all voiced a somewhat traditional viewpoint of media (which many online mainstream journalists are now confronted with) that the print version represents a 'more credible' form of journalism. Ortega said most of his writers wanted to be in the hard-copy first, but due to space constraints only the very best work went in the printed version, and everything else went online once it had gone through editorial processes. Bullock voiced similar sentiments to Arianna Huffington about the importance of people sitting down with his publication with a coffee, and said the internet 'would never take over the hard-copy' but would continue to build as a complement to the printed version. Lee is not particularly averse to the online versions and indeed, as an Indymedia collective member is clearly committed to the potential and ideals of empowered, citizens' publications. But she cannot help but feel that something extra is provided by holding the hard-copy of a publication together, as a team, and the broader community and social connection that this creates. Her words reverberate with our findings in the community broadcasting studies, which found that the *content* of community media was only as important, or perhaps not quite as important, as the cultural and community processes involved in producing it. Lee gains this sense of teamwork and community-building from publishing *The Indypendent* that she did not feel in the daily publishing ritual of Indymedia. And as a Generation Y'er, she is notably tired of the incessant 'need to be first' and continually in-action nature of social networks and news websites.

> ... there's a newer movement that's starting called the slow journalism movement and I love that idea because I think it's time for us to push back a little bit and just say, 'back off, we're not going to update our blog every five minutes and just wait until we produce the newspaper. Or just wait until we put out our website material every week'... We zoom around that fast and if you expect to be consuming news that fast, you're really only going to get material that's on the surface level... the whole Twitter and blogging and Facebook, it's all just like so demanding, it wears you thin.

Her frustration with the online world is tied to a broader call from alternative journalism for people to be active, and to participate in their communities. She says audiences and producers 'just need to get off the computer and go and engage in the world... go to the City Council, go to something where you're not wanting the newest news all of the time...'. Milan Rai also notes that there is a difference, for him, in making face-to-face contact with people and talking to them about the ideals of peace and the anti-war movement, which does not compare with handing over a URL for them to look up. Larry O'Hara from the UK's *Notes from the Borderland* feels the internet is having a 'deeply corrosive effect on political discourse in ways that I don't think people have even begun to manage [or] to quantify'. Lee also points to broader issues about journalistic quality and news accuracy which is being borne out, on a broader stage, by studies of online mainstream news websites which are finding that the 'pressure to be first' is often threatening 'the pressure to be right'. Online journalists and editors reporting on Australia's devastating bushfires in February 2009 told researchers they now tended to verify facts *after* the story had been published, rather than before as is journalistic convention (Gawenda and Muller, 2009: 12–13). It suggests a 'not wrong for long' attitude which contravenes the rigour of fact checking and accuracy that is supposed to form the basis of all good journalism (Johnston and Forde, 2009: 2011).

Jessica Lee from the *The Indypendent* notes a similar occurrence in the coverage of the November 2009 mass shootings at the US Fort Hood Military Base, the world's largest military base, which saw 12 people gunned down by a single shooter, an Army doctor and psychiatrist. Initial reports indicated there was more than one shooter, and that the doctor had been killed during the incident, which he was not. Lee recounts:

> The first facts that were reported, almost all of them turned out to be wrong and it was because everyone was rushing to publish the story before they even slowed down to really get into it...and then, you had people on Twitter, on Facebook that were just putting out of all sorts of mistruths. I don't think that serves our society very well. If you're considering journalism to be supports, checks and balances in our country or however it is described around the world, you need to let them go in and do their job and then the next day, or [if it's a pressing issue] in a few hours, they will have a story for you.

Milan Rai said he found much user-generated content or citizens' journalism was unreliable, but this was also the case with some hard-copy publications. It was always his job as editor, and that of his journalists, to use any information they received as a starting point only and to begin a process of verification and fact checking, regardless of where the information came from. There is something of an internet-weariness among some of the alternative journalists interviewed. I note the limitations of the study here, and the majority of journalists interviewed were not exclusively online bloggers and online news producers, although all of the journalists and editors interviewed had some presence and content on the internet, to varying degrees.

This has been a fairly lengthy way to say that it was an unexpected finding that some, in fact quite a few, people working in alternative journalism expressed reservations about the plethora of 'alternative' online media and the implications this has for perceptions of 'quality' alternative journalism. Still, many saw great empowerment potential in the internet, particularly as a tool for organizing activist groups and for providing publishing opportunities that might be impossible in the far more expensive hard-copy printing environment. *Crikey, The Huffington Post, The Onion, Salon.com, Slate, Politico, OpenDemocracy.org*, and an absolutely huge number of other mediated and unmediated political news sites are providing a broad range of new, high quality journalism. Particularly, research indicates the

value of the internet for alternative media is not just (or even primarily) in the content it produces, but, as with community broadcasting,
in the community it creates and the organization that it enables (Pepe
and Gennaro, 2009; Hyde, 2002; Kidd, 2003; Skinner et al, 2010).
And it is this organizational ability of the internet that we will pursue
now, primarily because it draws upon one of the primary themes of
this study as espoused by alternative journalists, which is the central-
ity of participation and activism to the work they do.

GetUp! (and out, and do something)

The Canberra Press Gallery is based in the nation's capital and
reports daily on the Australian Parliament, similar to the US
Whitehouse press gallery or the United Kingdom's Parliamentary
Press Gallery. Every June, they hold their Midwinter Charity
Ball. It is a big event, not for ordinary people but for politicians,
members of the press gallery and media executives. The crown-
ing event of the Midwinter Charity Ball is a light-hearted auction
which auctions off political leaders' time to the highest bidder.
Usually, corporate bidders and well-heeled lobby groups use the
opportunity to buy the ear, usually for a day, of a politician in the
senior ranks of Parliament – someone in a decision-making position. The money raised by the bids is given to charity. This year the
Ball and its auction made the front-pages of all Australian newspapers and most television and radio news programs for one reason:
an internet-based activist group GetUp!, which is based on the
United States concept *MoveOn.org*, had won the auction to buy
the time of the conservative Opposition leader Tony Abbott.[18] The
punchline was that they would force the Opposition leader, who
had promised to toughen refugee and immigration laws if elected[19]
to spend one day with an Afghan refugee.

   GetUp! (2010a) asked for donations for their bid from their
large email list of interested Australian citizens, who are regularly

---

18 Mr Abbott had offered bidders a one-day surfing lesson with him, as he is a
keen triathlete.
19 One of the Party's four key promises in the recent Federal election was to 'Stop
the Boats', referring to the policy of 'turning around' Australia-bound boats carrying refugees from various parts of Asia and the Middle East, usually coming
out of Indonesian ports. See, for example, http://www.liberal.org.au/Latest-
News/2010/10/28/Sixth-boat-in-a-week.aspx.

targeted with email campaigns for donations and action on a range of progressive political issues such as asylum seekers, climate change, Aboriginal social justice, and particular environmental campaigns. GetUp! asked its members:

> These opportunities [the winning bid at auction] are normally claimed by mining magnates and other corporate donors, but instead you can give that opportunity to a voice that wouldn't normally be heard in the corridors of power, with **the proceeds of the bid going to worthy charities (not to Mr Abbott)** [their emphasis].

The email campaign featured Riz Wakil, a former Afghan refugee who had spent nine months in Australia's Curtin detention centre, a prison-like facility for all refugees and asylum seekers who are awaiting immigration processing. The GetUp! email pleaded: 'If Tony Abbott becomes Prime Minister this year, he plans to take Australia back to [an] era of cruel and ineffective refugee policy that Riz experienced first hand.... If we want to change the refugee agenda in this election, we need to neutralize Tony Abbott's downward spiral on refugees'. GetUp! told members it had identified 'refugees with the courage to take a surfing lesson with Tony Abbott and over breakfast, share their powerful stories' (2010a) and wanted their list of members to contribute funds, as soon as possible, to help them win the auction.

When the time came for bidding, the GetUp! bid won the day with Tony Abbott for just over AUS$16,000.[20] The most obvious after-effect was not the surfing day that the refugee had with Tony Abbott, although this may have had some impact on Mr Abbott's views on refugees, but the intense media coverage that GetUp! received as a result of its successful bid which is a major aim of its campaigns. It was free mainstream media coverage for their issue, and Riz Wakil, an unlikely mainstream media source, was interviewed by a range of news and current affairs programs (GetUp! 2010b). Every major television station and all major morning newspapers, along with the national broadcaster, ABC-Radio and ABC-Television, ran with stories about the GetUp! coup[21].

---

20 The equivalent of about US$15,300 or €11,400.
21 Go to www.getup.org.au/campaign/TheWinningBid to see this campaign in detail; and to http://www.youtube.com/getupaustralia#p/u/0/tsPbVNsfFVE for a video summary of the mainstream media coverage gained.

The campaign was a prime example, and really, just the latest in a long list of successful attempts by GetUp! to mobilize people (or at least, get them to care enough to help GetUp! staff and volunteers do something) on contemporary progressive issues. This campaign to highlight the plight of refugees came on the back of other successful highly paid television advertising campaigns attempting, among other things, to expose the 'mistruths' of the coal industry in the climate change debate; and another which sought to highlight the biases of the 2008 Beijing Olympics broadcaster, Channel 7, by attempting to place a prime-time advertisement about the plight of Tibetans during the Opening Ceremony, which Channel 7 refused to run (GetUp! 2008).

GetUp! promotes itself as an 'independent, not-for-profit community campaigning group':

> We use new technology to empower Australians to have their say on important national issues. We receive no political party or government funding, and every campaign we run is entirely supported by voluntary donations[22] (GetUp! 2010c).

It was established by two Australians, Jeremy Heimans and David Madden, who had graduated from Harvard University's Kennedy School of Government and for its first four years was fronted by Executive Director Brett Solomon. Solomon 'moved on' to a new initiative in 2009, *Avaaz.org*, the new project of Heimans and Madden and four other 'social entrepeneurs'.[23] The GetUp! organization is now fronted and all its correspondence is signed by new National Director Simon Sheikh. GetUp! has the sort of financial support and audience following that many alternative journalism outlets can only dream about. They have 378,000 signed-up members[24] who receive their regular emails, and are often able to raise between AUS$50,000–$100,000[25] within a short space of time,

---

22 The words cited run as a regular 'rider' at the bottom of all GetUp! emails to members requesting support for particular campaigns.
23 http://www.avaaz.org/en/about.php.
24 Total Australian population is about 22 million, so the GetUp! membership represents just under 2% of the total population. Just by way of comparison, in the United States this would equate to around 5.25 million members; or 1.1 million members in the UK. *MoveOn.org* claims just over five million so the movements are directly comparable in terms of population reach.
25 US$47,000–US$93,000; €36,000–€72,000.

for particular television advertising campaigns, and novelty events such as the Midwinter Charity Auction which receive high levels of mainstream coverage.

The newer and far more international *Avaaz.org*, established in January 2007 is boasting 8.25 million members[26] which, it claims, makes it 'the largest global web movement in history' (http://www.avaaz.org/en/about.php). *Avaaz.org*, which was co-founded by global civic advocacy group Res Publica and the US *MoveOn.org*, operates in precisely the same way as GetUp! and claims to not just be involved in online advocacy but also to have assisted in the organization of 10,000 'rallies, flashmobs, vigils, marches and other online events' since 2007. *Avaaz.org*'s latest campaigns include a 1.2 million strong petition against whaling, and a petition aiming for 500,000 signatures against offshore drilling following the Gulf of Mexico oil spill disaster. The well-respected *Huffington Post* gave *Avaaz.org*[27] their 'Ultimate Gamechanger in Politics' Award' and the organization, which looks and feels the same as GetUp!, *MoveOn.org* and other similar online action groups, says their 'command of the tools of online organizing, and [our] ability to simultaneously field them in every part of the world, is unique' (Avaaz.org, 2010).

The key seems to be the immediate impact of the campaign – alternative news sites and publications attempting to raise that sort of money cannot do so, even with quite a loyal and large readership (the Australian online news magazine *New Matilda,* which closed in June 2010 after five years, is a case in point). The success that GetUp! experiences is due to its savvy use of new technologies such as email and Facebook which, similar to *Crikey's* daily emailed newsletter, target people during the day, usually progressively-minded citizens working in office environments. Both *Crikey* and GetUp! cleverly send most of their members emails close to lunchtime, when office workers are ready to take a break and see what is happening with online news sites, discussion lists and so on. Donations to GetUp! can be made for specific campaigns within a matter of five minutes through a secure internet site; a

26 Figures as at April 2011, and up from 5.5 million members only nine months earlier, in July 2010.
27 Avaaz means 'voice' in the Iranian Farsi language and, according to the *Avaaz.org* website, in several other Asian and Middle Eastern languages as well.

tax-deductible invoice is immediately generated by the system; and GetUp! provides all its members who feel strongly about a particular issue with a ready-to-go email that can immediately be posted out to a wide network of friends, discussion groups, news lists, Facebook pages and so on. Whether GetUp! would have the same level of success in a traditional print campaign, or through announcements on community radio, is almost rhetorical – they would not. The immediacy of the internet technology, the time of day and the way it targets people, and its discourse which makes members constantly feel part of a 'broader movement', is the key to its success.

Media use and political action

Boyle and Schmierbach (2009) note that while readership of traditional media such as newspapers has generally been shown to have a positive influence on traditional forms of political participation such as voting, writing letters to politicians, and donating money to political parties, there is less research conducted on how new media forms, and more traditional *alternative* journalism forms, may impact on levels of political participation such as protest. They draw on the example of GetUp!'s American equivalent, *MoveOn.org*, which Boyle and Schmierbach note have used their resources to reach out to large audiences, 'and exert influence on how they are presented in the mainstream media' (2009: 6). They note, however, that even well-supported groups such as GetUp! and *MoveOn.org* are not in full control of how the mainstream media represent their campaigns and, 'as such, there can be a distinct difference between the message the group would like to send and the one that is ultimately presented by the mainstream media' (2009: 6). The authors discover a strong connection between both traditional and protest political action, and the use of alternative media. This is an important finding not just for this discussion, but for the work as a whole and reinforces suggestions from alternative journalists that the provision of 'mobilizing' (Stanfield and Lemert, 1987) information positively affects audiences' willingness to act (also Schussman and Soule, 2005). This is the case regardless of whether the audiences received the information from a traditional 'print' alternative media outlet, or from an internet-based alternative site. Boyle et al also note that much research about the impact of new media on political activity has focused on its potential to involve people in traditional political actions, such as voting, donating to political parties and so on, but there is a significant gap in research which examines the impact organizations such as GetUp! and *MoveOn.org* might have on *protest* action, and non-traditional forms of political action (i.e. activism) that traditional media does not enable (Shoemaker, 1984; Schussman and Soule, 2005). They have found a positive correlation between the two, but note the field requires more work:

> As a variety of new technologies emerge online, making blogs and other individual channels of expression commonplace, researchers must consider how these tools facilitate non-traditional activity. Too often, investigations of such 'new' media focus on old, mainstream forms of political action (2009: 14).

Perhaps the biggest drawback of the wonderful potential of the online technologies is its limited international reach. Latest figures from 2010 indicate that while internet take-up is increasing, it still penetrates to only about 29 per cent of the world's population (Internet World Stats, 2010). So the community and citizens' media initiatives in India, Sri Lanka, Indonesia and Nepal that Tacchi and her team research and write about (2008); the Rodriguez team's projects in Colombia (2010); and the support for the development of community radio more broadly in emerging nations in the European Union (Council of Europe, 2009) remain extremely important. The online advocacy movement, epitomized by GetUp!, *MoveOn.org* and all its different incarnations, including a range of far more radical activist online organizing tools, are having a significant impact on the way developed countries and their citizens receive their political information and act upon it. Still, more than two-thirds of the world remains outside this realm and community-based media initiatives, hard-copy newspapers and more traditional forms of alternative journalism will continue to play an important role in those countries.

Chapter summary

I return to Bennett's earlier words, drawn upon in Chapter 2 in my discussions about the contribution of the internet to a 'new age' of alternative journalism. In essence, the internet, and in our case, alternative journalism on the internet, is a new way for people to communicate their message, organize community or political activity, and *form* specific communities of interest. However, it is, primarily, a new way of doing things – and is used in less than one-third of the world. In developed nations, it may certainly be a more *effective* way of doing things, and perhaps *The Huffington Post's* award to *Avaaz.org* as the 'Political Gamechanger' is warranted, but it does not essentially change what alternative journalism is or does. Bennett suggests the differences that internet technology makes are more the result of the 'human context' of the communications form, rather than the medium itself (2003: 19). Bennett's words also help us to understand the reservations expressed by some of the alternative journalists earlier, that in fact for them, as activists or journalists trying to convey their message in a credible, thought-provoking way, the plethora of material available on the internet may in fact be giving a heightened sense of credibility to more traditional forms. It is not how the internet does it e.g. open-source publishing, Facebook political groups, tweets from journalists and protesters etc but what the content is, and what the *impact* of the content is in connecting with audiences, forming communities and jump-starting civic participation. These three factors can be achieved by *any* media, and by any journalism, if it is done well. The internet is now a tool to assist alternative journalists to achieve this.

Chapter 6

Throwing out the bathwater (but not the baby): Objectivity, 'professionalism' and the economics of alternative journalism

The mainstream media characteristics that I have alluded to throughout this work currently dominate journalistic practice. As the early chapters point out, this has not always been the case but certainly, since the mid 1800s the notion of objective, professional journalism, which forms the basis of most contemporary understandings of 'journalism', have prevailed. Zelizer's analysis is comprehensive and appropriately pinpoints the various functions that dominant forms of journalism attempt to undertake in most democracies (2005). There is an understanding, though, that all Zelizer's six characteristics, and others that are identified by a variety of undergraduate journalism texts and attempts to define the craft/profession, are underpinned by a notion of fair, balanced, perhaps objective news. Curran (1991: 102ff) certainly sees that this form of journalism, with all its drawbacks, does play and should play a role in any contemporary democracy, *alongside* other forms of media such as adversarial and partisan media which is more closely aligned to the types of alternative journalism under discussion here. This work follows the model set by Curran which suggests a far more diverse and wide-reaching alternative journalism sector than currently exists. This chapter necessarily engages with the key mainstream journalism practices that we know and critiques them, in a somewhat brief manner as this has been done by many others far more comprehensively than I can do here (for example, McChesney, 2008; Bagdikian, 1983; Curran, 2005; Lewis, 2001; Hamilton, 2004; Schudson, 1995; Gitlin, 1980; Gans, 1979; Tuchman, 1978; Herman and Chomsky, 1988). I discuss this in the context of the practical findings that I will feature in this chapter, which is alternative journalists' views on objectivity and, connected to this, the economics of the industry. If we accept that the notion of objectivity and a type of journalistic professionalism arose as a direct result of the need for commercial media to appeal to the broadest possible audience, and this seems to be well-established, then it follows that non-commercialism in alternative journalism could perhaps be the very cause of its diversity. However, the findings show that it is not that simple, and there are some examples in alternative journalism of commercially successful, but still alternative, media outlets. The data from alternative journalists, proprietors and editors suggests that while many are wedded to the notion of 'alternative journalism as non-profit journalism', which is certainly one part of the sector, others are looking for ways to appeal to a broader audience, make a moderate living and grow the outlet, even if it does not mean reaping in millions of dollars.

This chapter is therefore designed to provide some inside knowledge for the alternative media sector about funding models that do and do not work, but first we must confront the commercial nature of most mainstream journalism and the professional norms which serve it.

Examining objectivity and 'professional ideology'

Judith Lichtenberg asserts that objectivity is one of the fundamental norms of journalism which is inextricably intertwined with the concepts of truth, fairness, balance, neutrality, and the absence of value judgements: 'in short... objectivity is a cornerstone of the professional ideology of journalists in liberal democracies' (1991: 216). But Lichtenberg recognizes objectivity has come under fire and sets out to defend the concept against its critics. She says the very criticism of the media as being unobjective or biased implies that objectivity is therefore possible (1991: 218). A more succinct argument in favour of the notion of objectivity is provided by Abramson, who identifies it as a simple 'commitment to telling the truth', and rejects the suggestion that it encourages bland, safe journalism (1990: 253; and indeed some in the alternative media are attempting to 'take back' this term by redefining it as truthful, credible journalism rather than the 'neutral' or 'detached' journalism that it has come to mean). Abramson views employment of 'objective' news principles as the only way the media can effectively act as a watchdog on the government (1990: 253). Denis McQuail also sees many benefits in the convention of objectivity, because it allows agencies of state and various interest groups to speak to the public without fear of undue distortion or intervention by the mediators (journalists). It also enables media outlets to distance their editorial content from advertising material (2010: 201). He argues objectivity has an affinity, 'in theory at least', to Habermas' model of undistorted communication in the public sphere (2010: 200). Objectivity is undoubtedly considered by some as a vital professional norm for journalists in Western democracies (Lichtenberg, 1991: 216; Westerstahl, 1983: 407; Esaisson and Moring, 1994: 272; Stovall, 2005: 33–35), although most, including McQuail (above) note that its development and acceptance is connected to the media's need to appeal to a wide market, for commercial purposes. Schultz points out that while the United States, Australia, Britain and Canada have accepted the development of objectivity as a by-product of the commercial media, the European intellectual tradition has always been more sceptical about claims to objectivity, arguing that objective or even neutral accounts of reality were not possible (Schultz, 1994: 44). Patterson says there are two reasons for this difference in attitude between Europe and the United States; firstly, the commercialization of the press and the necessity to reach the widest audience through non-partisan content came later in Europe than in the United States; secondly, continental Europe believed that objective or even neutral accounts of reality were not possible because individual biases would always determine the outcome of accounts of reality (Patterson, 1992: 5). This second claim has dominated much of the critical analyses of the mainstream media and objectivity. Udick suggests that while the 1949 United States Hutchins Commission identified the separation of fact from opinion as a major tenet of objective reporting, it also found the media should give context or meaning to facts. However, the only way facts can be given meaning is for the journalist to express opinion, as context requires 'a weighing of events and values ... it requires use of judgement' (Udick, 1993: 152).

Journalists and editors involved in the alternative press are also critical of the mainstream's claims to objectivity, and the bulk of the alternative press has rejected the 'neutrality' line and opted for open, advocacy journalism. Eric Utne, former editor of the bi-monthly collection of the 'best of the alternative press' in the United States, the *Utne Reader,* says the American media's pretences at objectivity are transparent. Utne says professional commentators are paired off in 'ritual combat', suggesting by their 'juxtaposition and heat' that they are offering real choices (1991: 2).

> If a Democrat ventures an opinion, reporters search for a contrary viewpoint from across the aisle 'for balance'. But this supposed choice and balance is illusory. Tweedledum and Tweedledee. No wonder Americans hate politics.

Brian Whitaker, one of the founding contributors to the alternative newspaper set up in the 1970s, the *Liverpool Free Press,* defended the newspaper's decision to reject objectivity, and clarified that this rejection did not mean the newspaper misrepresented the truth (1981: 105). The paper readily took sides, but not dishonestly – readers were aware of the political stance of the newspaper, and read it with that knowledge. Nelson says the British underground press of the 1960s and 1970s was vital to the public sphere, but these publications made no claims to objectivity and this, along with differences in language, style, colour and content, distinguished the alternative press from the 'hypocritical "objectivity" of Fleet Street' (Nelson, 1989: 47).

In many cases a publication that claims the notion of objectivity risks misleading its readers – newspapers 'are not a mirror of society', they are 'hardly mere neutral looking glasses' (Hollingsworth, 1986:

290; also Hamill, in Zelizer, 2005). Zelizer notes, though, that 'Journalism as a Mirror' is indeed one of the dominant six ways that journalists reference their work, implying journalism is a process of observation, without filtering processes, which reflects on 'objective happenings taking place in the real world' to the public (2005: 69). The European tradition suggests that a newspaper which is openly advocatory is more honest than one which claims complete objectivity. Thomas Patterson prefers that journalists retain loose links to political causes and movements, rather than attempt to claim 'objectivity'. He argues that a news system dominated by 'free' and independent journalists, detached from 'political moorings', produce news that underplays political ideas and is consensual, rather than competitive in content – a 'completely "free" press does not promote a wide-ranging political debate' (Patterson, 1992: 2–3). Patterson believes the competition over ideas produced by media that includes journalists with political ties encourages more vigorous debate, and more truly reflects the competition over ideas in the political arena and the broader public sphere (1992: 3). Bagdikian reinforces that objectivity has led news to be dominated by politically neutral subjects like crime and natural disasters at the expense of what he calls 'intelligent examinations into the causes of events' (Bagdikian, 1983: 132). The ongoing State of the News Media reports, generated by the United States Pew Project for Excellence in Journalism, make consistent findings that investigative and quality journalism is becoming increasingly difficult to produce in newsrooms that are becoming 'thinner and shallower' (Kovach, Rosenstiel and Mitchell, 2004: 27; see also Pew Project for Excellence in Journalism, 2003–2008, and go to *stateofthenewsmedia.com*).

The difficulty for the critics of objectivity is that it is so deeply entrenched as a professional norm of Western democratic journalism and while the market model dominates news media organizations, this will continue to be the case. Proponents of professionalism and objectivity in journalism place their faith in *individual* journalistic independence and commitment – if journalists are strong, and defend their independence and their integrity they will be able to combat commercial, editorial and proprietorial forces (Henningham, 1991: 3; Hadenius, 1983: 200; Schultz, 1994: 50). Charters of editorial independence and industrial action are two ways that supporters of the 'professionalism' of journalism believe journalistic integrity can be maintained within the commercial framework. Patterson's research found that more than two-thirds of journalists defined freedom of expression in terms of their own, and their news organization's rights rather than the public's right to diverse information which reflected a narrow professionalism which did not take account of journalists' place in the larger democratic scheme (1992: 15). Patterson also finds evidence that increased professionalism has caused greater homogeneity in news content. He blames professionalism for the failure of the news media to create a diverse marketplace of ideas. In his survey, United States journalists ranked highest on the professionalism index (determined by their attitudes to objectivity, impartiality, neutrality) and also ranked lowest on the diversity index (1992: 9). His international study of professional values across a range of countries found that, in the nations such as the United States, 'the same news stories are highlighted each day by the great majority of newspaper and broadcast organizations from coast to coast' (1992: 4). This narrowness can be attributed directly to the requirement for 'professional and objective' journalism, which forces news reporting to be driven increasingly by events rather than issues. Relatively minor editorial decisions such as which facts and events are more important do not constitute diversity of information, and are 'a far cry from a competitive marketplace of ideas' (Patterson, 1992: 4). Zelizer notes that the 'sixth sense' or 'nose for news' that most journalists use as a way of defining their work is a leading reference point for the industry (2005: 68), but Patterson interprets this as a common definition of news, developed out of professional training and experience which again, sees the same top stories appearing each day across a huge range of media outlets (1992: 4). Gurevitch and Blumler further argue that adherence to professional definitions of news values act as a powerful force for conformity and ensure journalists all arrive at the same decision when considering 'What is the most significant news today?' (1990: 282; Zhong and Newhagen, 2009).

Concerns about the rise of commercialism in newspapers extend back more than 50 years, when family-owned newspapers began to focus on profit, sometimes at the expense of editorial copy. I.F. Stone, a United States journalist who established the successful *I.F. Stone's Weekly* in 1953, wrote of the mainstream media:

> The fault I find with most American newspapers is not the absence
> of dissent. It is the absence of news. With a dozen or so honourable

exceptions, most American newspapers carry very little news. Their main concern is advertising. The main interest of our society is merchandising. All the so-called communications industries are primarily concerned not with communications, but with selling ... Most owners of newspapers are businessmen, not newspapermen. The news is something which fills the spaces left over by the advertisers. The average publisher is not only hostile to dissenting opinion, he is suspicious of *any* opinion likely to antagonize any reader or consumer (in Johnson, 1971: 6).

Indeed, anyone who has worked in newspapers is aware that the news is placed in the 'hole' that is left after paid advertisements have been placed, and eye-catching photographs have been put in. The advertisements drive how much space there is for news; the news does not drive how many advertisements can be run. Johnson and Wanta (1993), among others (Ruotolo, 1988; Schudson, 1995; McManus, 1994) reinforce the link between commercialism and homogeneity of media content and while many of these authors were writing before the internet as a communication and information medium developed, this type of analysis has continued well into the internet era (for example, and among many, McChesney, 2008; Hamilton, 2004; Anderson and Ward, 2007; Walley, 2002; Westin, 2001; McKinnon, 2006; Reeds and Colbourne, 2000; Lewis, 2001). James T. Hamilton's incredibly comprehensive economic study of US news media content shows intricately how market decisions clearly correlate with news content. Hamilton suggests that all recent trends in news media content are the result of a series of economic decisions by the major media companies (2004: 2) and offers an economic model for analysing recent trends in journalism and news production. Hamilton's central argument is that identified trends in the news media – such as the death of hard news, media bias, and the rise of celebrity – are usually attributed to poor ethical practice from journalists, failing news values, or 'misplaced values'. But his original research, based on content analysis, surveys of advertising companies to determine which demographic groups are targeted as a priority, and interviews with audiences to determine what topics appearing on the nightly news are most important to them, suggest that the trends identified are more due to economic choices than the human failings of the journalists and news producers (2004: 97ff).

In summary, the coupling of these two factors – professional 'objective' reporting and the commercial nature of the media – has led to a uniformity of reporting in the mainstream press and has caused most major media organizations to regularly report the same events in similar ways.

Alternative journalists' views on objectivity and commercialism in *their* news

In previous chapters I have alluded to the fact that many alternative journalists working today are journalists who used to work in mainstream outlets, but left disheartened; or are professionally trained journalists with progressive or more radical political views who prefer working in outlets where that can be expressed. In light of that, I was interested to discern how contemporary alternative journalists view the notion of objectivity, given that it forms the basis of 'professional' mainstream journalism. The need to investigate this was particularly salient in light of the literature, summarized (perhaps a little repetitively) above, which is presented to show that there is, indeed, quite significant concerns about the impact that objectivity has on the way news is presented, on news homogeneity, and the fact that objectivity is intrinsically linked to commercial imperatives. Essentially, I wanted to know – what do you think of the term 'objectivity'? And if you think it is important, what role does it play in your journalism? If it is not important, what other set of broad values guides your journalism?

Asked 15 years ago, the majority of alternative press journalists interviewed said objectivity was 'very important' to the work they did. At the time this result surprised me as I expected, even at that time when it was a relatively under-researched field, that there would be a general acceptance in the industry that alternative journalism equated with partisan, activist-driven or at least, openly subjective practices. The key, though, was in the way the press journalists defined objectivity which overwhelmingly rejected the notion of detachment and neutrality, but more focused on objectivity as the quest for truth (Forde, 1999). Kunda Dixit speaks of the importance for journalists not to throw out their humanity in the pursuit of objectivity, and says journalism cannot be 'blind to injustice' in its efforts to appear objective. An alternative press journalist in 1996 similarly explained to me:

> It's important that a journalist [tries] to discover the truth – neutral language is all rubbish. Journalists are human beings, everything they produce is subjective. There is a reality and a truth out there. The journalist's mission is to explain the reason for things. You can call a massacre a massacre. Call a rat a rat.

Another said:

> It's nonsense to treat the rich and powerful in the same way as ordinary people. I advocate speaking on behalf of the people who have no power. I don't believe in neutrality. Some things you don't have to balance. There's good and bad.

Almost to the number, the 73 journalists surveyed back then pointed to the importance of 'checking facts' in good journalism, regardless of whether they rejected the notion of objectivity or not. Many saw the verification of facts and solid research as the basis of objective journalism which was not neutral journalism but well-researched work which was able to come to conclusions. It was important to 'avoid coming to conclusions based on outcomes you would prefer rather than the facts as they stand, that's objectivity. Seeing the truth, regardless of whether it suits you or not'. Although I recognize different methodologies are at play, in 2010 we can still discern a similar approach to the underpinnings of alternative journalism. Interviewees were mostly likely to consider objectivity in terms of truthfulness, fairness and balance, with only a couple of journalists indicating that objectivity was a notion that they refused to engage with. Others saw that, in the broader media landscape, they were 'balancing things out' because they were acting as a counter-balance to mainstream representations of important social and political issues, but generally, objectivity was still a term that the alternative journalists I spoke to, related with. Jess Lee, editorial coordinator of Indymedia's free newspaper, *The Indypendent*, explains what it means to an alternative journalist:

> I think you can strive to be as fair as you can and be as well prepared for your stories in terms of understanding the complexity of issues and

histories...but ultimately at the end of the day, where you put your quotes in your stories, high or low in your stories show bias...so you just try to minimize that as much as possible and be honest about it.

She indicates this was a recent topic of discussion among some of *The Indypendent* journalists, as the principles of the organization recognize that professional, objective journalism is a large part of 'the problem' with mainstream media. Journalists from *The Indypendent* want to acknowledge their biases, and do not claim to be unbiased, because they are generally 'critical of things that happen in the world that cause suffering to people, and that as journalists we want to go out and investigate why this is happening'. Their journalists are engaged in the world, but we are 'able to step outside of that and be objective and pursue truth...our reporters are charged with finding truth and if that means that they are going to give extra quotes to an activist, where a mainstream journalist might not, then if they think they're treating the story well and going after truth, then I think that is fine'. Carlton Carl from the *Texas Observer* says objectivity is 'paramount' in the work his journalists do because in investigative journalism, it is counter-productive to spend weeks or sometimes months working on a story if, once it is published, it is found to have factual holes and biases. So for his journalists, objectivity is 'essential – that doesn't mean that there's not always going to be a decision by reporters and editors as to what to use in a story, what not to use. There's always going to be a choice as to what to cover'. But this did not affect the journalist's pursuit of objectivity, (which in Carlton's mind, meant truth and the facts) when covering a story.

Jon Bouknight says his community radio newsroom discourages volunteers with a 'particular axe to grind' although the station does try to encourage as many different voices as possible through their news and current affairs programming. The sector's not-for-profit status also legislatively means that it cannot be seen to be running a particular party-political line, so fairness in reporting (Bouknight calls it objectivity) is emphasized with all new volunteers. Jeff Clarke from US public broadcasting expressed similar sentiments. Peter Barr from Australian community radio news programming on the alternative youth station RTRfm in Perth, says objectivity is 'key, no matter what kind of organization you work for'. He said he doubted if working for a mainstream journalism outlet would enable him to be as objective as he is in his news production role at RTRfm and says despite his personal viewpoints, he does consult official sources such as police and government on certain issues which involve them.

Margaret Simons, a sometime mainstream journalist who primarily writes for independent news magazines in Australia and is a regular columnist for *Crikey,* said a 'slavishness to evidence', and an effort to do her very best with every story 'with integrity and with the truth' forms the basis of her practice. Objectivity, which she saw as a commitment to evidence and fact checking, was important and something to be preserved. Her words were echoed 15 years ago by another alternative press journalist who felt it took 'a certain intellectual vigour to try to be objective'. Milan Rai from the activist-based *Peace News* similarly talks about evidence, and 'fair use of all of the available evidence' as it is an important principle not to exclude anything just because it did not fit 'with your thesis...I think most people recognize reasonable uses of evidence and unreasonable uses of evidence and there's the kind of grey area where people disagree and that's fine...that's my interpretation of objectivity and I think it is a concept that is important to defend'. Tony Ortega from *Village Voice* in the United States gave a convincing account of how his publication, and presumably, others belonging to the relatively successful Village Voice Media alternative newsweeklies chain, considered objectivity and how it played out in the daily life of his journalists. He spoke of a regular commitment in his sector to longer-form, investigative journalism and there was an expectation that most of their newspapers engaged in this type of journalism regularly. But he saw that while objectivity, which he perceived as a sense of balance and fairness, was applied in the newsgathering stage, once in the writing stage the journalist was free to interpret the evidence as they saw it. I'll reproduce his words here, at length, as they summarize the views of many in the sector which consider objectivity closely related to a sense of evidence-based research and journalism which is not aiming for a 'false sense of balance':

> ...you're being objective in a sense that when a reporter goes into a story, he [sic] listens to everyone carefully, he tries to get as many different points of view as possible, looks at documents without any preconceptions and tries to gather information without any kind of agenda. That's when the objectivity should come in, as a reporter is

learning the situation and learning the story. Now here's the difference. We give a reporter a month, or two months, or three months
to gather that information. By that time, we trust that writer then to
write the story as it really is. In other words, by the time you've spent
months and months researching diseases caused by cigarettes and you
write a story about it, we don't want you to hold back out of some false
sense of balance. That's not being objective, that's just being untruth-
ful...That's what separates us from the dailies is we're not afraid to
say what we've learned and the dailies carry that sense of objectivity
too far and they end up with a 'he said, she said' story that doesn't do
anybody any good in the end.

I had heard something similar to Ortega's words in the mid 1990s,
when several alternative press journalists told me that good journalism – and yes, they didn't mind calling it 'objective' journalism – was analytical journalism which took sides based on a fair
consideration of all the facts.

There were some exceptions to this view and generally, the
radical outlets such as *SchNEWS* (UK), *People's World* (US),
Socialist Standard (UK) and *The Socialist* (US) felt they had license
to ignore any principles of objectivity due to the 'naked' biases of
more mainstream forms of journalism against most of the issues
they were confronting every day. Terrie Albano said her newspaper
was 'already taking sides' and they were quite up front about that;
Tristan Miller from the *Socialist Standard* in the UK said his publication was trying to convince readers to join the socialist movement and all their articles were slanted in that direction. For some,
this type of biased or loaded journalism was a response to existing
biases in the mainstream. For others, it was a simple, overt and
honest belief that objectivity was impossible. Billy Wharton from
The Socialist said political actors receiving mainstream coverage
were presenting their arguments 'very forcefully' and his publication was projecting ideas and campaigns that were 'kept so far out
of the mainstream media that we need to allow our writers to make
clear and forceful arguments'. Radical journalists from the mid
1990s similarly argued that they told the truth but 'in such a way
as to raise workers' awareness and self-confidence...The mainstream media does that all the time – it tells elements of the truth
in order to win an argument – but we're up-front about it'.

There is surely something of a line here, between the radical publications which either reject objectivity totally, or feel they have

license to be openly biased as a way of 'balancing the mainstream' in the broader media spectrum. The line is not that clear though, because some of the radical publications such as *Peace News* and *The Indypendent* were certainly in support of well-researched, evidence-based journalism as their definition and form of objectivity, as was the alternative youth community radio station RTRfm in Perth, Australia. So it is not an obvious demarcation of 'radical publications vs reformist'; or even 'professionally trained journalists vs untrained'. There were some trends, but there were numerous exceptions to them. The rejection of objectivity was not absolute among the radical publications; and nor was the acceptance of objectivity absolute among more traditionally trained journalists working in alternative outlets. This is the case in both the sample from the mid–late 1990s, among community radio journalists in the early 2000s, and again in 2009–2010. We will return to this issue and how it relates to the journalists' news values of activism, localism and 'providing context to the mainstream' that were discussed in Chapter 4, as we need to see if there are connections, or perhaps contradictions, between these two. However, in mainstream journalism the notion of objectivity is quite closely tied to issues of commercialism, as we saw earlier. Objective journalism arose primarily due to industrialization and the subsequent commercialization of the media and the marginalizing of radical voices (Hall, 1984: 36). So before I conclude this discussion, I want to consider alternative journalists' approaches to 'making money', or introducing commercial imperatives to their organization; and this discussion is surrounded by evidence from the editors, journalists and managers (in one case, the owner) about how they keep their outlet afloat. The final section of this chapter considers whether the notion of 'objectivity' in alternative journalism is in any way tied to commercial needs and aims. And what is alternative journalism's approach to commercial imperatives in their sector? Are the two incompatible?

Making alternative journalism 'work'

This sub-heading is probably a misnomer, but what I am trying to say is that there seems to be ways of funding alternative journalism that are more successful than others. Not necessarily more commercially successful – some excellent alternative journalism ventures have died a quick and painful death due to lack of resources for marketing and a general lack of funds – but journalism that is successful in the sense that it serves its community; it is connected to its community and audience; it is making an impact on people's 'civic' activity; it is making a significant contribution to public debate; and it is managing to keep the doors open and, sometimes, pay people for their work. The paid work is not essential in terms of defining their 'success' but most alternative journalists recognize that only, if only, they could be paid just a little more (than very little, or nothing) for slogging their hearts out everyday, they would be the happiest newshounds alive. It is significant that when I asked alternative journalists what was the biggest issue facing their industry today, their most common response was the impact of the internet and the way it has changed alternative media and communications; and their second most frequent response was how to survive financially, connected to how to grow their audience. In fact, issues of increasing circulation and struggling finances, when considered together, outweighed the comments about the impact of the internet. So it is a considerable issue in the industry today and is constantly on the minds of many alternative journalists, editors and producers.

Eric Beecher is an Australian journalist and media owner with a long history in what he prefers to call 'independent media' although his publications certainly fall into the category of 'alternative journalism' by my reckoning.[28] He is concerned that the label of 'alternative' marginalizes his mastheads and journalists too much, and presumably places them in the same stable as the radical press, online democratic movements such as Indymedia and so on. Either way, Beecher has either founded or helped develop a number of publications over the years, notably *The Eye* and *Crikey,* which have stood in competition to established mainstream media organizations and attempted to offer something editorially different. He has also run an independent publishing group, Text Media, which has since been sold to a major media ownership group (Fairfax) and now is proprietor of PMP, Private Media Partners. Beecher is a former mainstream journalist who became the youngest ever editor of one of Australia's flagship metropolitan newspapers, the *Sydney Morning*

---

28 *Crikey* was 'locked out' of pre-budget briefings by the Australian Treasurer in 2005, 2006 and 2007 because it was not considered to be part of the mainstream media. They have since been included due to their increasing audience reach.

Herald, at the age of 33. He had previously worked as a journalist at Melbourne's *The Age,* a quality broadsheet, and at London's *The Observer* and for a time at the *Washington Post.* After a three year stint as editor at the *Sydney Morning Herald* he was poached by Rupert Murdoch's News Ltd to be editor of his Melbourne *Herald.* This position he found untenable and after only two years there, quit and went to set up his own independent publishing firm (see Guthrie, 2010 for an insider's view on Beecher's time with Murdoch's News Ltd). It was always Beecher's goal to find a way to produce strong, quality journalism that had a large enough audience to sustain it in the marketplace. He has had some success with purely commercial ventures, and more recently with online industry-targeted magazines such as *SmartCompany.com.au, EurekaReport.com.au* and *BusinessSpectator.com.* There seems to be a recognition in the industry that Beecher undertakes these ventures to ensure his company stays afloat, but also as a way to fund what he really cares about, which is producing independent journalism. Indeed, industry sources seem to indicate that while *Crikey* is almost breaking even, it is still operating at a small loss, despite its strong readership and high-profile in Australia. Its continuation is assured, though, by Beecher's more successful commercially-oriented ventures.

When asked about the role of commercial imperatives in the daily life of *Crikey,* Beecher responded:

> Well I think it's critical in a sense...everyone knows [that] in my case and quite a few others, we've learnt from some fairly major and bitter mistakes that if you don't have viability, you don't actually have your outlet. So, it becomes a question of survival and if you ignore it, you do so at your peril. So the trick is to balance the principles of commercial viability alongside editorial integrity and meeting your journalistic mission...it's a bit of a balancing act.

The *Crikey* financial model is fairly unique. There are two content platforms. The first is a subscription-based daily email newsletter which contains about 25 original stories and columns. It is sent out at lunchtime to all paid subscribers – about 14,000[29] – and *Crikey's* research suggests that those paid subscribers send it on

---

29 When Beecher purchased *Crikey* from shareholder activist Stephen Mayne in 2005, the paid subscribers numbered 5,300.

to about 30,000 more 'squatters', or people who are reading the content but not paying for it. The second content platform is the website, which carries a small amount of the newsletter's content for free and also carries aggregated content which contains links to stories the *Crikey* staff have located that fit their readers' interests and the subject categories on the website. There are also a number of online-only bloggers, and both the emailed newsletter and the website carry advertising. Currently, Beecher cites the revenue at about 60 per cent subscription, and 40 per cent advertising with the publication sometimes making a very small profit which is put back into the business.

It is on this issue of commercial viability and economic impera-tives in alternative journalism that the sector is quite divided. I am sure there are many scholars reading these sections who are coming to the conclusion that Beecher's publications, due to their commercial nature, are not really alternative and some practition-ers would be thinking the same. Certainly, Beecher's publication is far more moderate in its politics and approach to activist news values, mobilizing the public and so on than many other alter-native or independent media outlets. What I want to discover is whether his concern to be commercially viable, even if it is just to pay the bills and wages, affects the type of journalism they do, the way they present it and the stories they cover. Tony Ortega from the Village Voice media chain in the United States addresses this issue regularly with the industry. While the Village Voice chain, consisting of 13 alternative newsweeklies across America, is com-mercially viable, Ortega claims this does not drive their journalism but rather, gives them the time and space to do it properly. Being commercially viable, according to Ortega, does not mean they cannot produce good, alternative journalism and producing good, alternative journalism should not mean that they always have to struggle financially. Ortega says his chain is regularly branded the 'evil empire' within the alternative media sector and he is becom-ing a little tired of it:

> I understand about what you mean by scale and I understand how people have concerns about the size of our company. I would just say to people in the alternative world, we seem like a large company, but in the media world, we're a tiny company. I mean we are 13 newspapers but our total revenue is probably less than what Time Warner spends on their car allowance. You know what I'm saying?

He says some in the industry feel that to be commercially successful indicates 'selling out' and goes against the spirit of the early
alternative weeklies, which arose from the 1970s counter-culture
movement. Indeed, one of the key editorial personnel in Village
Voice Media is Mike Lacey, who first established the *Phoenix New
Times* in 1970 (now a major masthead in the VVM chain) after the
Nixon government's incursion into Cambodia and the shooting of
university students at Kent State in a protest rally. The mainstream
Phoenix newspaper at the time had covered the incident poorly and
Lacey, along with colleague Jim Larkin, were inspired to begin the
Phoenix New Times with very definite activist, protest roots. Many
of the alternative newsweeklies today, including those in the VVM
chain, began similarly but now feature a high level of 'What's On'
news, gig guides, dining out options, reviews of local music and
so on. While independent and alternative journalism must be on
their agenda and featured in every issue for them to qualify as an
'alternative newsweekly', there is a recognition that their alternative journalism is funded by the strong revenues they receive from
the entertainment sections of the newspapers. With such a reliance
on advertisers, the potential for conflict, say, for example, a big
story broke about one of the *Phoenix New Times'* major entertainment advertisers, is ever-present. The chain has recently made a
decision, following the GEC, to syndicate some of its film reviews
with only three or four reviewers now employed across the whole
chain, rather than one in every city. For Ortega, these are the types
of decisions that need to be made if they want to continue to retain
good staff and do good alternative journalism:

> For me, the reason why I've stayed with these guys for 15 years is I
> really believe in that long-form journalism and also the way they treat
> people. There's this rather misconception about our company...they
> call us the evil empire. The truth is we actually pay better than just
> about any other company in this industry. We have people with very
> long tenures. Except for the very young editors-in-chief, I don't think
> you will find anybody that has worked for us less than 10 years. It's
> a company that values its employees and values what they do. We are
> doing this great alternative journalism across the country and we can
> afford to pay people decent wages. For so many people across the
> country, alternative journalism means working for next to nothing and
> we feel that's ridiculous. Why can't we do great investigative journal-
> ism, catch our daily newspapers out at their mistakes and still take
> home a decent pay cheque?

He cites the *Phoenix New Times'* coverage of an Arizona Sheriff, Joe Arpaio, who is labelled 'America's Toughest Sheriff' by mainstream media sources and who has also been criticized over alleged breaches of inmates' human rights. Ortega wrote 35 stories on Arpaio in four years at the *Phoenix New Times*, and won an award as Arizona Journalist of the Year in 1996 for his coverage.[30] Amnesty International (1997, 1998, 2000) launched an investigation on Arpaio, and cited Ortega's articles in their case. Alternative online site *The Huffington Post* reported in 2009 that Arpaio had gained infamy for 'reinstating chain gang labor and dressing predominately Latino inmates at his county jail in pink underwear, pink handcuffs, and striped jumpsuits' (Palevsky, 2009). Palevsky reports the Fox Reality Channel has offered Sheriff Arpaio a reality TV show entitled, 'Smile, You're Under Arrest', furthering his celebrity in Arizona where he has continued to be elected as Sheriff for 18 years, due to his high profile. Ortega recounts:

> ... investigating in 1997 and 1998 specific cases of ill-treatment of inmates, improper restraint and the death of one inmate in a restraint chair, as had been reported by Ortega. Amnesty investigated the Maricopa County jail again in 2002 following further reports of ill-treatment and the death of another inmate, a man with learning disabilities, who was allegedly hogtied and placed in a restraint chair.

While the local mainstream media has now turned around and gives more critical coverage of Arpaio (the *East Valley Tribune* won a Pulitzer Prize for their coverage of him and the Arizona *Republic* also condemns his work) for many years the mainstream continued to portray him as a popular sheriff who was simply 'tough on crime'. Ortega:

> The only thing he cares about, the single thing that obsesses him day and night is he wants to be on television. He wants to be in newspapers and everything he does is just about getting coverage and what used to drive me crazy is month after month, these journalists would fly into town, these mainstream journalists from newspapers and TV to say: 'Look at America's toughest sheriff. Isn't he amazing?' Not a single

---

30 See Ortega's 1997 articles, and go to http://www.phoenixnewtimes.com/related/to/Richard+Post/ for a list of Phoenix New Times articles on Joe Arpaio.

one of them would ever ask for a document or interview a jail guard and it was up to us to [challenge his record] ... So that was some of the most rewarding work I did ... but it's also frustrating because the guy is still there.

Benson offers support for Ortega, and condemns those critics who constantly push the line that critique and commercialization cannot exist together (2003: 111ff). Indeed, he argues that many AAN publications regularly contain the kind of 'mobilizing information' (Stanfield and Lemert, 1987; and see Ch 4) 'that is said to be missing from the mainstream press' (2003: 117). His analysis of San Francisco and Los Angeles-based alternative newsweeklies finds publications that are regularly producing strong political and investigative journalism which distinguishes them from local mainstream media. Benson concludes that while advertising-reliant alternative newsweeklies may not be 'more critical and oppositional than audience-supported [alternative] media', his research does provide evidence that 'the *most* advertising-reliant [alternative] media are not necessarily the most conservative and can even be quite progressive in all senses of the term' (original emphasis, 2003: 124).

Garneau has been among those to critique AAN for becoming a 'mainstream trade association', despite the evidence that some of its affilitates do provide strong alternative news (Garneau, 1993: 11). Schoonmaker (1987) and Prendergast (1990) confirmed 20 years ago that alternative newsweeklies were concentrating more and more on improving advertising levels. Indeed, following the era of the 1970s, when the radical political origins of the AAN publications began to shift, Schoonmaker noted at the 1987 AAN convention that there were more white, middle class faces in the audience than she expected (1987: 60).

However, Schoonmaker found that a large proportion of the alternative press had remained true to their roots and were providing a genuine alternative to the mainstream daily in their areas. She identified an increasing need for strong alternative publications 'in this age of *USA Today* and the sad trend it has spawned toward shorter, shallower, happier stories' (1987: 62). Ortega's claims, then, are not unsupported despite the regular criticism directed at the, undoubtedly, somewhat commercially-oriented US alternative newsweeklies.

Darryl Bullock from UK's *The Spark* says his readers are always assured that the publication runs no advertorial material, even though the publication is dependent on classified listings for some of its revenue. As a freelance writer for other publications he is regularly asked to 'drop' the names of advertisers into feature articles he is writing, as a way of improving their visibility and rewarding them for advertising. But readers of *The Spark* are always assured that none of their content in any way relates to the advertising received. Bullock says, 'It's massively important...it makes us unique and it certainly gives us integrity'. While readers might be reading the opinion of various journalists or freelancers who write for the publication, nothing in the copy is influenced by advertisers and there are no marked 'advertorials'. Community broadcasters do not take advertisements but are allowed, by leg-islation, to accept sponsorship announcements from local busi-nesses and community groups, which are paid. These are usually run at the end of programs, and not throughout, and Jeff Clarke from Northern Californian Public Broadcasting says this gives his journalists so much more time to tell their stories. His former col-leagues in commercial broadcasting are running between 14–15 minutes of commercials in a half-hour current affairs program, while his station runs 26 minutes in a half-hour slot; or 56 minutes of content in a one-hour slot – 'that extra length really allows you to tell a story a little more effectively'. The budget figures that Clarke cites for his NCPB organization are gigantic, and dwarf the figures we have collected from Australian community broad-casters (which I will look at in a moment). NCPB's total annual budget is 62 million dollars, of which 29 million comes from individual support and donations. About five million dollars, or eight per cent of their total budget comes through grants from the Corporation for Public Broadcasting, a statutory body which dis-tributes Federal funding to community and public broadcasters, and another nine million dollars comes from corporate sponsor-ship announcements and local foundational support. Due to the size of the organization and the number of staff, NCPB is also able to generate revenue from on-selling some of its content to other public and community broadcasters, and in royalties. They run a great deal of content from affiliate groups such as the Public Broadcasting Service (PBS) and National Public Radio (NPR), but about 18 per cent of radio content is entirely original; and about ten per cent of television content is original and locally-based.

Support from local foundations is not a model for funding in Australia or the UK in the same way it is in the States, but it is certainly one way that many alternative journalism ventures in the States have been able to maintain a 'not-for-profit' status but continue to meet overheads, wages, distribution and marketing costs, and so on. Bob Parry, from the Consortium for Independent Journalism which produces *ConsortiumNews.com*, says his original wage as negotiated with the outlet's board was somewhere around US$62,000, but he has never received 'anything like that' as a pay cheque. He is paid what is available, at the end of the month, after other costs have been met. The publication's structure was changed to not-for-profit status in 1999 to enable the organization to access donations, foundational grants and so on, and while Parry may not receive the pay cheque he is contracted to, he says the organization remains 'viable' and has been so since 1999. Carlton Carl from the *Texas Observer* recounts a similar situation for his not-for-profit newspaper, which pays 11 full-time staff, about 6–7 of which work in editorial, with the remainder working in production, business management, subscriptions and advertising. They receive money from subscriptions, foundational grants, larger donations from several well-to-do patrons and small gifts from readers. While Carl noted earlier that none of the staff would be working at the *Observer* for the good pay cheque, they are there to fulfil broader political and social aims and as long as they earn enough money to pay the bills, they will continue doing so.

Darryl Bullock's *The Spark* offered minimal payments to some of its more regular staff, but most still took on freelance and other writing work on the side to supplement their earnings from the publication. Still, he said they had not yet made a loss on a single issue in 17 years of operation; no mean feat for a glossy, colour magazine with a print circulation of 34,000 copies. Darryl explains:

> I think we're in a very unique position...We distribute ourselves, that makes us unique. We don't go through another agency. Every time an issue comes out, we set up in a couple of white vans and

take them to places where we know they will be picked up. It's a free publication, obviously we completely rely on advertising income but a section of the magazine, there's a 20-page directory where we list everything from local alternative health practice news through to yoghurt stalls and health food shops and that's all paid advertising and that's where our income comes from. I guess we probably turn over in excess of £200,000[31] a year, getting towards a quarter of a million [pounds].

Margaret Simons spoke of the importance of a 'benevolent proprietor' in independent publishing, a business person committed to independent journalism who is prepared to subsidize the apparently inevitable losses, often small ones, that an independent publication will make with other more profitable business interests. This was certainly the case for the popular *Nation Review* newspaper from the late 1960s–early 1980s in Australia which, despite its popularity and sometime notoriety, still struggled to attract sufficient advertising to meet costs. Its proprietor, Gordon Barton, a slightly leftish business person committed to the alternative lifestyle of the era, happily put some of his fortune into *Nation Review* which served as a training ground for many alternative journalists who have had a significant impact on the Australian news media landscape in the ensuing 30 years (satirical political journalist Mungo MacCallum, magazine managing editor Richard Walsh, political cartoonist Michael Leunig, feminist Germaine Greer, political writer Bob Ellis, journalist Phillip Adams, among many; Walsh, 1993). The *Crikey* model suggests similarly in that Beecher's successful commercial media ventures help to fund *Crikey* and he is prepared to wear those losses if it means the publication can continue to produce strong, independent journalism which fills the substantial gaps left by mainstream reporting.

Another model is evident in organizations which had certain funding, such as *People's World* which relied on a foundational grant from former members of the Communist Party of the United States, ex-unionists and so on. Editorial staff were entirely free to run the newspaper as they saw fit, within the political ideology of

---

31 About US$313,000; €234,000; AU$327,000.

their organization, without the constant worry of whether their appeal was broad enough to be sustained. They also ran an annual fundraising drive which usually raised around US$200,000. All the socialist publications tied to political organizations operated under this financial model with support from the political organization which was meagre but guaranteed, and which usually enabled some form of wage to be paid to key staff. Another similar, but less assured, model applies to publications such as *SchNEWS*. This follows a more classic alternative press model consisting of a small newspaper, run almost entirely by volunteers and activists which stays afloat because of its low overheads and costs. In many ways, *SchNEWS* has nothing to lose – they have a group of committed writers prepared to work for nothing, and like those radical publications attached to a political movement, are relatively free of any commercial concerns. Atton and Hamilton discuss similar political economic models existing in alternative journalism, labelling various types 'patronage', 'commercial support', and 'personal journalism' (2008: 27ff). I would add three more specific categories to this, and identify six diverse financial models operating in alternative journalism.

The classic model is the entirely volunteer-run publication with people working either while having other jobs on the side, studying, or 'in-between jobs'; second is the radical political publications and programs supported by specific political groups, often socialist, communist or anarchist; third is the US-based non-profit model which attracts foundational, trust, reader and some advertising support; fourth is the 'benevolent proprietor' who offsets the losses of their 'pet' alternative journalism project with more successful commercial ventures/old money; fifth is the hybrid most often seen in community broadcasting, a combination of state support with business and audience sponsorship; and sixth is the primarily commercial model which is a source of some consternation. It is an important issue, so although this has been discussed at some length already, let us look at it further.

The contradictions of economic imperatives in alternative and community journalism

One of the key findings from our 2001–2002 study of Australian community radio journalists, volunteers and station managers found that many stations were struggling financially as a result of Federal government funding decreases. While some of the larger stations, such as Melbourne's 3RRR, Radio Adelaide, RTRfm in Perth and those associated with guaranteed funding sources such as universities were in a reasonable financial position, other smaller locally oriented stations, particularly those in regional areas, were finding it difficult. We reported at the time (Forde, Meadows and Foxwell, 2002):

> ...as a result of funding decreases, stations are finding it increasingly difficult to remain afloat without significantly adjusting content to attract a larger audience. Some stations feel this is forcing them to adopt more commercial formats, which is against the principles of community radio as outlined in the *Broadcasting Services Act* (1992).

Further there was a sense in the sector that they were under increasing pressure to rely less on assured government funding sources and more on sponsorship and donations from local business and individuals, and this was affecting content choices being taken by managers on a daily basis. In order to show their relevance to community, the stations had to show reasonable levels of support from their audiences but at the same time, due to their non-profit status, they were not able to show significant audience numbers which might be considered a threat to the local commercial broadcaster who may have paid millions of dollars for their license (sometimes more than 100 million Australian dollars). Community radio in Australia attracts its funding from several sources: sponsorship announcements (similar to local advertisements); subscription fees; paid training programs; on-selling programming; and government funds which, for most, represent less than ten per cent of their total revenue which is very much in line with the figures provided by the US public and community broadcasting sectors (Pierson, 2009; Clarke, 2010 – see appendices). Community radio managers suggested government advertising in community media could be increased as a way for government to support the sector, but without providing direct 'hand-outs'. Indeed, the point was made by one station manager that many commercial media organizations would suffer significantly, in a financial sense, if government advertising was withdrawn:

> ...you wouldn't want to be pretending that the government doesn't give a lot of money to mainstream commercial media because it gives a hell

of a lot of money to them and to the ABC [the national public broad-caster in Australia]...They give millions to the ABC, they give a lot of money to commercial media in various ways and they give a teeny weeny little bit to community radio in retrospect.

One of the most interesting connections between the money that goes to commercial media is government advertising contracts. I always think it's ironic if you sit all through this year watching the number of International Year of the Volunteer ads playing on television on every station, and the amount of money that a private media company is being paid to make those and televisions stations are being paid to broadcast those, and we could just have a little bit of that because we are volunteers. I don't think we get nearly enough of [that] government information con-tract advertising (Adelaide Focus Group, 2001 – see Appendix C).

It is situations such as this which highlight the inherent contra-diction between commercial imperatives – simply, the need to make money from the product – versus the aims of community and alternative journalism to serve a niche audience and/or to report the truth and the bare facts without concern for whether a broad audience will like it or not. Here is where alternative jour-nalism conflicts with the basic principles of the free market. The free market model would dictate that if a product cannot attract enough demand, it does not deserve to exist in the market. In terms of journalism, this philosophy has been applied to the 'news product' on many occasions primarily by media ownership groups to Royal Commissions, parliamentary hearings, and so on (Royal Commission, Canada, 1981: 27; Swan and Garvey, 1991: 6). Henningham puts this argument particularly strongly – 'In the case of newspapers, a democratic-capitalist society must accept the final judgment of readers as to whether any title deserves to survive' (1991: 2). There are significant holes in this argument. Firstly, and as a myriad of others have pointed out, journalism and news are not like any other product in the free market such as pegs, mowing services or computers – these are products that people can choose to buy or not. Information and news can of course be sold as a product, but the requirements of democracy are far more robust and complicated than a simple 'audience-demand' model suggests. The European media subsidy policies, which are discussed in Chapter 7, are based on this assumption. Our community media audience studies showed that to evaluate community broadcasting only in terms of its audience reach was entirely missing the point – their value was far more in their proc-esses of community creation and their importance as a cultural resource. There is also a need for ideas to be aired which may not be popular, but which may shed important light on an aspect of an issue currently under discussion in the public arena.

In a simple example, in Australia at the moment our newspapers are awash with a fear campaign about the 'boat people' – asylum seekers arriving in leaky boats from Indonesia and other parts of south-east Asia, hoping to be accepted as refugees in Australia. With the range of wars occurring at the moment, this is an international trend and a concern reflected in many countries in Europe and the United States (Larson, 2006; Reimers, 1998; Milhelj, 2004). The Australian newspaper headlines are variously screaming, 'They're Here' (see Dibben, 2010) (as though the refugees are poltergeists, or aliens); 'Refugees, come on down' (as though this is a game show and the refugees are being 'invited' in by 'soft' legislation); and ' "Thousands" of refugees queueing up' (see Staff Writers and Wires, 2009) (although the story went on to say that there were 'no specific figures'). The overall impression is that Australia's borders are significantly threatened by these 'illegal boat people' and the discourse is inherently connected to anti-Muslim sentiments more evident since the 9/11 attacks. It is a populist view of what is occurring – most people believe it to be true (see Refugee Council of Australia, 2010 for case studies of inaccurate and misleading coverage of asylum-seekers and refugees), and it sells newspapers and advertising space because it attracts audiences. Of course, the facts are quite different. Boat arrivals make up just over two per cent of Australia's total immigration intake, and most of the arriv-als turn out to be legitimately asylum-seeking which is an action protected under international law. More than 93 per cent of our immigrants are not asylum seekers or refugees, and arrive by plane (Asylum Seeker Resource Centre, 2010). In addition, Australia takes far fewer refugees and asylum seekers than most other devel-oped nations in the world. This is being reported in alternative media outlets, and *Crikey* has presented these figures on several occasions (the alternative newspaper *Green Left Weekly* has also reported real figures, Fletcher, 2010). However, even though many mainstream journalists and editors apparently read *Crikey,* these figures are not in any way making it into any significant sections of the mainstream media. The figures are certainly not reflected in the headlines and have in no way affected the dominant discourse surrounding refugees. I would suggest that for mainstream daily newspapers, nightly commercial television, or commercial radio news, to run such figures would immediately lose them a significant chunk of their audience because it would too directly threaten the dominant discourse about refugees that much of the audience has been fed most of their lives. In a way, the mainstream commercial media has boxed itself into a corner. It has, over time, established a set of 'rules' about how certain groups in society are covered and now, despite facts and evidence to the contrary, it is finding it difficult to push down those stereotypes because it will lose it audience, which equals advertisers, which equals profit. Certainly, this lack of informed opinion within the public sphere as a whole enables existing power and social structures to continue. And so we will continue to see immigration portrayed as a 'threat to our way of life'; Indigenous peoples as a 'problem that can't be solved, no matter how much money you throw at it'; and protest action as small, marginalized groups of violent young activists who have no real connection to society at all (unless they belong to farming or logging sectors, in which case they are ordinary people forced to take to the street to fight for their jobs and their livelihood). The list goes on, and see, variously Glasgow Media Group, 1976; Meadows, 2001; Romano, 2004; McKinnon, 2004; Klocker and Dunn, 2003; and Burrows, 2004.

Based on this analysis, what we might expect to see is that *if* a profit motive dominates an alternative media outlet, then that will also affect the news they choose to cover. Carlton Carl, from the *Texas Observer* which operates differently to many of the commercial AAN publications due to its non-profit status but which still relies on a level of advertising support, says the publication must publish whatever 'truth' or information it comes across, regardless of how this affects advertisers and local supporters. He believes that many of the AAN publications have become 'quite establishment themselves' because they rely on large circulations to sell advertising, although he notes all the publications cover some level of local politics and social issues. His own newspaper has links with local progressive politics and regularly runs a progressive line, but Carl says he reiterates to journalists that progressive candidates and office-holders are just as open to scrutiny as anyone else. These are words only, I know, and we might find many mainstream journalists and editors would espouse similar claims to independence and 'seeking the truth'. But the proof is in the pudding – *Crikey*, despite its need to survive commercially, runs the figures about refugees prominently, in its lead story, which goes against the majority of people's beliefs about refugees and boat people. The mainstream newspapers do not. This decision will forever marginalize *Crikey's* readership to a select group of progressive-thinking, generally left-leaning audience (which it is, borne out by their own market research). However as an alternative news organization, it will do. It is enough.

What I am saying here is that in my experience, and based on in-depth qualitative interviews I have conducted with alternative journalists in the US, the UK, and Australia; surveys of 350 community radio journalists, station managers and volunteers in Australia; and a combined quantitative/qualitative interview with an additional 73 alternative press journalists and editors, even when the need to survive commercially exists in alternative media it is secondary to the content and to the process of creating that content. Importantly, the 'commercial imperative' is not framed by a need to make significant profit, or indeed any profit, it is more a need to survive, to be able to pay the bills, some wages and usually, to put anything remaining back into the outlet through better marketing, more journalists, better facilities and so on. I believe it is counterproductive to suggest that the need to survive on some level commercially, to appeal to enough of an audience just to pay the bills, is antithetical to alternative journalism. Alternative journalists and their editors and owners/boards do not want to be consistently on the margins. They want to increase their audiences, not to make more profit or sell more advertising, but so their message and their journalism is reaching more people. So their politics and their attempts to reinvigorate civic life, to encourage activism, to enable people to get up and act on 'the truth' of any particular story is absorbed by a broader group. It is a basic desire to have a real impact on people's minds and that is what drives it, regardless of the funding model at play.

Summary

This chapter has canvassed a fairly broad range of issues, beginning with alternative journalists' views of objectivity and its role in their

work; and moving on to a consideration of commercial imperatives and funding models in the sector. I am tying those two concepts together because I want to know if alternative journalists and
those that set the 'framework' for their processes use the concept
of objectivity to attract a broader audience, in the same way that it
is used in commercial journalism. The answer, always with one or
two exceptions, is no. The irony is, though, that the mainstream
terminology of 'objectivity' is key to some of the alternative journalism that occurs today. But it is a far more sophisticated and
considered objectivity than we might attach to the term instinctively. It is not at all related to notions of neutrality or detachment,
but is solidly grounded in concepts of truth-seeking, fact checking,
verification of sources and being honest about personal or other
issues that might cause bias in reporting. In a sense, it seems that
objectivity is 'the baby' and all the other notions that have attached
themselves to it, such as impartiality, neutrality, detachment, and
of course professionalism, can be thrown out and are not central
to this journey. If seeking to ferret out the truth, to get to the real
story, to give a voice to people who are disenfranchized belongs to
anyone, it belongs to alternative journalism.

This chapter has also made an important point that the commercial imperatives that exist in some alternative organizations,
and it is only some, are secondary to the content they produce and
to the processes that go into producing that content. Some mainstream journalists might argue this also, but there is too much evidence to the contrary for their arguments to be sustained (Carlson,
2009; Bennett, Lawrence and Livingstone, 2007; McChesney,
2003; 2008; Bagdikian, 1983; 2004; Benson, 2003; Murdock,
1982). Alternative journalists, on the other hand, regularly talk
about taking cuts in their wages, taking a second job, moving to
not-for-profit status, and 'just paying the bills' as normal parts of
their working life and techniques that are used to make their outlet
'viable'. Essentially, commercial success in alternative journalism,
for the most part, does not mean making a significant profit but
means making enough money to pay the journalists and other
staff, distribution costs, rent and facilities. If there is anything left
over, it will generally be put into marketing, more staff or better
facilities as a way to expand the outlet and its audience. There is
no denying that alternative journalists do not want to remain on
the margins and they are constantly looking outwards to find other

sources of potential funds, other ways to keep their integrity and their message intact, but to broaden the group who hears it. This type of 'commercialism', I argue, which is really a far more modest attempt to be *viable*, is one that is entirely consistent with the spirit and ideology of alternative journalism. For most, it provides a way forward to make significant inroads into dominant discourses about a range of issues confronting contemporary societies.

The next chapter moves away, for the moment, from the focus on the journalists and examines the policy environment that alternative, community and radical journalists operate within. While policymakers and scholars regularly point to the legal frameworks, ownership policy and regulatory measures that impact on the practices of mainstream journalists, so we might consider that policy specific to community media forms may also have some affect on the way community and alternative journalists carry out their work – or indeed, whether they are able to carry it out at all.

Chapter 7

The global policy environment for alternative and community media forms

This chapter acknowledges an increasing and well-founded trend to consider what the new forms of global media policy might look like. While I am focusing on as many areas of international media policy as possible, I do this all within the general framework of alternative and community media, and consider the shape of policy which supports these forms. Despite the sense that we are now in uncharted territory with the unregulated internet and all its communal potential and content, there remains significant scholarship which suggests the 'nation-state' will continue to play a role in developing specific media policies for a long time to come. Certainly, however, the shape of global alternative media policy at this juncture is unknown, despite some interesting indications from the Council of Europe (Lewis, 2008; Council of Europe, 2009). Raboy identifies the difficulty in talking about global media policy frameworks and as with all good points, his is simple. Studying global media policy raises a new and fundamental problem of definition – 'What are we talking about here?' (2007: 343). Unlike its conventional 'national' counterparts, global media policy is not 'made' in any clearly definable political space, and it involves an assortment of players. He argues that where media policy has always been difficult to grasp as an object of study, global media policy is even more ambiguous. 'Unquestionably, a global framework for media policy is emerging, although its contours are not yet clear' (Raboy, 2007: 343).

> This situation poses a particular challenge not only to internationalizing media studies, but far more importantly, to the ongoing development of citizenship and democratic public life...Generally speaking, the study of media policy can be tied to a broader political project to place the question of media policy on the public agenda, as progressive politics come to be redefined in keeping with the new political challenges of globalization (Raboy, 2007: 343–44).

Of course, the key issue is the way that new media cross nation-state boundaries, the traditional 'borderline' for regulatory regimes. Governments fear they will lose political and economic sovereignty if they participate in devising policy which will affect their own country along with neighbouring nations and perhaps, nations well beyond their own continent. Cultural identities are also threatened by such a notion but Stein and Sinha call for the pursuit of effective legislative frameworks 'both nationally and internationally' in order to 'animate global media systems' (2002: 426). Van Cuilenberg and McQuail identify that the most recent period of media policy development, which they more specifically refer to as communications policy, comes following a public service model framework which existed until the 1980s. Into the 1990s, media convergence, telecommunications and satellite technology signalled the '(relative) disengagement of the state' in many policy frameworks, 'and the treatment of media content and communication more as a commodity than a democratic resource' (Bailey, Cammaerts and Carpentier, 2008: 52; van Cuilenberg and McQuail, 2003). McQuail noted that this new 'third phase' of communications policy, which takes account of telecommunications and new media, still has social, political and economic goals as its main guide, but that these priorities have been reordered. 'Economic goals take precedence over the social and political' (McQuail, 2010: 239).

This chapter first considers the relevance of media policy in the globalized communications era, and goes on to consider two types of currently existing and established alternative media policy: the seemingly-outdated but well-supported newspaper subsidies system in Scandinavia which fosters local, as well as alternative and radical newspapers; and the community broadcasting policy model in Australia. Recent EU discussions on an emerging European-wide approach to community media are also canvassed and an overview of the United States' approach to community broadcasting policy is included. I will summarize with a reconsideration of the ideological frameworks which govern most media or communications policymaking, which remain even in this 'global media policy' era.

A place for media policy?

There are important considerations in thinking about the development of appropriate global media policy, one of which is the suggestion that there is 'no more place for public policy in the "information society"'. International intergovernmental agencies play a part role, as does the corporate sector which operates as a 'powerful policy-making actor, in unregulated areas, through technical innovation'. And importantly, civil society must be dealt with 'inclusively before any policy process can claim legitimacy' (Raboy, 2007: 344–45). There is a kind of recognition that 'the public', presumably due to the rise of citizens-generated media, community media, and internet activism should now be a primary policy consideration. Certainly the 'public interest' has always been a part of media policy discourse but in many ways, this has fallen by the wayside in recent years and given over to concerns about the importance of the free market 'naturally' shaping the media industry. Katz says both media and broadcasting sectors specifically have been restructured away from public service obligations, and approaches placing greater dependence on market forces are evident (2005: 251). Schmuhl and Picard (2005) identify the underlying tenets of the US approach to media policy which are based on the libertarian principles espoused first by Milton, then Rousseau, and later John Stuart Mill, primarily arguing that the 'unfettered marketplace' will naturally bring social and economic benefits. Any constraints and controls on the market are undesirable because they 'preclude achievement of benefits' (Schmuhl and Picard, 2005: 142), and the market has inbuilt, but unseen, self-correcting mechanisms which will ensure freedom and diversity. This principle, intended to apply to commerce and business, was translated across to the discussion and dissemination of ideas, based on the principle that only when individual citizens have the right to free expression, and the right to be heard, is true libertarian philosophy in action (2005: 143). While this simplifies libertarian philosophy somewhat, it is certainly the principle which underlies any governmental decision we see to take a 'hands-off' approach to the media.

The US stance was emphasized during the New World Information and Communication Order (NWICO) policy debates which occurred, roughly, between 1976–85. Sosale returns to an evaluation of these UNESCO-led debates, which emphasized the great divide between, essentially, the European interventionist approach to media policy and the United States' belief in the ability of the free market to naturally regulate. Indeed, when the United States pulled out of the NWICO dialogue in 1984, followed swiftly by the UK in 1985, 'the debate lost the momentum that it had achieved in the decade of 1976–85' (Sosale, 2003: 377; Roach, 1987: 36). Sosale says the MacBride Round Tables held between 1989–98 ensured that, despite its end, the main principles of the NWICO debate have continued to stay on global policy agendas. Essentially, the NWICO debates contained allegations of 'authoritarianism' from those opposed who were primarily, as Golding points out (1977), Western journalists driven by professional ideology (also Ojo, 2002: 1). Roach argues the United States' withdrawal from UNESCO as a result of the NWICO debates was a straightforward attempt to push the US view on government control of the media – that is, to have no role (1987: 36). Sosale says NWICO proponents were searching for a solution to the 'apartheid in global communications' which, to be corrected, required redefinitions of professional practices and ethical parameters in journalism (2003: 378). Sosale summarizes:

> While many opponents to the new policy frequently let their opposition to the role of the state overshadow the variety of suggestions offered by proponents...the latter did not adequately account for the full implications of state intervention in citizens' 'right to be informed' (2003: 379).

Within the revised policy environment proposed by NWICO, the 'imbalanced world communicative order' which saw Third World nations ignored and marginalized sought to be redressed through a re-working of journalistic practices such as gate-keeping, and the encouragement and creation of a more appropriate climate of public opinion, particularly among First-World audiences (Sosale, 2003: 381). The United States' opposition to the tenets of the NWICO debates is not surprising, given their historical hands-off approach to any form of media regulation which is, arguably, unsurpassed in any other developed democracy (for a thorough critical analysis of the US withdrawal from UNESCO and NWICO, see Preston, Herman and Schiller, 1989). Streeter notes that any suggestion of broadcasting media policy in the United States that might favour notions of public service or question the basic premises of what he calls the corporate-liberal foundations are off the political agenda completely – 'broadcast policy supports the principles of corporate liberal broadcasting by legitimizing those principles without calling them into question' (Streeter, 1996: 115; also Lewis, 2001: 168–69).

In more contemporary times, European media scholars have expressed concern that the free market tenet is now dominating much global media policy discussion in that continent also, and we will look at that in the closing sections of this chapter. It is useful to note here that despite the relatively 'unregulated' internet, other parts of the media landscape which *are* able to be regulated in the interests of public service and citizens' rights to diverse information are increasingly attracting a non-interventionist approach. Balcytiene notes that, in the small Balkan states, the new free market model is so highly valued that an entirely non-interventionist approach has been taken. Indeed, this is a trend she identifies across much of the European Union – '[i]n the wider European media politics, too, a general tendency towards neoliberal policy promoting deregulation, competition and openness can also be observed' (2009: 46).

In the ensuing sections, my focus is on existing and potential policy that might affect alternative and independent journalism. While Atton and Hamilton frame their discussion of 'policy' in terms of the 'definitions, intentions and goals' of alternative journalism – and indeed industry structures and personal philosophies do form part of the 'policy' of the sector (Atton and Hamilton, 2008: 63) – the focus here is on a broader understanding of legislative policy which impacts upon journalism. To begin with, let us look back to previous policy incursions to assess their impact on our primary focus here, the alternative and independent media.

State-based subsidies

The nature of public funding to various types of media is as diverse, perhaps, as the alternative media sector itself. Options range from the government-run and controlled systems found in authoritarian regimes, right through to public service broadcasting models well-established in the United Kingdom, Australia and Canada, to government-supported community media models, and finally to systems like 'press subsidies' which support smaller daily, alternative and radical political outlets in many parts of northern Europe. In the latter three guises, the policy occurs within an essentially democratic system with an overall 'public interest' aim. It is, in many ways, an interventionist stance which suggests that the corporate model will not provide all that democracy requires. The United States takes a different view and, apart from its public and community broadcasting sector which does receive some public funds, there is no national public broadcaster as in most other developed democracies.

In this section I wish to use the Swedish press subsidies system as an example of how an interventionist media policy works. The Swedish example is selected primarily because it is a well-established system and I have, in the past, conducted research and interviews with journalists and editors there about the subsidies system (Forde, 2000a; 2000b). This discussion examines past and existing media policies which are designed to offer information diversity and which in practice may also impact on the development of a robust and *better resourced* alternative and independent journalism. Weibull notes that when the Swedish Social-Democratic government introduced the subsidies system as a way of mitigating the anti-democratic effects of the free market, it was 'regarded in many other Western countries as a dangerous government intrusion into the free press' (2003: 89). Indeed, the conservative forces in Swedish society argued strongly against the development of the policy in the late 1960s when it was introduced, suggesting that state intrusion into the market was not in accordance with freedom of the press; and that it also 'harmed the big papers by changing the conditions of competition' (Weibull, 2003: 93). Other nations with a background in the free market-liberal tradition have consistently rejected press subsidies because of the apparent threat they pose to media freedom. Each British Royal Commission on the Press (see under Royal Commission on the Press, Great Britain: Ross, 1947–49; Shawcross, 1961–62; McGregor, 1974–77), the Canadian Royal Commission on Newspapers (Kent Royal Commission, 1981), and the Australian parliamentary inquiry into the print media (House of Representatives, 1992) received submissions advocating the establishment of subsidies as a way of combatting the trend towards ownership concentration. While they variously found the public interest to be poorly served by increasing monopolization and by falling journalistic standards, none suggested government-provided subsidies to rectify the situation. The US Hutchins Commission also examined issues of press diversity but did not consider government-imposed interventions. All have rejected press subsidies because of the implications of government money being provided to assist the press – there must be some 'quid pro quo', it is assumed (Brown, 1974: 80). But the Swedish perspective is that press ownership and structure is regulated in order to protect the right of *citizens* to access diverse information, rather than the free market approach of protecting the right of *business* to operate without regulation (Weibull and Anshelm, 1992; Department of Culture, Sweden, 1994).

The subsidies took a variety of forms, both direct and indirect, general and selective, but the detail is not important here (for an excellent overview of the way the system operates practically, see Weibull, 2003; Gustafsson, 2007; Gustafsson and Hadenius, 1976; Hadenius, 1983; 1985). The strength of the party-political press in Sweden, and indeed in much of Europe, formed the basis of the subsidies system as it was considered important to the cultural and political life of the country to keep alive a plurality of political voices. The Swedish public is highly involved and integrated into the political system, with one of the highest levels of non-compulsory voter turnout in the Western world at around 82 per cent in 2006 and more than 90 per cent turnout in the 1970s (Suine, 1987: 398; IDEA, 2010[33]). Additionally, their newspaper

---

33 The IDEA website (Institute for Democracy and Electoral Assistance), based in Sweden, lists voter turnouts for a range of compulsory and non-compulsory voting systems around the world. Its figures indicate US voter turnout regularly sits around 47–50%; but with a large number of voting-age but unregistered voters, actual turnout might be more like 38% in 2006. The UK has a similar non-compulsory voting system, as with Sweden and the US, and voter turnouts there improve on the US figures with a turnout of 61% of registered voters in 2005 (58% of the total number of voting-age people).

Australia, with its compulsory voting system, regularly sees voter turnouts around 94–95% as registered, non-voters are fined if they fail to vote (IDEA, 2010, see http://www.idea.int/vt/ for individual country statistics).

readership figures are extremely high, with 489 newspapers read per 1,000 people, compared to an average of only 190 per 1,000 people in the European Union as a whole[34] (Gustafsson, 2007: 4). The various parties – Social Democrats, the Farmers Party (later the Centre Party), and the Communist Party – ran daily newspapers in most major towns with their editorial stances clearly enunciated in the late 1960s, when the system was first considered and introduced. The more conservative Liberal Party, on the other hand, had only loose ties to the liberal press which operated only where the market demanded it (Weibull, 2003). The subsidies system proved particularly successful in keeping alive many of these small, political newspapers which, over time and through processes of journalistic professionalism, became less clearly tied to particular parties. They still remained in the market as 'secondary' daily newspapers providing competition for the larger, higher-circulation daily. Certainly, the need for the subsidies system is probably in part due to the size of the Swedish media market, a 'small state' as suggested by Balcytiene (2009) and Puppis (2009) with a fairly dispersed population of around 9.2 million.

After just over 30 years of operation and around the turn of this century, the subsidies system was entirely 'up for discussion', with a recognition within policy circles that it was not strengthening any of the 'secondary' newspapers in their market. It had kept alive a number of publications, but they continued to struggle and were reliant on the subsidies to survive as daily newspapers. It was undoubtedly *slowing* the death of many outlets, and was ensuring a plurality of voices in some of the larger markets (Ots, 2009; Weibull, 2003):

> Even though many of the problems are recognized, changing the system runs up against some practical problems. Cutting the subsidies will eventually mean that an unknown number of the daily newspapers that receive support will disappear, blood that few politicians wish to have on their hands (Ots, 2009: 384).

---

34 UK newspaper readership is considerably higher than in Australia (210 copies distribution per 1,000 people) and the US (240), with 332 copies distributed per 1,000 adults.

In 1998, the Swedish 'Presstödsnämnden', the statutory body established to independently administer the subsidies, was providing more than 530 million Swedish Kronor[35] (70 million US dollars) in direct subsidies to newspapers. Some of this was comprised of seed funding for new publications to start-up, but the bulk was to ensure the survival of a 'secondary' paper in particular markets where they were threatened. By 2010, this figure had increased slightly to 551 million Swedish Kronor[36] (80 million US dollars) following a review of the Press Subsidies system in 2006 (subsidy figures reported by the Swedish Press Subsidies Council, Presstödsnämnden, 2011). Karl-Erik Gustafsson's 2007 analysis of the press subsidies system, commissioned by the Press Subsidies Council, reinforced the important place of daily newspapers in the contemporary social and political life of Swedes. Due to the size of the market, he concluded it was unlikely that the 15 cities which still boasted two daily newspapers would have them if it were not for the subsidies system. Importantly, he also recognizes that the system has not meant that the dominant position of the primary daily in an area is at all threatened or changed by the existence of the subsidies. He writes:

> Selective press subsidies are an unusual form of support, but then the daily press is an unusual industry. Newspaper publishing is not like just any other business. Daily newspapers often have dual roles: they play an important part in the democratic process while at the same time representing key media in the commercial system (Gustafsson, 2007: 57).

Mart Ots notes that the Swedish model has attracted considerable interest as a possible path to a more heterogeneous media landscape but that the policy now is at a crossroads in that decisions about increasing reliance on subsidies or making way for something new need to be made (Ots, 2009: 376; Couldry and Curran, 2003: 9). Ots argues that a dramatic injection of funds into the subsidies system will surely strengthen some publications, and perhaps allow new ones to begin; but policymakers are considering the alternative option which is a reduction in the subsidies and a stronger

---

35 Approx. €55 million; AUS$82 million.
36 Almost €60 million; and AUS$84 million.

reliance on market forces which might 'distribute resources and reshape the media landscape' (2009: 384). Weibull observes that the subsidies system did not 'in any way change the structure of the newspaper market' although it did function 'relatively well for a long time' (2003: 104). Couldry and Curran suggest that any state subsidy measures 'have only a limited effect in redressing the concentration of media power unless they are linked to community structures and practice' (2003: 10). But Ots suggests the most favourable policy option now is public service content funds, directed at any media – print, broadcast, digital or online – because it is 'potentially holistic and not bounded to specific delivery platforms, production competencies, or institutions'. Instead, it can apply a 'public interest' test to content and deliver special funding for specific programming and outlets, which presumably, and based on Curran and Couldry's assessment, would suggest that an increasing number of community and alternative media outlets instinctively connected to their audiences might benefit. Gustafsson, in his report to the Press Subsidies Council in 2007, is far more upbeat about the impact of the subsidies system and is convinced it must remain. He says there is 'no cause to review' the grounds for the original decision to introduce press subsidies or the way they are designed because 'Both as a means and as a method, the support system has served its purpose well' (2007: 59). The diversity evident in the Swedish *daily* newspaper market is what distinguishes it from other countries, and, as in public service radio and television, 'selective press subsidies are a way of guaranteeing diversity in the daily press industry'. So the jury is out, but there is evidence that state subsidies to newspapers are achieving some of their basic aims in keeping alive daily newspaper diversity, even if it has not been an unmitigated success in encouraging new publications to emerge.

Where the subsidies system really shines, however, is in a sector of the landscape that is given minor consideration in most of the assessments of the subsidies. This is in its support of what the Swedish system refers to as 'one-day' newspapers, or weeklies. Localized versions of these weeklies, sometimes chain-owned, sometimes independent, have increased from 15 in number when the subsidies system was introduced to about 50 today (Gustafsson, 2007: 31). Chains have certainly developed among these local, community-based commercial newspapers for whom the subsidies provide additional resources and a type of 'reimbursement' for their high printing costs. In addition to these local weeklies, political movements have also been able to establish weeklies through the production subsidies offered by the Council. Gustafsson says while a number of the leftist organizations of the 1970s 'had qualms about accepting support from the state' initially, many existing and new political movements started up their own radical and activist newspapers due to the subsidies. Three of those newspapers, *Internationalen, Proletaren,* and *Offensiv* survive through to today, with production support. Two of the larger (minority) political parties, the Greens and the Christian Democrats, have also been able to keep alive weekly newspapers (Gustafsson, 2007: 33). The principle underlying the policy was delivered by political science research, commissioned by the third Swedish press inquiry, which 'found that in an opinion-making context these one-day publications had the role of supplementary newspapers and helped maintain diversity' (Gustafsson, 2007: 32). In neighbouring Norway, the socialist newspaper *Klassekampen,* launched in 1969 as a magazine was able to re-launch in 1973 as a weekly, and then a daily in 1977 with the assistance of subsidies. It still operates as a daily newspaper alternative in Oslo (Gustafsson, 2007: 33).

Significantly, subsidies have enhanced the growth and opportunity for ethnic newspapers in the Scandinavian region. The largest three, a Finnish-language weekly, Estonian-language weekly and Spanish-language weekly targeting all Latin-speaking migrants publish with the assistance of production subsidies. Gustafsson points out that the ideology of the subsidies system is that while many of these newspapers may not be competing in the circulation or advertising market, which by some frameworks is the *only* market, they are competing in the *opinion* market which is equally as important within Swedish media policy (Gustafsson, 2007: 34).

There is of course an argument that newspaper diversity is irrelevant in the global media age, and certainly much discussion of global media policy pays scant regard to the various lines drawn between traditional media formats. The subsidies system serves its purpose in our discussion, however, as a sample of an interventionist media policy – opposed by free market ideology and supported by social democracy – designed to counter the forces of the commercial market. It is also useful to know that there are examples of media subsidies systems operating in healthy democracies which provide resources and a viable future for many politically diverse and non-commercial outlets. The subsidy system's strength, while up for discussion in terms of the daily newspaper market, seems quite certain for the weekly political, radical and ethnic communi- ty-based publications which have formed the basis of much of the discussion in *Challenging the News*.

To continue this investigation of policies specifically for alterna- tive and community media, there are examples of broader media policy frameworks which operate in a system less overtly commit- ted to the social-democratic model – the community broadcasting model in Australia. In this section, I also want to consider recent community media policy discussions occurring in the EU.

Third-sector media policy

Cammaerts argues that while many community radio discourses, theories and policies are oriented towards developing countries and emerging democracies, community radio stations in the West are often forced to operate in the margins. He suggests that espe- cially in countries with a strong public service broadcasting tradi- tion, community radio is only a fairly recently recognized distinct media space and struggles for 'legitimacy', particularly on the FM band, with more established public and commercial broadcast- ers (2009: 648). Tacchi notes that the South African broadcasting system, dominated by the monopoly state-controlled South African Broadcasting Corporation until the 1990s, is struggling to sustain a viable community broadcasting sector. She notes South African community radio, particularly those stations servicing black com- munities, 'is largely under-funded and struggling to survive' (2003: 2185). Australia also has, like the United Kingdom, quite a strong public broadcasting tradition with the Australian Broadcasting Corporation established as a national broadcaster (radio and tel- evision) in 1932 and 1956 respectively. The Special Broadcasting Service, a second national public broadcaster funded entirely by government and monitored by a statutory authority was formed in 1980 as a national radio service and 1984 as a national televi- sion service. In addition to this long tradition in national public broadcasting, the community radio sector in Australia is one of the oldest *official* community broadcasting sectors, beginning in 1973 with the allocation of some low-powered FM licenses and officially enshrined in legislation, following four years of broadcast, in 1978. The first licenses followed significant campaigning by leftist, student, ethnic and classical music enthusiasts and the first full-time community radio station, 2MBS-FM (a classical music station) went to air in 1974.[37] Many authors have attributed the birth of the community radio movement in Australia to the reformist Whitlam Labor government (Seneviratne, 1993; Rosenbloom, 1978). Thornley (1995) gives equal credit to both the Coalition (conservative) and Labor governments, but notes the first licenses were granted during the Whitlam Labor era. In its short history, the community radio sector has experienced phenomenal growth. In 2010, the Australian Communications and Media Authority listed 346 community radio broadcasters, including a number of remote networked Indigenous community stations. In comparison, there are currently 273 commercial radio licenses. The fundamental philosophy involving both the rights of groups to broadcasting opportunities and the obligations of democratic governments to provide an environment conducive to public participation, still underpins the community radio sector.

According to Australian broadcast policy, a 'community' may be defined in terms of interest, geographical or cultural boundaries. However defined, enabling local access to the airwaves is a consistent and central theme of community radio. The commitment to 'democratizing' the airwaves is particularly evident in the sector's Code of Practice (required under section 123 of the Broadcasting Services Act 1992). Among other principles, the code clearly states the sector's responsibility to 'seek to widen the community's involvement in broadcasting and to encourage participation by those denied effective access to, and those not adequately served by other media'. Of course, this is a key feature of community radio that differentiates it from commercial media. The capacity of community radio to provide access to groups not adequately served by mainstream media is a consequence of both their 'local community' and 'not-for-profit' status: operating on a not-for-profit basis

---

37 The United States had preceded this legislation by about ten years, introducing the Public Broadcasting Act of 1967 to formalize a framework for a national public network, although Pacific Radio in Berkeley had been broadcasting since 1948 with the support of university-based resources (Bailey et al, 2008: 55). The establishment of community and 'public' broadcasting in the US was even more important, given there was and still is no national public broadcaster.

frees community broadcasters to pay less attention to audience measurement and more attention to their community's profile and needs. To illustrate, in late 2000, the City Mayor of Shepparton in Victoria approached 3ONE, the resident community station, asking if they could secure an Arabic speaker as quite a number of Iraqi asylum seekers had moved into the area and there was a need for communication (Francis, 2000). The station identified a bilingual presenter who was able to broadcast for short periods each day in Arabic to the asylum seekers, providing information about their status in Australia and giving them news from their home country. This is just one example of the niche services community radio offers its communities – services that cannot be and will not be provided by their commercial counterparts. Duty to diversity is articulated in the sector's Code of Practice in which the sector has a manifest mission to 'present programs, which contribute to expanding the variety of viewpoints in Australia and enhance the diversity of programming choices available to audiences'. This resolution is particularly important in Australia where geography and the 'tyranny of distance' mean regional coverage and perspectives are vital to, and appropriate for, many communities.

Australian broadcasting policy requires that community stations be not-for-profit; represent the community they have been licensed to represent; and significantly, encourage their communities to participate in station operations and program content (Thompson, 1999: 23). In line with this, community radio stations see their listeners as potential volunteers. By advocating the participation of citizens in local broadcasting and thus supporting the community by broadcasting issues and ideas of immediate relevance to their everyday existence, community radio has established itself as a real and relevant 'alternative' to other radio services in many Australian cities and towns. The sector as a whole is represented by the Community Broadcasting Association of Australia, an advocacy body that represents the sector in funding and policy debates with government and provides a range of services to its members. Community broadcasters pay an annual membership fee which assists with the operating costs of the organization. Funding to the sector is channelled through the Community Broadcasting Foundation, similar to the Corporation for Public Broadcasting in the United States, which receives the government funding allocation and then makes independent decisions about how different stations might be allocated funds. In both the United States and Australia, certain funds are set aside to assist specific Indigenous broadcasters and ethnic language broadcasters to offer specialized cultural programming.

While (in the vast majority of cases) not commanding comparable audiences to commercial media, community radio performs a vital task in the Australian community enabling representation in the public sphere for those who would otherwise be denied access. There is further evidence that the strong involvement and engagement of volunteers in Australian community radio, and especially in Indigenous and ethnic radio sectors, is bringing down the barrier in audience-producer relations (Forde, Meadows and Foxwell, 2009), a trend which was once unique to community radio but which is now evident in broader new media initiatives (Platon and Deuze, 2003). It was interesting for us, as researchers, to discover that in many ways the concept of 'alternative media' does not adequately encapsulate the purpose and operations of community radio. While within the framework of this book all community radio stations in Australia would qualify as 'alternative' due to their ultra community-based and non-profit status, it is certainly a tag that many localized community stations resist. Cammaerts (2009: 648) identifies that community radio movements in many nations had limited lobbying power and were usually positioned as 'rogue or unprofessional amateurs' within the broadcasting community and this is a label that many established stations, particularly, now reject. This trend had been highlighted in the past 15 years, as commercial radio stations have closed down in regional areas, leaving community radio to be the only provider of a local service and thus, suddenly servicing a large, diverse audience.

Rodriguez (2002: 79) urges researchers to move beyond definitions of community media that rely on what it is not, to an analysis of the 'transformative processes they [media] bring about within participants and their communities'. In our initial report on community radio in Australia, we echoed Rodriguez's (2001; 2002) observations along with those by other community media specialists (Rennie, 2002; Tacchi, 2002; Couldry, 2002; van Vuuren, 2002) and suggested that the 'transformative' roles played by these stations within their communities should become a focus for governments and policymaking bodies (Forde, Meadows and Foxwell, 2002). Certainly, Cammaerts reinforces that current regulatory

models and typologies do not properly reflect on, or accommodate, the historical struggle of participatory radio – 'nor do these
models and typologies fully recognize the valuable democratic role
that community radio plays' (2009: 648). A report produced by
AMARC, the international representative body for community
broadcasters, noted the important role local radio stations could
potentially play in the development of excluded and marginalized communities in West African countries (Mamadou, 2008).
The report highlights the incredibly broad role that community
broadcasting, if properly supported, could play in promoting good
governance, defending human rights, contributing to poverty education, and fighting against HIV/AIDS (Mamadou, 2008). These
roles, so important to nations included in the report such as Benin,
Burkina Faso, Cameroon, Ghana, Chad, and Liberia, move far
beyond community media as an 'alternative to the mainstream'
and recognize the integrated and holistic place that community
media can play in communities, if supported by policy.

Tacchi notes that international development agencies champion
community radio as a tier of broadcasting that 'gives a voice to the
voiceless and provides an important channel for local development
and the enactment of citizenship' (2003: 2183). The world's largest
democracy, India, has only recently enshrined local community
radio in legislation despite the opportunities it offered for enacting
citizenship and civil society in many disadvantaged rural and urban
areas (Tacchi, 2003: 2183). In advising on the sorts of measures that
Indian policymakers might look to in structuring community broadcasting legislation for their own country, Tacchi points out that evidence from the Australian sector suggests guaranteed and consistent
state support has been crucial to its success (2003: 2187). She notes
that while the Australian sector, now 'mature' by international
standards is looking for and finding innovative ways to sustain itself
(running cultural festivals, live gigs, training programs, fundraising drives, engaging local small-scale businesses, giving volunteers
on-air opportunities and so on), early state support to the Australian
sector, and to any new sector, is essential. She concludes:

> State support in terms of adequate legislation and funding, especially
> in the early stages of the development of community radio in India is
> clearly the key to the development of effective citizens' media (2003:
> 2187).

Briefly, and to provide some comparison with the Australian developments, the US community broadcasting industry has had to
fight a tougher battle to stay on the airwaves. Bailey et al note
that during the 1970s, when a plethora of alternative radio stations
emerged after the 1967 legislation formalizing the sector, both
commercial and public broadcasting organizations fought persist-
ently against the presence of alternative radio (2008: 55). While
public and community broadcasters now have much in common,
sharing the bottom 20 per cent of the US spectrum with 'blurred
lines' between the two sectors (Pierson, 2009), community radio
was initially considered a great threat to both existing public and
commercial broadcasters. Indeed, the licensing body, the Federal
Communication Commission, revoked all low-power licenses in
1978, forcing any community broadcasters to buy an expensive 100
watt license if they wished to continue operation. Only the larger,
financially viable stations survived, consistent with the 'liberal ideology at the heart of US media policies' (Bailey et al, 2008: 55).
Volunteer-based stations have struggled to attract support in the
United States which bases its funding model partially on stations
proving some commercial viability (even though they do have a
non-profit status). In 1996, the Grassroots Radio Coalition was
formed to lobby against the increasing commercialization of US
public radio. Attempts to re-introduce low-power FM licenses have
essentially failed out of political concerns that they might affect the
market position of commercial licensees (Bailey et al, 2008: 56).
Streeter's point, made earlier, about the absolutely unquestioned
place of the corporate liberal model governing US broadcasting
policy confirms the basis of this decision (1996).

European policy and community media

In the European context, key indicators of trends in policy can
be found in three fairly recent documents: a study of European
community media commissioned by the European Parliament
(European Parliament, 2007); Peter Lewis's report commissioned
by the Council of Europe on social cohesion and community media
(Lewis, 2008); and the most recent 'Declaration of the Committee
of Ministers on the Role of Community Media in Promoting Social
Cohesion and Intercultural Dialogue' which grew out of Lewis's
study (Council of Europe, 2009). Community media, as identified

by the European Parliament, has a similar remit and definition to that applied and explained by the Broadcasting Services Act in Australia, and detailed above (European Parliament, 2007: iii). The EP found there was 'currently momentum' in the development of community media across the union, although the application of policy and public recognition of the sector varied considerably from one country to the next (EP, 2007: iii–iv). The report noted that community media could assist the European Union to meet a range of policy targets and initiatives, particularly in the areas of media pluralism and diversity, media literacy's role in fostering active citizenship, local culture and social cohesion, along with policy objectives in racial equality and non-discrimination of minorities. They generally concluded that those nations which had established community media sectors enshrined in legislation, with guaranteed funding from government bodies had higher levels of participation and recognition in their communities. Resonating with Tacchi's earlier advice to Indian policymakers, the 2007 report suggested that 'dedicated funding support can help the sector to develop the capacities needed to operate in a more continuous and sustainable fashion' (2007: v).

Policy approaches vary considerably across Europe with some, such as Ireland, adopting a market approach to the community media sector to encourage stations to show market sustainability; others such as The Netherlands have an established formula to provide state funds to assist in the operation of their well-established community media sector (EP, 2007: 11–13). The Parliament also notes a 'considerable number' of community radio stations in a country such as Portugal, but only one has a legal license under broadcasting initiatives to support student-based radio stations – the rest are pirates (2007: 16). The diversity in the sector suggests a uniform European policy on community media is not possible, but some common ground in policy objectives can be found. In recognition of the importance of digital and internet formats to the future of community radio the Parliament recommended the establishment of a European-wide internet-based community media portal, a media policy which, if not global, is certainly crossing national boundaries and represents a 'supranational' structure. While the Parliament generally recognizes most community policy will need to come from national governments, they do indicate that a European-wide approach to representation and interactions with the European Parliament would be a desirable objective for the sector. Other policy suggestions included integrating community media more intimately into the European Union's communications strategies which would enable the Union to connect more closely with local groups; and highlight the sector's role in achieving EU policy objectives (European Parliament, 2007: 51–54). These final recommendations were a trigger for the report later commissioned by the Culture and Education Committee, authored by Peter Lewis which generally found that community media was playing a key role in social cohesion and citizenship 'particularly for minority ethnic communities and refugee and migrant communities' (Lewis, 2008: 5) which is a broad EU policy objective. Lewis plainly states, based on past research and current policy discussions:

> A supportive legislative and policy infrastructure is the critical condition for sustainable community media. A further condition is the existence of an organisation which is representative of the sector and is at least partially supported by the state (2008: 15).

Policy funding models are recommended to be based on something similar to the Australian and UK case, where a range of funding sources are drawn upon – government support, sponsorship, training programs, indirect grants for health and other welfare initiatives, fundraising events and membership drives, station subscriptions and so on (Lewis, 2008: 22–23). In response to the Lewis report, the Declaration, which was adopted by the Committee of Ministers in February 2009, declared its support for the sector 'with a view to helping them play a positive role for social cohesion and intercultural dialogue' and recommended that the EU further examine various policy options and funding models that might enable a strong community media sector to exist. The Declaration notes the preference to combine direct and indirect funding to the sector 'while duly taking into account competition aspects' (2009: 3) which one would presume means ensuring commercial operators are not significantly affected in a negative way by the presence of a local community broadcasting service. The Declaration makes a series of statements in support of the sector and is clearly intended as an overview document to provide both the Union and individual member states with some guidance as to the shape that their evolving community media policy might take.

The umbrella over EU community media policy seems to be social cohesion and intercultural dialogue, and the Declaration suggests any policy should 'review codes of professional ethics or internal guidelines [to] ensure [those overarching guidelines] are respected' (Council of Europe, 2009: 4).

To summarize what we have said up to this point, we can say that community broadcasting policy models in Australia and many parts of Europe (and now emphasized by the Council of Europe's support for the sector), and press subsidies models in Scandinavia, suggest a model of government (public) support for community, local, political and radical media ventures that makes them viable as community/local organizations; that does not impact on the ability of commercial media businesses to carry out their commerce; and that ensures not just a competitive commercial marketplace but a competitive marketplace of *opinion* and *ideas*. Furthermore, and importantly, audience research informs policymakers that such support for community, local or alternative media ventures is not only justified by the content they produce (i.e. the opinion and ideas), but the opportunities they offer to audiences and communities to organize, produce, learn, and create.

Global trends

Examples from Australia, Sweden and the European Union can give us an idea of trends in those areas but there are also broader 'umbrellas' we can detect that have an impact on specific nation-based policies. Waltz notes that communication is often conceived of as a commercial operation, 'not a civic good or a civil right' (2005: 131). Indeed, this is certainly the policy framework that has guided much media policy in first-world democracies and which now, it seems, is beginning to dominate discussion about the future of global media policy within the European Union. Balcytiene examines the 'highly prized' nature of the free market in three small Balkan countries, emerging from the Soviet era (2009). Now that certain bans and restrictions have been removed, any attempt to regulate any part of the market including cross-media ownership, broadcasting regulations and so on, are considered a backwards step and will not be taken. The author argues, though, that past experience suggests content diversity can only be promoted and achieved through 'moderate intervention' such as subsidies for culture and minority media (Balcytiene, 2009). Bardoel and d'Haenens also note that, in many countries, the government has taken a more critical stance towards public service broadcasting in recent years. Recent regulatory changes at both national and EU levels 'undoubtedly show a tendency to favour a market-oriented approach' (2008: 339) although the recent Declaration in favour of community media suggests, at least, a mixed-model which combines some form of government support with concern for the impact on the commercial market. Jiménez and Scifo note 'two complementary but often opposed flows of interests' in developing community media policy – firstly market deregulation, and secondly the necessary defence of democratic principles and the cultural role of community media (2010: 136). Syvertsen offers a comprehensive analysis of the trend against public broadcasting in the Norwegian environment, and believes the push began in the 1980s from private media interests who had made a concerted and successful effort to remove barriers to entry for all commercial broadcasters, to the point that the commercial sector now dwarfs publicly regulated broadcasters. Indeed, European publishers and the private television companies with some support from the EU Competition Directorate have argued that publicly regulated broadcasters distort competition and that the license fee in many cases constitutes illegal state aid. These interests argue in favour of a more limited remit for publicly owned broadcasters and a system whereby public funding is allocated only to clearly specified 'public service tasks' (Syvertsen, 2003: 162). She notes a shift not just in policy directions following pressure from private interests, but that larger segments of the public perceive that the demise of publicly funded and regulated media might express greater liberalization or democratization. She explains this shift primarily in terms of 'the influx of postmodern and neoliberal sentiments':

> ... sentiments that in turn may have profound implications for the type of 'cultural policy' regulation of which the public broadcasting model is a part. Public broadcasting regulation, like European cultural policy in general, is clearly based on the view that some cultural products are more valuable than others and that it is necessary to protect these through regulation and support. A more postmodern attitude presumes, however, that these value judgments are based on traditional taste and cultural hierarchies that may no longer be viable and that it

is therefore not self-evident why these cultural forms should continue
to be protected (Syvertsen, 2003: 163).

Indeed, in terms of public (not community) broadcasting policy,
if increasing pressure is put on public broadcasters to prove significant audiences they will clearly be moving closer to a commercial model of operation, which will mean their content offering
does not differ significantly from a commercial offering. This is
Steinmaurer's primary concern, echoing those of a growing number
of scholars who have identified an 'economic rationale' ideology
settling over much developing EU media policy, replacing 'cultural
and political objectives' (2009: 84; also Bardoel and d'Haenens,
2008; Balcytiene, 2009; Syvertsen, 2003; Costa e Silva and Sousa,
2009: 97–98). The large public broadcasters cannot claim the connection to community and engagement of audiences as participants
that the third sector can, and so any policy shifts to move national
public broadcasters closer to a market-viable approach will certainly
change the unique nature of public broadcasting. The Netherlands'
Scientific Council for Government Policy, in reporting on future
media policies, concluded that the public interest or pluralism in the
media should no longer be looked at in terms of a single medium
or sector such as broadcasting or the press, but should include the
full supply of content and its use via other media, whether public
or private, on the basis of important social functions (Bardoel and
d'Haenens, 2008: 339). In this view, the public interest is served
first by the functions of a high quality news service and the formation of public opinion and social debate, and, to a lesser extent,
by the functions of arts and culture and specialized information.
Bardoel et al cautiously see a positive future for public broadcasting in Europe although suggest the future of the sector, as an independent, government-supported policy model is not assured (2008:
350–51). McQuail argues despite the 'no policy' approach that
Britain has always taken to its press, communications, particularly
in the global information age, are so political that they will always
be 'extensively politicized, in one way or another' with opposing
ideologies clashing over policy directions (2000: 33).

Waisbord and Morris suggest that this era of globalization,
which witnesses the movement of information and commerce
across national boundaries, has been touted by proponents of liber-
alism as containing great democratic prospects. The globalization

of media technologies, essentially, 'makes it possible to bypass government controls' as the state (government), is the 'bogeyman of information democracy' (2001: viii). They note that the 'states' are becoming increasingly invisible in media policy debates because they are jammed, uncomfortably, between the global and local, the only two spheres that are registering in media policy debates (2001: ix). This helps explain the considerable focus the European Union has given to a developing community media policy, albeit within a cautious framework that still seeks to protect the rights and profits of commercial operators. This latter tendency stems from the fact that the United States 'wields more influence in shaping international communication policies than any other state', while Europe also plays a significant role, dwarfing the contribution of developing nations and the Third World in global policy debates (Waisbord and Morris, 2001: xvi). Chakrakvartty and Sarikakis argue that the post-World War Two project of 'national development' and modernization of Third World economies and cultures were very much 'at the heart of the most significant struggles in the field of global communication policy' and provide an interesting lens through which to consider the state's role in representing the public interest (2006: 24).

Summary

The tension between the various versions of 'how to' conduct media policy in a democracy remain,[38] despite the impact of globalization. Individual nations' ideologies and interpretations of 'freedom of the press' and 'the marketplace of ideas' continue to frame media policy even though there are increasing trends which indicate some national borders, at least, are 'virtually' coming down. The United Nations' Working Group on Internet Governance in 2003 explored the public policy dimensions of internet governance but as Dwyer notes, the issue of how and in whose interests the internet is regulated 'is an ongoing power struggle' (2007: 53). It

---

38 Hallin and Mancini offer a three-tiered model to media policy – the Mediterranean/polarized model which reflects a high degree of state control; the corporatized model (north/central Europe) in which commercial and public service media are combined; and the North Atlantic liberal model in which the market clearly dominates the system (2004).

is a struggle which, in part, reflects ongoing tensions about the right of corporations versus the right of citizens (Dwyer, 2007: 54). Vick notes that whenever democratic countries regulate media, 'they engage in a precarious balancing act', attempting to juggle a diversity of interests and ideologies (2001: 3). Policymakers, he points out, regularly make subjective judgements about freedom of speech which is enshrined in most constitutions, but the interpretation of which varies greatly from nation to nation (2001: 3). This analysis highlights how a healthy, socially democratic nation such as Sweden can enshrine in legislation press policies which intervene in the free market by keeping afloat publications which, audiences and circulation would dictate, should close. It also explains why the United States' policy framework, which certainly includes community broadcasting but no national public broadcaster, will continue to reject suggestions of any form of government support for the sorts of publications discussed within the pages of this book. Indeed, the United States' position on media policy is no more keenly demonstrated than in the nature of a large section of their alternative media, which, as discussed in Chapter 6 is significantly more commercial than any others. In the same way, the US 'public' broadcasters (which really take the form of a 'community' broadcaster anywhere else), boast chains of ten television stations and 15 radio stations, with operating budgets exceeding 60 million dollars per year. They, too, have taken on a commercial face in light of the low levels of government support and reflect the culture, national ideology and 'distinct regulatory paradigm' (Bailey et al, 2008: 53) from which they have sprung. Within the laissez-faire ideology, this (albeit limited) commercialism in the alternative media is a positive outcome. Other perspectives, grounded more solidly in the European social-democratic tradition which to some extent is transplanted to Australia through its connections with Britain and public broadcasting, favour an interventionist approach which sees government *step into* the market in order to create public spaces, public spheres, for alternative, community, radical and local media that the rough-and-tumble of the market cannot, in most cases, provide nor protect.

Chapter 8

Concluding thoughts: The nature of alternative journalism

Analysis to date of alternative journalism, in all its various guises and descriptions, has been limited but it covers fairly broad territory. Like many before me, I have referred to the plethora of terms used to describe the content and processes exhibited by those who work for (again) alternative, community, radical, grassroots, citizens', street or niche media. However, if we are to give this field real meaning, and to be able to identify what it is alternative journalists do, and why they do it, and what that may mean for broader concerns, we need to be more discerning about the media we include within our definitions. By and large, alternative media journalists are driven by the need to, either, provide context to news already covered in the mainstream so that readers and audiences might be better informed; or to provide information to their audiences which will overtly encourage them to take part in democracy, in civic society – to participate, to *do something*. These motivations have been consistent across time and they were revealed in a study of Australian alternative press journalists 13 years ago; Harcup's case study similarly found the importance of contextualized reporting in coverage of the 1981 riots in Yorkshire (2003); publications such as the *Phoenix New Times* which were foundational members of the Association of Alternative Newsweeklies were established

to motivate readers against the oppression of the radical politics
of the 1960s and early 1970s (Spear, 2009; Ortega, 2009 – see
Appendices); the Indymedia movement and other alternative online
publishing initiatives are clearly geared towards organizing, mobilizing and motivating large groups of people in particular campaigns
(Platon and Deuze, 2003; Hyde, 2002; Downing, 2003); and of
course the nineteenth century and early twentieth century radical
press, spurred on by the threat of world wars, conscription, and
the rise of leftist political movements were consistently calling their
readers 'to arms' and to the streets (Turner, 1969; Kessler, 1984;
Kornbluh, 1964; Miraldi, 1995; Curran, 1978). Media historian
Lauren Kessler identifies a key difference between the motivations
of the alternative media and the dominant mainstream outlets. It is
an obvious difference, but the essence of what it is to be alternative
is not reinforced enough. Kessler found that throughout American
history, groups had published alternative publications not because
of a dedication to journalism necessarily, but as a means to reach
people with ideas, to organize and to promote issues and causes
they believed in (1984: 42).

Much has been made about the changes brought to alternative
media by the rise of the internet and digital technologies, and the
significant technological changes are undoubtedly one of the key
triggers for increasing audience and scholarly attention in this field.
Curran initially sees the internet as just the latest in a long line of
new technologies touted to democratize the media, and argues that
hope around these technologies was inevitably and always short-
lived – 'New technology has not fundamentally changed the underlying economic factors that enable large media organizations to
maintain their market dominance' (2003: 227). Curran's cynicism
is reassessed, though, through his study of the *OpenDemocracy.org*
site which he says is helping to redefine journalism primarily due to
the technology it uses. And so, we return to earlier arguments about
what alternative journalism really is: whether it is something that is
'ever-changing', always responding to its counter (the mainstream)
which defines it or whether it is something more distinct.

The evidence of what it is alternative journalists do would
suggest that alternative journalism is something quite distinct,
and something quite definable. Certainly, it is no harder to define
alternative journalism than it is to define mainstream journalism
which, it seems, is a broadly understood term. What the research

here shows, and I believe it is simply a mirror of research that has gone before, is that while the external circumstances *surrounding* alternative media and alternative journalism may change – the technology used; the politics of the day; changing culture and so on – the essential underpinnings of alternative journalism have remained the same for at least the 150 years since there began a distinct 'radical' versus 'liberalist/commercial' binary. It devalues alternative journalism to suggest that it has no real core, no enduring set of values or no clear identity. That identity is comprised of its commitment to motivating its audiences to take part in civic society; to know the key issues in the dominant public sphere and to critique them and provide information to audiences which 'fills the gaps' and contextualizes what the dominant media glosses over; to uncover untold stories and to represent the unrepresented, the voiceless, the 'downtrodden' (Downing, 2003), and to have an overriding sense of social responsibility.

Alternative journalism and the public sphere

The policy sections of this book also pointed to the crucial role that a range of community, independent and alternative media outlets are playing in diversifying the broader public sphere. Fraser, in her expansion on Habermas' work, notes the importance of layered and overlapping public arenas operating as something of their own, self-contained public spheres (1999: 126); and Squires refers to these as 'multiple, co-existing' and 'subaltern' spheres, particularly within the context of the African-American public sphere in the United States (Squires, 1999: 3; 2009). Public sphere theories suggest that the ultimate aim of the discussion and discourse that occurs within these 'counter-public spheres' is for it to enter the broader arena; to have an impact not just on the communities that initiated and created it, but on the larger, 'dominant' group as well. Policy discussions then, such as those occurring within the European Union, would appear to support this broader goal of fostering a strong, well-resourced 'community' public sphere. While the United States model would generally suggest that the liberal marketplace will accommodate the existence and development of smaller public spheres, more interventionist policies, such as those identified in the Scandinavian region, are directed towards more overtly *facilitating* the development and operation of those counter-publics. In tying structure to policy, Curran argues for the growth of more adversarial media, which have the potential to make the media 'more representative' (2005: 126):

> It is therefore healthy for the media system to include partisan and adversarial media. These are often more ready to voice maverick or dissenting opinion than mainstream media because they cater to minorities and are unconstrained by the 'fair and balanced' norms of objective journalism.

Curran cites the example of the online news site *OpenDemocracy. org* as a contemporary embodiment of multiple public spheres, particularly relevant in the global age which reinforces specialist communities, 'with specific forms of knowledge, organized interests, established NGO's, and well-trodden paths to multilayered power' (2003: 239). In this, he is describing the increasing emergence of multifarious alternative and community media forms – perhaps, as Benhabib conceptualizes it, as a series of glass balls 'with a smooth circumference, even if the boundaries are transparent' (interviewed by Wahl-Jorgensen, 2008: 963). Within their own public spheres, alternative journalists are unquestionably fulfilling an educational and/or mobilizing function. Their broader aim is to transplant this function to a larger audience, to see their own impact within the alternative public sphere move across the 'transparent' boundary to other (larger) spheres of discussion and debate. Along with their recognized aim to work within their own communities, to create morale and confidence in their own communities – indeed, to *create* communities – this conception of alternative journalists as attempting to reproduce their impact in the broader public sphere is key to their processes.

The politics of the economy

I do not believe that any assessment of the work of alternative journalists, or any journalism, can be complete without considering the broader political and economic structure that they work within. This includes studies of mainstream journalists' ethics, professional values and processes. It stems from the general notion of media power as 'one of society's main forces in its own right'; an institution which holds 'an increasingly central dimension of power in contemporary societies' (Couldry and Curran, 2003: 4).

Importantly, alternative journalists have a key role to play in this notion of media power. Chapter 2 noted Couldry and Curran's assessment that rather than the classic 'Fourth Estate' role that much analysis suggests journalists should fulfil, it is, in fact, of key importance that *someone* is watching the watchers; that media power itself must be monitored, assessed, critiqued, and challenged (2003: 3). Alternative journalists provide that critique.

The somewhat unfortunate side of this consideration of the role of alternative journalism in the political economic structure is that the only reason they are now considered *alternative* – when in the past radical and working class media formed the *mainstream* – is due to the economic structures which arose from the mid 1800s onwards to usurp the traditions of journalism as they existed at the time. The rise of a commercial media, with its need to appeal to a broad mass audience which has been discussed at length in *Challenging the News* forced a type of radical journalism to the margins, and made it the 'alternative'. It is this very commercial, mass-appeal form that alternative journalists, for the most part, now challenge and attempt to thwart as a way to regain a stronghold on debate in the contemporary public sphere. Just as they should. McChesney lucidly argues that the structures which govern contemporary dominant forms of journalism will never allow an effective, truthful, mobilizing type of rich journalism to emerge. It is not in its nature:

> A political economic analysis stresses that the reasons for lousy journalism stem not from morally bankrupt or untalented journalists, *but from a structure that makes such journalism the rational result of its operations* (my emphasis, 2003: 324).

McChesney says a political economy analysis of media does not assume, as other analyses might, that 'the existing media system is natural or inevitable or impervious to change' (2008: 12). The structure of media and the presence of media power has developed as a result of 'policies made in the public's name but often without the public's informed consent'. Political economy links our media and communications systems to our economic and political systems; and for many radical alternative journalists this is their bread and butter. Not only are political economy scholars drawing these connections, but alternative journalists are identifying and challenging these connections in their daily work. Chapters which examined alternative journalists' news values and perceptions of their role in society identified their drive to challenge and critique the mainstream as a motivating professional force. Their critique of mainstream media coverage of political and social issues *shapes* some of their own content and processes. In truth, their assessment of mainstream practices is not the entirety of what they do. Still, it is the case that the alternative journalist's role as an on-the-ground, daily or weekly reminder of the connections between politics, economy and media power is central to their work. While such discussions are 'off-limits' (McChesney, 2008: 342ff) to mainstream journalists, they often take front and centre in alternative journalism news.

Atton and Hamilton give attention to the political economy of alternative journalism specifically, and also identify the more foundational aspects of the concept (2008: 23ff). As it relates to alternative journalism, *critical* political economy 'enables a greater understanding of the nature and implications of relationships between the role of journalism, how journalism is organized and practiced, and whose interests are served' (2008: 25). Curran intricately draws the connections, over a long period of time, between capitalist principles and the media (2002) and, like many before, sees an innate connection between capitalism 'and the production and reception of the media' (Steel, 2009: 222). Indeed, new technology, like the advent of mass communications before it (Curran, 1982), offers many things to alternative journalism but also offers established media organizations the opportunity to 'colonize' far more successfully than more poorly resourced alternative journalism efforts (Cammaerts, 2008). News Ltd, Time Warner, even large public broadcasters such as the BBC are able to cross-promote, market, and run promotions so that 'their dominance reflects the enormous resources at their disposal' (Curran, 2003: 234).

Political economy focuses on the role of the state and corporations and explains a great deal about the operations of the contemporary media system but it cannot fully recognize and account for the contributions of alternative and community media journalists. Political economy points to the significant limitations of commercial media and it is undoubtedly the commercial corporate structure of much news and journalism today that is the source of weakening democracies. I have tried in this book, however, not to paint a simple picture of 'commercialism is bad', for I do not think it achieves a great deal. Streeter suggested in his work on commercial television: 'My central question is not, "Is it good or bad to organize electronic media on a commercial basis?" but rather, What does it mean to organize commercial broadcasting in that way?' (1996: xi). Similarly, in my discussions about commercial and corporate structures in *Challenging the News* I wished to focus on what the implications of the dominance of corporate media are for the broader journalism industry, rather than to reach simple conclusions that commercial journalism is faulty and doomed. I believe this is well-established by a plethora of excellent media analysts. Indeed, political economy tells us that such structures are so ingrained and pervasive, and their impact on culture so complete, that they will not be demolished any time soon. What I do want to focus on, though, in these concluding thoughts, is how alternative processes are operating outside this dominant structure; and the contributions those alternative processes (carried out by alternative and independent journalists) are having on their communities, politics and certainly, mainstream public debate. In a sense a broad-brush analysis of our political economic system, while providing an overarching framework, cannot penetrate far enough to examine the cultural aspects – 'the universe of beliefs, myths, and practices that allows a highly unequal media system to seem legitimate'. And notably:

> Beliefs in the media's central place in social life can be effectively challenged only by *alternative* frames...any lasting challenge to media power requires a different social practice. Contesting media power thus ultimately means developing new forms of communication... (Couldry, 2003: 41).

In their 2003 work, Couldry and Curran note that their definition of 'alternative media' is somewhat less 'political' than the formulations of Downing (2001) and Rodriguez (2001), whose considerations deal more explicitly with either radical political media or empowering citizens' media. Couldry and Curran prefer the 'more flexible *comparative* term, since it involves no judgments about the empowering effects of the media practices analysed. What we bring together here may or may not be media practice that is politically radical or socially empowering...' (2003: 7). Atton and Hamilton follow this definition for their work (2008: 2). While most analysis of alternative media production recognizes an implicitly political umbrella to the work of the alternative media there is a rejection that alternative journalism, per se, needs to be *overtly* political or, at the very least, to have 'public sphere debate' at its core. I believe the evidence presented in *Challenging the News* suggests otherwise, and it is here that John Downing's work becomes more relevant to my analysis of alternative journalism. In his 2001 work Downing is dealing almost exclusively with radical and social movement media, and my considerations are far broader than that. Indeed, the preceding pages have shown that many of the journalists included in this work reject the tag 'alternative' and instead prefer 'independent', in an obvious effort to distance themselves from radical and adversarial journalism. Nevertheless, the work they do is political and has similar overarching aims to the work of the radical journalist, even though their ultimate aims are a little more moderate – for example, making the public more aware of racism in their society, as opposed to the radical journalists' aim to usurp the entire power structure. We must still see their commensurate aim though, which is to inform, educate and where appropriate, encourage action. Downing draws together some key discussions of this book – the process of alternative media production (in my context, journalism) and the marrying of that process to action. Through 'dual activity by radical media makers and radical policy activists', there is a possibility that a zone, a public sphere, might be created that is 'worth inhabiting' (Downing, 2001: 394). I believe this work has shown that many alternative journalists have created a public sphere that they feel is certainly worth inhabiting – even though the realm they have created does not have the quantity of participants, the breadth of reach or the long-range impact that they aim for. Still, and without wishing to look at alternative and independent journalists through rose-coloured glasses, there is ample evidence that the work they are doing is unique, is carrying on an important tradition of politically-based journalism and is attempting far more successfully than other forms to meet the demands of journalism that democracy makes.

This analysis accounts for the *content* of alternative journalism, but what of its processes? I have reported elsewhere with colleagues (Forde, Meadows and Foxwell, 2009) that the collapse of the audience-producer boundary in Indigenous and ethnic community broadcasting has enabled the concept of empowerment

(Grossberg, 1987) to become an accurate descriptor of what it is community media does. Local community media producers, who may or may not have political goals or beliefs as the basis to their production, are empowered by the 'cultural citizenship' facilitated by their community media outlets:

> This absence of a defined audience-producer boundary highlights the potential of these media to empower citizens and their communities both at the level of the local...and as a crucial element of the broader democratic process (2009: 128).

Certainly, the processes of the diverse range of alternative and community *media* productions suggest an overarching political aim – to influence public opinion, to enter public debates, to inform people, to create an active community with these preceding goals – is not an essential component. The process of community empowerment that occurs through media production is a satisfactory goal as it attempts to (and may) disrupt media power. I return to my comments made at the start of this book, however, that broader media production, and the aims of that production are not quite what we are dealing with here. Journalism is what is at stake, and we might see that as a far more specific set of practices connected implicitly to democratic processes. Essentially, the link between journalism, politics and society is important. If mainstream media journalism favours the politically and economically powerful, which political economy tells us it does, then the formulation of a public sphere which combats that discourse is an overtly political action. It was certainly political in the 1850s, and earlier, when the radical working class press was more overtly representing the interests of ordinary people against the growing established power of commercial media, and it remains political today. Alternative journalists' work, has a political basis – the process of forming alternative public spheres, containing (among other things) alternative journalism is itself a political act. It is important to keep hold of that in theorizing what it is alternative journalists are doing.

Mobilize, localize, contextualize

To reiterate, if we focus on the journalistic practices at work in alternative news organizations, and the stated motivations of those who work for such outlets through time, we can begin to formulate an identifiable set of practices which are defining traits of the alternative journalist. An important part of this process is to accept that any form of alternative journalism must include some fulfilment, or an attempt to fulfil, a broader democratic purpose – otherwise we must include Britney Spears' online fanzines (because she gets such a bad run in the mainstream media) in our discussions and this defeats the purpose of acknowledging the contribution that alternative journalists have made and continue to make. This is not to say that some cultural fanzines, or ezines, do not contain alternative journalism, but that if the term 'alternative', or 'radical' or 'independent' is to mean anything, it must be anchored to something of a political and democratic purpose, as moderate as that might sometimes be. While alternative journalists are often defined as 'amateurs', and this definition has certainly gained weight with the rise of blogging and citizens' media, I suggest that this definition only applies if we choose to use the 'professional' traits of mainstream journalists (objectivity, training in formal writing, understanding of hard news forms, and so on) as a reference point. If we identify a range of other characteristics, based on what it is that alternative journalists have *always done*, we begin to see a set of professional traits unique to this sector. The evidence suggests the following set of characteristics exist in most forms of alternative journalism and are essential components of the craft:

Firstly, alternative journalists are committed to encouraging their readers to participate, in broader social campaigns and political activity. This motivation drives much of their journalism, is the reason why they entered the industry and is most likely the reason why they continue to do their work, despite the lack of financial and other rewards. This strong commitment to a political (democratic) purpose and to a quite traditional understanding of journalism as that which enhances democracy and civic life, rather than stifles it, is a key, unique trait of alternative journalists as a group.

Secondly, alternative journalists prioritize local news or news immediately relevant to their specific/community audience over other news, and it is this focus which often facilitates strong community connections and the blurring of the audience-producer boundary. This trait accounts for much community media journalism and is certainly a common thread in community broadcasting research, both into the sector itself and its audiences. It is also evident in studies of locally-based alternative community newspapers; and any outlets which are representing specific 'lifestyle' communities which sit outside mainstream culture. The community/alternative journalist's immersion in their community i.e. their identification as an 'ordinary community member', facilitates interaction with and involvement from the community in the media outlet.

Thirdly, alternative journalists choose stories which represent 'the untold', or 'the scoop', often about the unrepresented, the voiceless, the downtrodden that their audience will not have seen or read about anywhere else. This is another key driving motivation for the alternative journalist. It relates to their need to 'fill the gaps' left by the mainstream and report on the unreported. It also relates to a desire to represent the powerless, those outside existing media and political power structures, and to give them a voice. In some contexts, this trait relates to a time-honoured journalistic tradition to 'scoop' other journalists – to provide an exposé that no-one else has but in the alternative journalism context it is related to exposing the failings of the dominant power structures.

Fourthly, alternative journalists understand the key issues/news canvassed by the dominant media, and they critique that news and its processes. This is one characteristic that is inherently linked to the mainstream media, and which relies on following up and completing existing news stories or providing it with fuller context. It relates to the alternative journalist's critique of the mainstream as politically biased, commercially constrained, and encumbered by its principles of professional detachment, neutrality and the requirement to demonstrate no overt subjective judgement regardless of the issue. Within this trait, many alternative journalists see it as their role to balance out the mainstream's biases, hence finally achieving what they consider to be an 'objective' account of an issue.

It is important to recognize that these traits of alternative journalism can be exhibited by professionals and amateurs; by journalists working for both commercial and not-for-profit ventures; by journalists who espouse 'independence' and by those who espouse absolute partisanship; by volunteers as well as full-time paid workers. These factors do not determine whether a journalist is 'alternative', or not – it is the instinctive commitment to the defining characteristics above, enunciated by the journalists themselves, that is what makes alternative journalism.

I research in this field because I find interactions with alternative and independent media journalists to be thought-provoking and inspiring. I particularly find that, in an environment which is perpetually negative about the future of democracy and the role of good journalism in it, alternative journalists provide a grounding and a confidence that others cannot. For the most part they are frustrated by their lack of audience and lack of resources but their commitment to the task at hand does not falter. This study has attempted to show that what alternative journalists are doing today is doing what they have always done, but what many of their mainstream counterparts forgot about, and left behind, sometime back in the early 1900s (or perhaps earlier). Patterson suggests that news journalists need to remember and know 'their place in the larger democratic scheme' (1992: 15), and the evidence suggests this is something that alternative journalists hold dear. They have not given up their purpose, as activist journalists, educator journalists, citizen journalists, *critical* journalists. The working class and radical press, the socialist journalists of the late nineteenth and early twentieth century and their successors through the counter-culture movement and beyond have carried out their work in a similar way, albeit in an ever-changing environment. And this new batch of alternative journalists who can utilize internet technology and other advances that have the potential to make their work more efficient and more effective will continue to do what their predecessors have always done – use information and communications to challenge, to analyse and to mobilize.

Appendices

Fieldwork and research methodologies

Appendix A: Background to interviewees and publications, 'Rethinking Journalism' project, 2009–2010

Peter Barr, news and talks producer at RTRfm community radio in Perth, Australia

Peter Barr has been working in community radio for the past 15 years; predominantly for RTRfm in Perth.

RTRfm is a community radio station based in Perth broadcasting to most of the wider metropolitan area targeting primarily a youth audience.

Eric Beecher, Publisher of *Crikey*, Australia

Eric Beecher started his career in newspapers as a journalist on *The Age* in Melbourne. He was Australia's youngest ever editor of a metropolitan daily newspaper when he was appointed editor of the respected *Sydney Morning Herald* at age 33. He left the mainstream media in the 1990s to start his own independent publishing house.

Well-known in Australian political, media and business circles, *Crikey's* influence extends beyond its subscriber base, and is a widely read daily emailed newsletter and website covering major news and current affairs.

Margaret Simons, Freelance journalist, Australia

Margaret Simons is an award-winning freelance journalist and the author of seven books and numerous essays and articles. She maintains a blog on journalism and the media at The Content Makers and is *Crikey's* regular contributor and commentator on media issues.

Jeff Clarke, President and Chief Executive Officer of the NCPB in Northern California

Jeff Clarke was appointed President and CEO of KQED Public Broadcasting in June 2002. A Wisconsin native, Clarke has a broadcasting career that spans 44 years with more than 31 years in public broadcasting.

NCPB is a large public broadcasting non-profit organization, delivering television, radio, internet and education network content.

Jon Bouknight, Volunteer at Radio Station KPOV-LP FM 106.7 in Bend, Oregon

Jon Bouknight has been a teacher for the past 25 years. He has never worked as a practising journalist, but does teach radio production at community college.

KPOV-LP is a non-commercial, low power radio station in Bend, Oregon, broadcasting at two watts on 106.7 FM. The station airs a variety of syndicated news and talk programming along with some programming of local origin.

Tony Ortega, Editor-in-Chief, Village Voice, New York.

Tony Ortega took up his current position at the *Village Voice* in April 2007. Prior to his career with the *Village Voice* he was the editor of the Broward-Palm Beach *New Times* and has had a long career in the US alternative newsweekly sector.

The *Village Voice* is an alternative weekly newspaper from New York, founded in 1955. It is now the leading masthead in a 13-strong chain of alternative newsweeklies in the States.

Bob Parry, Editor of ConsortiumNews.com

Bob Parry covered Washington for more than three decades for news organizations including the Associated Press, Newsweek and Bloomberg, before establishing the online investigative publication *ConsortiumNews.com* in the mid 1990s.

ConsortiumNews.com was formed in 1995 by former CIA analyst Ray McGovern and Bob Parry after they founded the Consortium for Independent Journalism in Arlington, Virginia. The online investigative news website became a not-for-profit operation in 1999.

Richard Karpel, Executive Director, Association of Alternative Newsweeklies

Richard Karpel was an executive director of AAN from 1995–2010. He works in the management and representative aspects of the alternative newsweekly industry in the United States and has since become the Executive Director of the American Society of Newspaper Editors.

The Association of Alternative Newsweeklies (AAN) is the trade association of alternative weekly newspapers in North America. AAN provides services to a large number of generally liberal or progressive weekly newspapers across the United States and in Canada. AAN has 132 members, all non-daily free-circulation papers distributed in major metropolitan areas of North America.

Scott Spear, Executive Vice President, Village Voice Media

Scott Spear joined the alternative newsweekly chain New Times as Director of Marketing in 1980. He served as general manager of the *Phoenix New Times* in 1981 and was named publisher of that paper in 1989.

Village Voice Media is a privately held corporation headquartered in Phoenix, Arizona. The company owns the *Village Voice*, founded by the 'New Journalists' in 1955. In 1995, Village Voice Media merged with the New Times Media Corporation, another major publisher of alternative newsweeklies to form a 13-masthead chain.

Billy Wharton, Editor of The Socialist

Billy Wharton is a writer and activist whose articles have appeared in the *Washington Post*, the NYC *Indypendent*, *Spectrezine* and the *Monthly Review Zine*.

The Socialist is the official magazine of the Socialist Party USA, published in print and also available online.

Carlton Carl, CEO and Executive Publisher, The Texas Observer

Carlton Carl has worked for the *Houston Chronicle*, briefly for the *New York Times*, and has worked as a freelance journalist and media advisor for non-government agencies, community groups and politicians.

The Texas Observer was established in 1954 and is a not-for-profit organization. The Observer is a member of the Association of Alternative Newsweeklies and specializes in progressive social and political issues, and investigative journalism.

Terrie Albano, Editor, People's World, Chicago

Terrie Albano is a Communist Party USA activist and has been active in grassroots political and labour organizing for more than 25 years. In the early 1990s, she was National coordinator of the Young Communist League USA. She is a writer.

The *People's World* is a national, grassroots newspaper and the direct descendant of the *Daily Worker*. *People's World* reports on and analyses struggles for workers' rights, peace, equality, social and economic justice, democracy, civil liberties, women's rights, and protection of the environment. As of early 2010, it has stopped hard-copy weekly publishing, and now appears as an online daily publication.

Carol Pierson, President and CEO, National Federation of Community Broadcasters

Carol Pierson worked as the President and CEO of the NFCB from May 1996 until February 2010. She is now the Treasurer of the Media and Democracy Coalition in the San Francisco Bay Area.

The National Federation of Community Broadcasters is a national alliance of stations, producers, and others committed to community radio. NFCB advocates for national public policy, funding, recognition, and resources on behalf of its membership.

Jessica Lee, General Coordinator of The Indypendent

Jessica is a journalist involved in both the Indymedia movement, and New York City's hard-copy newspaper loosely associated with Indymedia, *The Indypendent*. She helps lead *The Indypendent's* 'Basic Journalism' reporting workshop series. In 2007, her investigative reporting of the pending Violent Radicalization and Homegrown Terrorism Prevention Act won an award with Project Censored, as a top story not covered by the mainstream media.

The Indypendent is the newspaper project of the New York City Independent Media Centre, which is affiliated with the global Indymedia movement (indymedia.org), NYC IMC sponsors three other volunteer projects: the children's newspaper IndyKids, the IndyVideo news team and the NYC IMC open-publishing website (nyc.indymedia.org).

Larry O'Hara, Editor of NFB Magazine

Larry O'Hara is a regular contributor to Robert Ramsay's *Lobster* magazine. *Notes from the Borderland* (NFB) is described as 'a parapolitical investigative magazine'. The magazine was first published in 1997. The political perspective of NFB is Left/Green.

Darryl Bullock, Contributor, The Spark

Darryl Bullock is a freelance writer who works for *The Spark* and also writes for other UK magazines on food and lifestyle issues.

The Spark was established in 1993, and operates as a viable quarterly colour glossy magazine focusing on ethical and environmental issues. Now printing 34,000 copies an issue and with a readership of more than 100,000, *The Spark* distributes around Bristol and Bath, throughout Gloucestershire, Somerset and Wiltshire.

Milan Rai, Editor of Peace News magazine/Peacenews.info

Milan Rai is a British peace campaigner best known for being arrested on 25 October 2005 next to a London war memorial, the Cenotaph, for refusing to cease reading aloud the names of civilians killed in Iraq in the course of Britain's most recent war, alongside fellow activist Maya Evans.

Peace News, established in 1936, is written and produced by and for activists, campaigners and radical academics from all over the world.

Tristan Miller, General Secretary of the Socialist Party of Great Britain

Tristan Miller helps administer the Socialist Party's internal and external affairs, and is involved in both management and some writing for the monthly newspaper, *The Socialist Standard*.

The Socialist Standard has been published without interruption since 1904. The publication focuses on socialist advocacy and Marxian analysis of current events, particularly those affecting the United Kingdom.

John Hodge, Contributor to SchNEWS, Brighton

John Hodge has been working in alternative media for around 15 years and was a founding editor of the West Australian satirical magazine, *Lies*, before heading to the UK in the mid nineties. As

well as his involvement in writing, editing, graphics and web production for *SchNEWS*, he is involved in several other alternative
media including Indymedia UK and other publications.

SchNEWS is a free weekly publication operating from Brighton,
England, which has been running since November 1994. The
main focus is environmental and social issues/struggles in the
UK – but also internationally – with an emphasis on direct action
protest, and autonomous political struggles outside formalized
political parties. The politics of its writers are predominantly
anarchist.

Appendix B: Fieldwork and method, *Community Media Matters:
An Audience Study of the Australian Community Broadcasting
Sector,* 2007

Metropolitan and regional radio focus groups:

Artsound, Canberra
Valley FM, Tuggeranong Valley
2QBYN, Queanbeyan
2TVR, Tumut, NSW
2BAY FM, Byron Bay
2FBi, Sydney
2SER, Sydney
3RRR, Melbourne
3CR, Melbourne
3GDR, Melbourne
Fresh FM, Bendigo
7THE Sound of the City, Hobart
EDGE Radio, Hobart
4ZZZ, Brisbane
4MBS, Brisbane
4FCR, Fraser Coast Qld
Radio Nag, Yeppoon
6CRA, Albany WA
6RPH, Perth
Sonshine FM, Perth
6RTR, Perth
8KTR, Katherine
Radio Adelaide

ROX-Fm, Roxby Downs SA
5TCB, Bordertown SA

Indigenous community radio and television focus groups:

Radio Larrakia, Darwin
3KND, Kool 'n' Deadly, Melbourne
Bumma Bippera Media, Cairns
98.9FM Murri Country, Brisbane (formerly 4AAA)
Radio Goolarri, Broome
CAAMA, Alice Springs
TEABBA, Darwin
Umeewarra Media, Port Augusta

Indigenous community face-to-face interviews:

Batchelor College
BRACS Festival, Alice Springs
Laura Cultural Festival, Cape York
Palm Island
Townsville
Torres Strait Cultural Festival, Thursday Island
BRACS Festival, Woorabinda
Yuendumu Sports Festival
Maningrida Music Festival
Beagle Bay, Kimberleys
Djaridjin, Kimberleys
Anangu-Pitjantjatjara-Yankunytjatjara lands, 25th anniversary of
    land hand-back, Umuwa

Ethnic community radio focus groups:

Macedonian program, Plenty Valley FM, Victoria
Vietnamese youth program, 3CR, Melbourne
Sudanese program, 3ZZZ, Melbourne
Turkish program, 3ZZZ, Melbourne
Tongan program, 5Ebi, Adelaide
Serbian program, TEN73 Border FM, Albury-Wodonga
Filipino/Tagalog program, 104.1 Territory FM
Indonesian program, 104.1 Territory FM
Chinese Youth program, 4EB Brisbane
Greek Seniors program, 4EB Brisbane

Community television focus groups:
Channel 31, Brisbane (Briz-31)
C31, Melbourne
Channel 31, Adelaide
Access 31, Perth
TVS, Sydney

Appendix C: Fieldwork and method, *Culture Commitment Community: The Australian Community Radio Sector,* 2002

The fieldwork for the project involved several stages:

Telephone Survey of Station Managers
Telephone Survey of General Volunteers
Telephone Survey of News and Current Affairs Volunteers
Focus Group Discussions involving Metropolitan and Regional Centres in each state
Cumulatively 350 survey interviews conducted.

Focus groups with station managers and senior employees/volunteers were carried out in Brisbane; Townsville; Canberra; Sydney; Bathurst; Darwin; Hobart; Melbourne; Warrnambool; Adelaide; Port Augusta; Perth; and Albany, yielding 35 hours of transcribed discussion.

Interviewees were also conducted with sector bodies, such as the Community Broadcasting Association of Australia, the National Ethnic and Multicultural Broadcasters Council, Radio for the Print Handicapped Australia, the Community Broadcasting Foundation and the Association of Christian Broadcasters.

Appendix D: Fieldwork and method, *Reinventing the Public Sphere: The Australian alternative press industry,* 1996–97

A total of 73 editors and journalists from the following publications were interviewed throughout 1996–97. A quantitative survey was conducted with all participants, and additional extended comments were provided by most. All survey interviews were anonymous. Note the publication details below were correct as of 1998 and I have left them in that format to indicate their status at the time the research was conducted:

Adelaide Review: Independent political comment monthly, edited by former Liberal Party staffer Christopher Pearson, owned by private company. Circ. 41,500.

Anarchist Age: Anarchist comment on current issues, published by Anarchist Media Institute and Libertarian Weekly Workers for a Self-Managed Society. Circ. undisclosed.

Arena Magazine: Left comment on current political issues, published bi-monthly by Arena Publishing Pty Ltd. Circ. 2,500.

The Big Issue Australia: Fortnightly left-ish comment on current social issues, established by Anita Roddick of The Body Shop. Circ. 10,000.

The Bug: Irregularly published political satire magazine, published by mainstream journalists in Brisbane. Circ. 5,000.

Eureka Street: Social justice-oriented monthly published by Jesuit Publications. Circ. 6,000.

The Guardian: Weekly left-wing newspaper published by Communist Party of Australia. Circ. undisclosed.

Green Left Weekly: Weekly left-wing newspaper cooperatively owned, formerly associated with Democratic Socialists. Circ. 6,000–8,000.

Impact: Monthly A4 publication on current social and welfare issues, published by Australian Council of Social Services. Circ. 1,100.

In The National Interest: Right-wing comment on current political issues, now closed but reopened as Wake Up Australia. Published by a private individual. Circ. stated to be 20,000.

Koori Mail: Fortnightly national Indigenous newspaper, published by collective of five Aboriginal communities. Circ. 6,000.

Land Rights Queensland: Monthly Queensland Indigenous newspaper mainly focused on Native Title, published by FAIRA Aboriginal Corp. Circ. 10,000.

Neighbourhood News: Monthly publication with left-wing perspective on current social issues, focusing on Brisbane's West End community. Circ. 3,000.

New Dawn: Bi-monthly magazine with conspiracy angle, features on general political and social issues. Circ. 20,000.

New Internationalist: Monthly international publication with some Australian content, focusing on Third World and development issues, owned by a cooperative trust. Circ. 14,000.

News Weekly: Fortnightly conservative comment on social issues and politics, published by National Civic Council. Circ. 11,800.

Nexus New Times: Bi-monthly magazine similar to *New Dawn,* conspiracy theory and features on current social issues. Circ. 27,000.

NuWave Newspaper: Community newspaper produced every six weeks by young people with a focus on news and current affairs. Some input from local Youth Bureau. Circ. 5,000.

Peace 2000: Bi-monthly newsletter focusing on nuclear disarmament and peace issues, published by community group. Circ. 500.

People's Equality Network: Irregularly produced newsletter criticizing mainstream coverage of women's issues from an anti-feminist perspective. Circ. 900.

Quadrant: Monthly conservative magazine published by a private company with prominent conservative contributors and editor. Circ. 6,000.

The Queensland Independent, formerly *The Weekend Independent:* Monthly newspaper produced by University of Queensland journalism students and staff, general and investigative news distributed to local community. Circ. 7,000.

The Republican: Weekly independent newspaper with left-ish perspective on current news and events, closed August 1997. Circ. undisclosed.

Socialist Worker: Fortnightly newspaper focusing on recent news issues published by International Socialists' Organization. Circ. 1,500.

The Stirrer: Small monthly newsletter with social justice perspective on news and current affairs, some philosophical material. Circ. 50.

Sydney City Hub: Weekly news and lifestyle newspaper published by former US alternative newsweekly editor. Circ. 25,000.

UNITY: Bi-monthly newsletter with news and comment on international issues. General social justice and aid news. Circ. 2,000.

X-Press Magazine: Weekly music and political street paper, leftish/youth perspective on topical issues, high advertising content. Circ. 39,000.

References

Abramson, J.B (1990). 'Four criticisms of press ethics', in Lichtenberg, J (ed), *Democracy and the Mass Media,* Cambridge University Press: Cambridge.

Agre, P (2002). 'Real-time politics: The internet and the political process', *The Information Society,* 18(5): 311–31.

Amnesty International (2002). UNITED STATES OF AMERICA: The restraint chair. How many more deaths?, Amnesty International, available at http://www.amnesty.org/en/library/asset/AMR51/031/2002/en/2cff6ca9-d890-11dd-ad8c-f3d4445c118e/amr510312002en.pdf, retrieved June 8, 2011.

Amnesty International (1997). UNITED STATES OF AMERICA: Ill-treatment of inmates in Maricopa County jails, Arizona, Amnesty International, available at http://www.amnesty.org/en/library/asset/AMR51/051/1997/en/a7debf26-e9dd-11dd-90b2-a9da8ab8e550/amr510511997en.pdf and retrieved June 8, 2011.

Amnesty International (1998). United States of America: Rights for All, published by Amnesty International and available online at http://www.amnesty.org/en/library/asset/AMR51/035/1998/en/0440cd04-da99-11dd-80bc-797022e51902/amr510351998en.pdf.

Anderson, H (2005). 'Agitate educate organise: The roles of information-based programming on 4ZzZ', *3CMedia,* 1: 58–72.

Anderson, P and Ward, G (2007). 'Introduction', in Anderson, P and Ward, G (eds), *The Future of Journalism in the Advanced Democracies,* Ashgate: London.

Armstrong, M (1990). 'The industrial workers of the world in Australia', *Socialist Review,* 2: 65–83.

Association of Alternative Newsweeklies (2009a). *AAN Membership Guidelines 2009,* accessed June 2009 at http://aan.org/alternative/Aan/index.

Association of Alternative Newsweeklies (2009b). *Easy Reader,* accessed 8 July 2009 from http://aan.org/alternative/Aan/ViewCompany?oid=oid%3A24.

Asylum Seeker Resource Centre (2010). *Asylum Seeker Fact Sheet and Myth Buster, 2010,* Asylum Seeker Resource Centre: Melbourne, accessed 20 September 2010 from http://www.asrc.org.au/media/documents/myth-busters.pdf.

Atton, C (2009). 'Why alternative journalism matters', *Journalism,* 10(3): 283–85.

Atton, C (2009a). 'Alternative and citizen journalism', in Wahl-Jorgensen, K and Hanitzsch, T (eds), *The Handbook of Journalism Studies,* Routledge: New York, 265–78.

Atton, C (2007a). 'Alternative media in practice', in Coyer, K, Dowmunt, T and Fountain, A (eds), *The Alternative Media Handbook,* Routledge: Oxon and New York, 71–77.

Atton, C (2007b). 'A brief history: the web and interactive media', in Coyer, K, Dowmunt, T and Fountain, A (eds), *The Alternative Media Handbook,* Routledge: Oxon and New York, 59–65.

References

Atton, C (2004). *An Alternative Internet: Radical Media, Politics and Creativity,* Edinburgh University Press: Edinburgh.

Atton, C (2003). 'What is alternative journalism?' *Journalism,* 4(3): 267–72.

Atton, C (2002). *Alternative Media,* Sage: London.

Atton, C and Couldry, N (2003). 'Introduction to special issue', *Media, Culture and Society,* 25: 579–86.

Atton, C and Hamilton, J.F (2008). *Alternative Journalism,* Sage: London.

Australian Government House of Representatives Standing Committee on Communications, Transport and the Arts (2001) *Local Voices: An Inquiry into Local Radio,* Parliament of the Commonwealth of Australia: Canberra.

Australian Press Council (2008). *State of the News Print Media in Australia Report,* accessed 2 July 2009 at http://www.presscouncil.org.au/snpma/snpma2008/ch07_2_snpma2008.html.

Avaaz.org (2010). 'About us', accessed 5 July 2010 from http://www.avaaz.org/en/about.php.

Bagdikian, B (1983). *The Media Monopoly,* Beacon Press: Boston.

Bagdikian, B (2004). *The New Media Monopoly,* Beacon Press: Boston.

Bailey, O, Cammaerts, B and Carpentier, N (2008). *Understanding Alternative Media,* McGraw-Hill Open University Press: Berkshire, England.

Balcytiene, A (2009). 'Market-led reforms as incentives for media change, development and diversification in the Baltic states – A small country approach', *The International Communication Gazette,* 71 (1–2): 39–49.

Bardoel, J and d'Haenens, L (2008). 'Reinventing public service broadcasting in Europe: prospects, promises and problems', *Media, Culture & Society,* 30(3): 337–55.

Barker, G (2009). 'The Crumbling Estate', *Griffith Review,* 25: 117–23.

Bathily, A (2004). *Community Radio in Senegal Today,* Association Mondiale des Radiodiffuseurs Communautaires (AMARC)/Africa: Johannesburg, South Africa.

Bear, A (1983). 'The Emergence of Public Broadcasting in Australia', *Australian Journal of Communication,* 4: 21–28.

Bennett, W.L (2003). 'New media power: The internet and global activism', in Couldry, N and Curran, J (eds), *Contesting Media Power: Alternative Media in a Networked World,* Rowman & Littlefield Publishers: Lanham, Maryland, 17–37.

Bennett, W.L, Lawrence, R and Livingston, S (2007). *When the Press Fails: Political Power and the News Media from Iraq to Katrina,* University of Chicago Press: Chicago.

Benson, R (2003). 'Commercialism and critique: California's alternative weeklies', in Couldry, N and Curran, J (eds), *Contesting Media Power: Alternative Media in a Networked World,* Rowman & Littfield: Lanham, Maryland, 111–27.

Bouknight, J with Reisfar, T, Ficher, M and Clouart, C (2008). *Handbook for the KPOV Citizen Journalism Team,* KPOV 106.7FM: Bend, Oregon.

Boyle, M.P, and Schmierbach, M (2009). 'What makes a protester? The role of mainstream and alternative media in predicting mainstream and protest participation', *Communication Quarterly,* 57: 1–17.

Breed, W (1955). 'Social control in the newsroom: A functional analysis', *Social Forces,* 33(4): 326–35.

Brown, R.U (1974). 'Shop talk at thirty: Press subsidies', *Editor & Publisher,* 107(19): 80.

Buckley, S and Hartland, K (2009). 'Broadcasting success story at risk', Open Letter to the Prime Minister, Rt. Hon. Gordon Brown, 20 July 2009. Received by email, 21 July 2009.

Burgmann, V (2009). 'The Industrial Workers of the World in Australia: Achievements and Limitations', presented to *Laborism and the Radical Alternative: Lessons for Today* conference, Melbourne, Australia, May 2009.

Burgmann, V (1985). *In Our Time: Socialism and the Rise of Labor, 1885–1905,* Allen & Unwin: Sydney.

Burrows, E (2010). 'Tools of resistance: The roles of two Indigenous newspapers in building an Indigenous public sphere', *Australian Journalism Review,* 32(2): 33–46.

Burrows, E (2009). *Writing to be Heard: The Indigenous Print Media's Role in Establishing and Developing an Indigenous Public Sphere,* unpublished PhD thesis, Griffith University, June 2009.

Burrows, E (2004). 'Bridging our differences: Comparing mainstream and Indigenous media coverage of Corroboree 2000', *Australian Journalism Review,* 26(1): 175–90.

Calhoun, C (1992). 'Introduction', in Calhoun, C (ed), *Habermas and the Public Sphere,* MIT Press: Massachusetts.

Cammaerts, B (2009). 'Community radio in the west. A legacy of struggle for survival in a state and capitalist controlled media environment', *The International Communication Gazette,* 71(8): 635–54.

Cammaerts, B (2008). 'Critical reflections on the participative nature of blogs', *Working Paper No. 62,* American University in Paris: Paris.

Carey, J.W (1989). *Communication as Culture: Essays on Media and Society.* Boston: Unwin Hyman.

Carlson, M (2009). 'Review of "When the Press Fails: Political Power and the News Media from Iraq to Katrina"', *Journalism: Theory, Practice and Criticism,* 10(2): 261–70.

Carpentier, N, Lie, R and Servaes, J (2003). 'Community Media: Muting the Democratic Media Discourse?' *Continuum: Journal of Media & Cultural Studies* 17(1): 51–68.

Castells, M (1996). *Rise of the Network Society, The Information Age: Economy, Society and Culture,* Volume 1, Blackwell Publishing: Massachusetts.

Castells, M and Talens, A (2010). 'When our media belong to the state: Policy and negotiations in Indigenous-language radio in Mexico', in Rodriguez, C, Kidd, D and Stein, L (eds), *Making Our Media: Global Initiatives Toward a Democratic Public Sphere,* Hampton Press: Cresskill, NJ, 249–70.

Chakrakvartty, P and Sarikakis, K (2006). *Media Policy and Globalization.* New York: Palgrave Macmillan.

Collins, S and Rose, J (2004), 'City voice: An alternative to the corporate model', *Pacific Journalism Review,* 10(2): 32–45.

Cock, P.H (1977). 'Australia's alternative media', *Media Information Australia,* 6: 4–9.

Cook, T (2005). 'The functions of the press in a democracy', in Overholser, G and Jamieson, K.H (eds), *The Press,* Oxford University Press: New York, 115–19.

Comedia (1984). 'The alternative press: The development of underdevelopment', *Media Culture & Society*, 6(2): 95–102.

Compton, J (2000). 'Communicative politics and public journalism', *Journalism Studies*, 1(3): 449–67.

Costa e Silva, E and Sousa, H (2009). 'Keeping up appearances. Regulating Media Diversity in Portugal', *The International Communication Gazette*, 71(1–2): 89–100.

Couldry, N (2003). 'Beyond the hall of mirrors? Some theoretical reflections on the global contestation of media power', in Couldry, N and Curran, J (eds), *Contesting Media Power: Alternative Media in a Networked World*, Rowman & Littlefield Publishers: Lanham, Maryland.

Couldry, N (2002). 'Mediation and alternative media, or relocating the centre of media and communication studies', *Media International Australia incorporating Culture & Policy*, 103: 24–31.

Couldry, N and Curran, J (2003). 'The paradox of media power', in Couldry, N and Curran, J (eds), *Contesting Media Power: Alternative Media in a Networked World*, Rowman & Littlefield Publishers: Lanham, Maryland.

Council of Europe (2009). *Declaration of the Committee of Ministers on the Role of Community Media in Promoting Social Cohesion and Intercultural Dialogue*, Adopted by the Committee of Ministers, 11 February 2009 at the 1048th meeting of the Ministers' Deputies.

Coyer, K, Dowmunt, T and Fountain, A (2007). *The Alternative Media Handbook*, Routledge: Oxon and New York.

Cranitch, T (2006). *Personal interview with the author*, recorded 6 June 2006.

Curran, J (2005). 'What democracy requires of the media', in Overholser, G and Jamieson, K.H (eds), *The Press*, Oxford University Press: New York, 120–40.

Curran, J (2003). 'Global journalism: A case study of the internet', in Couldry, N and Curran, J (eds), *Contesting Media Power: Alternative Media in a Networked World*, Rowman & Littlefield: Lanham, Maryland.

Curran, J (2002). *Media and Power*, Routledge: London.

Curran, J (1991). 'Mass media and democracy: A reappraisal', in Curran, J and Gurevitch, M (eds), *Mass Media and Society*, Edward Arnold: London.

Curran, J (1978). 'Capitalism and control of the press, 1800–1975', in Curran, J, Gurevitch, M and Woolacott, J (eds), *Mass Communication and Society*, Edward Arnold: London.

Curran, J (1978a). 'The press as an agency of social control: An historical perspective', in Boyce, G, Curran, J and Wingate, P (eds), *Newspaper History from the Seventeenth Century to the Present Day*, Constable: London.

Dahlgren, P (1996). 'Media logics in cyberspace: Repositioning journalism and its publics', *Javnost/The Public*, 3(3): 59–71.

Dahlgren, P (1991). 'Introduction', in Dahlgren, P and Sparks, C (eds), *Communication and Citizenship*, Routledge: London and New York.

Davenport, T (2004). '*The Appeal to Reason*: Forerunner of Haldeman-Julius Publications', *The Big Blue Newsletter*, 3: 6–21, accessed 3 March 2010 from http://www.marxists.org/history/usa/culture/pubs/hjcc/2004/0800-hjcc-bbn03.pdf.

Davis, S (2000). 'Public journalism: The case against', *Journalism Studies*, 1(4): 686–89.

Department of Culture, Sweden (1994). *The Daily Press in the Media Landscape of the 1990s*, First Report, 1994 Parliamentary Commission on the Press.

Deuze, M (2006). 'Ethnic media, community media and participatory culture', *Journalism*, 7(3): 262–80.

Deuze, M and Marjoribanks, T (2009). 'Newswork', *Journalism*, 10(5): 555–61.

Dibben, K., Kearney, S. and Knowles, K. (2010) ' "THEY'RE HERE": Refugee crisis hits home! As Christmas Island overflows boat people are enjoying shopping trips in Queensland', *The Sunday Mail* (Qld), 28 March, p.1. http://www.crikey.com.au/2010/03/29/theyre-heeeeeeeere/.

Dixit, K (1994). 'Global news – A view from the south', *Who's Telling the Story* conference publication, Community Aid Abroad: Victoria.

Downing, J (2003). 'The Independent Media Centre movement and the anarchist socialist tradition', in Couldry, N and Curran, J (eds), *Contesting Media Power: Alternative Media in a Networked World,* Rowman & Littlefield Publishers: Lanham, Maryland, 243–57.

Downing, J (1984). *Radical Media: The Political Experience of Alternative Communication,* South End Press: Boston, Massachusetts.

Downing, J, with Villarreal Ford, T, Gil, G and Stein, L (eds), (2001). *Radical Media: Rebellious Communication and Social Movements*, Sage: Thousand Oaks, California.

Dwyer, T (2007). 'New media: The policy agenda', in Nightingale, V and Dwyer, T (eds), *New Media Worlds: Challenges for Convergence,* Oxford University Press: Melbourne, 37–59.

Easy Reader (2009). 'Three decades of independent reporting', accessed 8 July 2009 from http://www.easyreader.info/.

Edwards, J and Newbery, A (2007). *BBS Media Survey 2008*, Brumfield Bird & Sandford Pty Ltd: Brisbane.

Esaisson, P and Moring, T (1994). 'Codes of professionalism: Journalists versus politicians in Finland and Sweden', *European Journal of Communication*, 9: 271–89.

European Parliament (2007). *The State of Community Media in the European Union*, European Parliament Committee on Culture and Education: Brussels.

Ewart, J (2002). 'Overlooked and underused: How Australia's first public journalism project treated women and Indigenous people', *Australian Journalism Review* 24(1): 61–82.

Fitzgerald, T (1972). '*Nation:* Giving it a stir', *Funeral tribute for George Munster.* National Library of Australia: MS 7995. Records of the magazine 'Nation', accessed April 2006 from http://john.curtin.edu.au/fitzgerald/biography/nation.html.

Fletcher, J (2010). 'Elections 2010: A festival of cruelty towards refugees?', *Green Left Weekly,* 11 April 2010 accessed 6 July 2010 from http://www.greenleft.org.au/node/43605.

Forde, S (2010). 'The lure of the local: Giving community broadcasting audiences what they want', *Pacific Journalism Review,* 16(1): 178–91.

Forde, S (2000a). 'Freedom of the press and government press subsidies: Swedish journalist's views on subsidies in 1999', *Australian Journalism Review*, 22(1): 106–117.

Forde, S (2000b). 'The end of the press subsidies "experiment" in Sweden?', *Media International Australia*, 95: 107–15.

Forde, S (1999). 'Journalistic practices and newsroom organisation in the independent and alternative press', *Australian Journalism Review*, 21(3): 60–79.

Forde, S (1998). 'Monitoring the establishment: The development of the alternative press in Australia', *Media International Australia*, 87: 114–33.

Forde, S (1997a). 'A descriptive look at the public role of the Australian independent alternative press', *AsiaPacific Media Educator*, 3: 118–30.

Forde, S (1997b). 'Characteristics and ethical values of Australia's independent press journalists', *Australian Studies in Journalism*, 6: 104–26.

Forde, S, Foxwell, K and Meadows, M (2009). *Developing Dialogues: Indigenous and Ethnic Community Broadcasting in Australia*, Intellect Books: Bristol.

Forde, S, Foxwell, K and Meadows, M (2003). 'Through the lens of the local: Public arena journalism in the Australian community broadcasting sector', *Journalism*, 4(3): 317–42.

Forde, S, Foxwell, K and Meadows, M (2002). *Culture, Commitment, Community: The Australian community radio sector*, Brisbane, Griffith University, available at http://www.cbonline.org.au/index.cfm?pageId=14,40,3,835.

Foxwell, K, Ewart, J, Forde, S and Meadows, M (2008). 'Sounds like a whisper: Australian Community Broadcasting hosts a quiet revolution', *Westminster Papers in Communication and Culture*, 5(1): 5–24.

Fountain, N (1988). *Underground: The London Alternative Press, 1966–1974*, Routledge: London.

Francis, B. (2000). 'Ethnic Funds Good For Everyone', *CBX*, November, 17.

Fraser, Nancy (1999). 'Rethinking the Public Sphere: A Contribution to the Critique of Actually Existing Democracy', in C. Calhoun (ed.) Habermas and the Public Sphere. Cambridge: MIT Press, 109–142.

Gans, H (1979). *Deciding What's News: A Study of CBS Evening News, NBC Nightly News, Newsweek and Time*, Random House: New York.

Garneau, G (1993). 'Going mainstream? Alternative newspapers beef up association for PR, lobbying', *Editor & Publisher*, 126(25): 11–12, 66.

Garnham, N (1986). 'The media and the public sphere', in Golding, P, Murdoch, G and Schlesinger, P (eds), *Communicating Politics: Mass Communication and the Political Process*, Leicester University Press: Leicester.

Gawenda, M and Muller, D (2009). The Black Saturday bushfires: How the media covered Australia's worst peace-time disaster, Centre for Advanced Journalism, University of Melbourne: Melbourne, accessed 12 March 2010 from http://www.caj.unimelb.edu.au/__data/assets/pdf_file/0003/328008/bushfire_report_with_exec_summary_November_2009.pdf.

GetUp! (2010a). 'Get Abbott on board with refugees', email to members, 16 June 2010.

GetUp! (2010b). 'Wow – the press literally have not stopped calling!', email to members, 18 June 2010.

GetUp! (2010c). 'Video: We haven't talked about this', email to members, 26 March 2010.

GetUp! (2008). Email to members, 12 August.

Gillmor, D (2006). *We The Media: Grassroots journalism by the people, for the people*, O'Reilly Publishing: California.

Gitlin, T (1980). *The Whole World is Watching: Mass Media in the Making and Unmaking of the Left*, University of California Press: Berkeley.

Glasgow Media Group (1976). *Bad News*, Routledge: London.

Glasser, T (2000). 'The politics of public journalism', *Journalism Studies*, 1(4): 683–86.

Glasser, T and Craft, S (1998). 'Public Journalism and the Search for Democratic Ideals', in Liebes, T and Curran, J (eds), *Media, Ritual and Identity*, Routledge: London and New York, 203–18.

Glessing, R.J (1970). *The Underground Press in America*, Indiana University Press: Bloomington.

Golding, P (1977). 'Media professionalism in the third world: The transfer of an ideology', in Curran, J, Woollacott, J and Gurevitch, M (eds), *Mass Communication and Society*, Edward Arnold: London.

Golding, P and Murdock, G (1991). 'Culture, communication, and political economy', in Curran, J and Gurevitch, M (eds), *Mass Media and Society*, Edward Arnold: London.

Gordon, J (2009). 'Introduction', in Gordon, J (ed), *Notions of Community: A Collection of Community Media Debates and Dilemmas*, Peter Lang: Bern, Switzerland, 11–14.

Gray, R (1970). 'Introduction', in Glessing, R.J (ed), *The Underground Press in America*, Indiana University Press: Bloomington.

Griffen-Foley, B (2003). 'Media', *Australian Book Review*, March: 45–47.

Grossberg, L (1987). 'Critical theory and the politics of empirical research', in Gurevitch, M and Levy, M (eds), *Mass Communication Review Yearbook*, Volume 6, Sage: London, 86–106.

Gunaratne, S (1996). 'Old wine in a new bottle: Public versus developmental journalism in the US', *AsiaPacific Media Educator*, 1(1): 64–75.

Gurevitch, M and Blumler, J (1990). 'Political communication systems and democratic values', in Lichtenberg, J (ed), *Democracy and the Mass Media*, Cambridge University Press: Cambridge and New York, 269–89.

Gustafsson, K-E (2007). *The Market Consequences of Swedish Press Subsidies*, Swedish Ministry of Culture: Stockholm.

Gustafsson, K-E and Hadenius, S (1976). *Swedish Press Policy*, The Swedish Institute: Stockholm.

Guthrie, B (2010). *Man Bites Murdoch: Four decades in Print, Six Days in Court*, Melbourne University Press, Melbourne.

Haas, T (2007). 'Public journalism: An agenda for future research', *AsiaPacific Media Educator*, 18: 185–97.

Haas, T and Steiner, L (2006). 'Public journalism', *Journalism*, 7(2): 238–54.

Habermas, J (1989). *The Structural Transformation of the Public Sphere*, trans. by Burger, T with Lawrence, F, Massachusetts Institute of Technology: Massachusetts.

Hadenius, S (1985). *Swedish Politics During the 20th Century*, The Swedish Institute: Stockholm.

Hadenius, S (1983). 'The rise and possible fall of the Swedish party press', *Communication Research*, 10(3): 287–310.

Hall, S (1984). 'The rise of the representative/interventionist state 1880s–1920s', in McLennan, G, Held, D and Hall, S (eds), *State and Society in Contemporary Britain: A Critical Introduction*, Polity Press: Cambridge.

Halleck, D (2002). *Hand-held visions: The impossible possibilities of community media*, Fordham University Press: New York.

Hallett, L (2009). 'The space between: Making room for community radio', in Gordon, J (ed), *Notions of Community: A Collection of Community Media Debates and Dilemmas*, Peter Lang: Bern, Switzerland.

Hallin, D (1989). *The 'uncensored war': The media and Vietnam*. University of California Press: Berkeley.

Hallin, D.C and Mancini, P (2004). *Comparing Media Systems: Three Models of Media and Politics*, Cambridge University Press: Cambridge.

Hamilton, J (2004). *All the News That's Fit to Sell: How the Market Transforms Information into News*, Princeton University Press: Princeton, New Jersey.

Hampton, M (2008). 'The "Objectivity" ideal and its limitations in 20th Century British journalism', *Journalism Studies*, 9(4): 477–93.

Harcup, T (2003). 'The unspoken – said: The journalism of alternative media', *Journalism*, 4(3): 356–76.

Henningham, J.P (1996). 'Australian journalists' professional and ethical values', *Journalism and Mass Communication Quarterly*, 73(1): 206–18.

Henningham, J.P (1995). 'Journalism in the USA and Australia: Some comparisons', *Australian Journal of Communication*, 22(1): 77–91.

Henningham, J.P (1991). *Submission to the House of Representatives Select Committee on the Print Media*.

Herman, E and Chomsky, N (1988). *Manufacturing Consent: The Political Economy of the Mass Media*, Vintage: London; and Pantheon: New York.

Hirst, M (2009). 'Book Review, *Alternative Journalism* by Chris Atton and James F. Hamilton', *Global Media Journal, Australian Edition* 3(1), accessed 16 February 2011 from http://www.commarts.uws.edu.au/gmjau/v3_2009_1/pdf/m_hirst_BR.pdf.

Hollingsworth, M (1986). *The Press and Political Dissent*, Pluto Press: London.

Hopkin, D (1978). 'The socialist press in Britain, 1890–1910', in Boyce, G, Curran, J and Wingate, P (eds), *Newspaper History from the Seventeenth Century to the Present Day*, Constable: London.

House of Representatives Standing Committee on the Print Media (1992). *Final Report*, Australian Government Publishing Service: Canberra. Note: AKA 'The Lee Inquiry'.

Howley, K (2009). 'Notes on a theory of community radio', in Howley, K (ed), *Understanding Community Media*, Sage: Thousand Oaks, California.

Howley, K (2005). *Community Media: People, Places and Communication Technologies*, Cambridge University Press: Cambridge.

Huffington, A (2009). *Opening Remarks of Arianna Huffington for the Senate Subcommittee on Communications, Technology, and the Internet's Hearing on 'The Future of Journalism'*, accessed 10 July 2010 from http://iwncenter.com/pdfs/HuffingtonTestimonyFutureofJournalism.pdf.

Hyde, G (2002). 'Independent Media Centers: subversion and the alternative press', *First Monday*, 7(4), accessed 18 February 2010 from http://firstmonday.org/htbin/cgiwrap/bin/ojs/index.php/fm/article/view/944/866.

IDEA (Institute for Democracy and Electoral Assistance) (2010). *Voter Turnout figures*, accessed 23 September 2010 from http://www.idea.int/vt/.

Internet World Stats 2010 (2010). *Internet Usage Statistics*, accessed 5 April 2011, at http://www.internetworldstats.com/stats.htm.

Jankowski, N (2003). 'Community media research: A quest for theoretically-grounded models', *Javnost*, 10(1): 1–9.

Jiménez, N.R and Scifo, S (2010). 'Community media in the context of European media policies', *Informatics and Telematics*, 27(2): 131–40.

Johnson, M (1971). *The New Journalism: The Underground Press, the Artists of Nonfiction, and Changes in the Established Media*, University Press of Kansas: Kansas.

Johnson, S (1991). 'Resistance in print I: *Grassroots* and alternative publishing, 1980–84', in Tomaselli, K and Louw, P.E (eds), *The Alternative Press in South Africa*, Anthropos: Bellville.

Johnson, T.J and Wanta, W (1993). 'Newspaper competition and message diversity in an urban market', *Mass Communication Review*, 20(3 & 4): 136–47.

Johnston, J and Forde, S (2011). 'The silent partner: News agencies and 21st century news', *International Journal of Communication*, 5: 195–214. Available at http://ijoc.org/.

Johnston, J and Forde, S (2009). ' "Not wrong for long": The role and penetration of news wire agencies in the 24/7 news media landscape', *Global Media Journal*, Australian Edition, 3(2), accessed 30 April 2010 from http://www.commarts.uws.edu.au/gmjau/2009_3_2_toc.html.

Johnstone, J.W.C, Slawski, E.J and Bowman, W.W (1976). *The News People*, University of Illinois Press: Urbana, Illinois.

Katz, Y (2005). *Media Policy for the 21st Century in the United States and Western Europe*. Cresskill: Hampton Press.

Kessler, L (1984). 'Up the creek without a paddle', *The Quill*, 72: 40–44.

Kidd, D (2003). 'Indymedia.org: A new communications commons', in McCaughey, M and Ayers, M.D (eds), *Cyberactivism: On-line Activism in Theory and Practice,* Routledge: New York.

King, E (1997). 'The impact of the internet on journalism: An Introduction' *Electronic Journal of Communication*, 7(2), accessed 16 February 2011 from http://www.cios.org/www/ejc/v7n297.htm#Introduction.

Klocker, N and Dunn, K (2003). 'Who's driving the asylum debate?', *Media International Australia*, 109: 71–92.

Kornbluh, J (1964). *Rebel Voices*, University of Michigan Press: Michigan.

Kovach, B, Rosenstiel, T and Mitchell, A (2004). 'A crisis of confidence: A commentary on the findings', in Pew Research Center for the *People & The Press: Press Going Too Easy on Bush: Bottom-Line Pressures Now Hurting Coverage, Say Journalists*. Pew Research Centre: Washington D.C., 27–32.

Landers, K and Agence-France Presse (2009). 'Gunman kills 12 in Texas shooting rampage' *ABC News*, accessed 5 July 2010 from http://www.abc.net.au/news/stories/2009/11/06/2734789.htm.

Larson, S (2006). 'Asylum-seekers as seen through letters to the editor in Australia and the US', *Australian Studies in Journalism*, 16: 147–68.

Leamer, L (1972). *The Paper Revolutionaries: The Rise of the Underground Press*, Simon and Schuster: New York.

Lester, L and Hutchins, B (2009). 'Power games: environmental protest, news media', *Media Culture Society*, 31: 579–95.

Lewis, J (2001). *Constructing Public Opinion: How Political Elites Do What They Like and Why We Seem To Go Along With It*, Columbia University Press: New York.

Lewis, P (2008). *Promoting Social Cohesion: The Role of Community Media,* Report prepared for the Council of Europe's Group of Specialists on Media Diversity, Media and Information Society Division, Directorate General of Human Rights and Legal Affairs, Council of Europe: Strasbourg.

Lewis, P.M (1976). *Bristol Channel and Community Television,* London: IBA.

Lichtenberg, J (1991). 'In defense of objectivity', in Curran, J and Gurevitch, M (eds), *Mass Media and Society,* Edward Arnold: London.

Linder, L (1999). *Public Access Television: America's Electronic Soapbox,* Praeger Publishers: Westport, CT.

Lister, M, Dovey, J, Giddings, S, Grant, I and Kelly, K (2003). *New Media: A Critical Introduction,* Routledge: London.

McAuliffe, K.M (1978). *The Great American Newspaper: The Rise and Fall of the Village Voice,* Charles Scribner's Sons: New York.

McChesney, R (2008). *The Political Economy of Media: Enduring Issues, Emerging Dilemmas,* Monthly Review Press: New York.

McChesney, R (2003). 'The Problem of Journalism: a political economic contribution to an explanation of the crisis in contemporary US journalism', *Journalism Studies,* 4(3): 299–329.

McChesney, R (1999). *Rich Media, Poor Democracy: Communication Politics in Dubious Times,* University Illinois Press: Illinois.

McKay, G (2010). 'Community arts and music, community media: Cultural politics and policy in Britain since the 1960s', in Howley, K (ed), *Understanding Community Media,* Sage: Thousand Oaks, California.

McKinnon, K (2006). 'Five major trends', Ch 2, State of the News Print Media Report, 2006, http://www.presscouncil.org.au/snpma/ch02.html, Australian Press Council: Sydney.

McKinnon, K (2004). 'Chairman's Foreword', in *Annual Report No 28,* Australian Press Council: Sydney, 3–6.

McManus, J.H (1994). 'The elaborate compromise: A model of commercial news production', paper presented to the *1994 International Communication Association Annual Convention,* Sydney, Australia, July 1994.

McQuail, D (2010). *Mass Communication Theory,* 6th edition, Sage Publications: London.

McQuail, C (2000). 'Media Policy – Premature obsequies?' in Tumber, H (ed), *Media Power, Professionals and Policies,* Routledge: London, 13–34.

Mamadou, O (2008). 'Community radio and broadcasting landscape in Benin', in an AMARC compilation, *Citizen Empowerment for Good Governance through Community Radios in Western Africa: Legislative and Policy Frameworks,* AMARC (World Association of Community Radio Broadcasters): Africa, 4–5, accessed 23 September 2010 from http://africa.amarc.org/documents/livre_AMARC_OSIWA_EN.pdf.

Manne, D (2004). 'The usual suspects', *Dateline,* The *Texas Observer,* 4 November 2004, accessed 5 July 2010 from http://www.texasobserver.org/archives/item/14396-1792-dateline-the-usual-suspects.

Mathes, R and Pfetsch, B (1991). 'The role of the alternative press in the agenda-building process: Spill-over effects and media opinion leadership', *European Journal of Communication,* 6(1): 33–62.

McPhedran, Ian (2010). "Wave of refugees fast becoming a tsunami", The Daily Telegraph (Sydney, Australia), 20 March 2010, available at http://www.dailytelegraph.com.au/news/opinion/wave-of-refugees-fast-becoming-a-tsunami/story-e6frezz0-1225842984932.

Meadows, M (2009). 'Electronic dreaming tracks: Indigenous community broadcasting in Australia', *Development in Practice,* 19(4): 514–24.

Meadows, M (2008) 'Beyond the mainstream: journalism, community and democracy', refereed paper presented at the *Comparative Journalism Studies Conference,* University of Tasmania, 25–27 June.

Meadows, M (2001). *Voices in the Wilderness: Images of Aboriginal People in the Australian Media,* Greenwood Press: Westport.

Meadows, M, Forde, S, Ewart, J and Foxwell, K (2009). 'A catalyst for change: Australian community broadcasting audiences fight back', in Gordon, J (ed), *Notions of Community: A Collection of Community Media Debates and Dilemmas,* Peter Lang: Bern, Switzerland, 149–72.

Meadows, M, Forde, S, Ewart, J and Foxwell, K (2009a). 'Transformative processes in community journalism', *Journalism,* 10(2): 155–170.

Meadows, M, Forde, S, Ewart, J and Foxwell, K (2007). *Community Media Matters: An Audience Study of the Australian Community Broadcasting Sector,* Griffith University: Brisbane. Available at http://www.cbonline.org.au/index.cfm?pageId=51,171,2,0.

Merritt, D (1995). *Imagining Public Journalism: An Editor and Scholar Reflect on the Birth of an Idea,* Roy W. Howard Public Lecture No. 5, School of Journalism: Indiana University.

Merritt, D (1995a). *Public Journalism and Public Life: Why Telling the News is Not Enough,* Lawrence Erlbaum Associates: New Jersey.

Milhelj, S (2004). 'Negotiating European identity at the periphery: media coverage of Bosnian refugees and "illegal migration"', in Bondebjerg, I and Golding, P (eds), *European Culture and the Media,* Intellect: Portland, Oregon.

Miraldi, R (1995). 'Charles Edward Russell: Chief of the muckrakers', *Journalism & Mass Communication Monographs,* April, 150: 1–27.

Molnar, H and Meadows, M (2001). *Songlines to Satellites: Indigenous Communication in Australia, the South Pacific and Canada,* Pluto Press: Leichhardt.

Murdock, G (1982). 'Large corporations and the control of the communications industries', in Gurevitch, M, Bennett, T, Curran, J and Woollacott, J (eds), *Culture, Society and the Media,* Methuen: London.

Nelson, E (1989). *The British Counter-Culture, 1966–73: A Study of the Underground Press,* Macmillan: London.

Nerone, J (2009). 'The death (and re-birth?) of working-class journalism', *Journalism,* 10(3): 353–55.

Neville, R (1995). *Hippie Hippie Shake,* Heinemann: Melbourne.

Nightingale, V and Dwyer, T (2007). *New Media Worlds: Challenges for Convergence,* Oxford University Press: Melbourne.

Nolan, S (2001). 'Half a century of obscurity: The Age 1908–1964' *eJournalist,* Special issue on proceedings from the Australian Media Traditions Conference, 1(2): 1–9 and accessed October 1, 2010 from http://ejournalist.com.au/v1n2/nolan.pdf.

References   199

Officer, R, Kenyon, F and Morton, D (1991). *News Ltd Submission to the House of Representatives Select Committee on the Print Media, Part II.*

Ojo, T (2002). 'Post-NWICO debate: Image of Africa in the Western Media', *Media in Transition 2: Globalisation and Convergence*, 10–12 May 2002, Massachusetts Institute of Technology, Cambridge, Massachusetts, accessed 8 July 2010 from http://web.mit.edu/cms/Events/mit2/Abstracts/TOjo.pdf.

O'Lincoln, T (1993). *Years of Rage: Social Conflicts in the Fraser Era*, Bookmarks: Melbourne.

O'Lincoln, T (1985). *Into the Mainstream: The Decline of Australian Communism*, Stained Wattle Press: Sydney.

Ortega, T (1997). 'Jailers show a paraplegic who's boss', Phoenix New Times, January 23, 1997, accessed from http://www.phoenixnewtimes.com/1997-01-23/news/jailers-show-a-paraplegic-who-s-boss/, 10 February 2011.

Ots, M (2009). 'Efficient Servants of Pluralism or Marginalized Media Policy Tools? The Case of Swedish Press Subsidies', *Journal of Communication Inquiry*, 33(4): 376–92.

Palevky, M (2009). 'Sheriff Joe Arpaio separates mother from children, immigrant crackdown', *The Huffington Post*, 16 January 2009, accessed 22 September 2010 from http://www.huffingtonpost.com/2009/01/16/sheriff-joe-arpaio-sepera_n_158660.html.

Pappas, C (2011). 'Arianna Huffington: The cookie who cared', *The Huffington Post*, 14 February 2011, accessed 15 February 2011 from http://www.huffingtonpost.com/dr-cheryl-pappas/arianna-huffington-the-co_b_820521.html.

Paterson, C (2006). 'News Agency Dominance in International News on the Internet', Papers in International and Global Communication, Centre for International Communications Research, No 01/06, accessed 1 February 2009 from http://ics.leeds.ac.uk/papers/cicr/exhibits/42/cicrpaterson.pdf.

Patterson, T (1992). 'Irony of the free press: Professional journalism and news diversity', *American Political Science Association* meeting, Chicago, September 1992.

Pavarala, V and Malik, K.K (2010). 'Community radio and women: Forging subaltern counterpublics', in Rodriguez, C, Kidd, D and Stein, L (eds), *Making Our Media: Global Initiatives Toward a Democratic Public Sphere*, Hampton Press: Cresskill, NJ, 95–113.

Pavarala, V and Malik, K.K (2007). *Other Voices: The Struggle for Community Radio in India*, Sage Publications: Thousand Oaks, California.

Peissl, H and Tremetzberger, O (2008). *Community Media in Europe: Legal and Economic Contexts of the Third Broadcast Sector in 5 Countries*. English Summary. Accessed http://www.communitymedia.eu/images/publications_books/2008_rtr_community_media_in_europe_eng.pdf.

Pepe, A and Gennaro, C (2009). 'Political protest Italian-style: The blogosphere and mainstream media in the promotion and coverage of Beppe Grillo's V-Day', *First Monday*, 14(12), accessed 18 February 2010 from http://firstmonday.org/htbin/cgiwrap/bin/ojs/index.php/fm/article/view/2740/2406.

Perry, P.F (1977). 'Alternative magazines and the growth of the counter culture', *Media Information Australia*, 6: 10–13.

Pew Project for Excellence in Journalism (2009). The State of the News Media: An Annual Report on American Journalism, published by the Pew Center, accessed from http://www.stateofthemedia.org/2009/index.htm, 27 April 2009.

Pew Project for Excellence in Journalism (2008). The State of the News Media: An Annual Report on American Journalism, published by the Pew Center, accessed from http://www.stateofthemedia.org/2008/, 20 June 2008.

Pew Project for Excellence in Journalism (2007). The State of the News Media: An Annual Report on American Journalism, published by the Pew Center, accessed from http://www.stateofthemedia.org/2007/, 20 June 2008.

Pew Project for Excellence in Journalism (2006). The State of the News Media: An Annual Report on American Journalism, published by the Pew Center, accessed from http://www.stateofthemedia.org/2006/, 18 August 2007.

Pew Project for Excellence in Journalism (2005). The State of the News Media: An Annual Report on American Journalism, published by the Pew Center, accessed from http://www.stateofthemedia.org/2005/, April 2006.

Pew Project for Excellence in Journalism (2004). State of the News Media, 2004, accessed from http://www.stateofthenewsmedia.com/2004/, 10 August 2004.

Platon, S and Deuze, M (2003). 'Indymedia journalism: A radical way of making, selecting and sharing news?' *Journalism*, 4(3): 336–55.

Prendergast, A (1990). 'The profitable alternatives', *Washington Journalism Review*, July–August, 12: 26–27.

Presstödsnämnden (Press Subsidies Council, Sweden) (2011). 'Press subsidies', accessed 15 February 2011 from http://www.presstodsnamnden.se/Presstod.htm.

Preston, W, Herman, E.S and Schiller, H (1989). *Hope and Folly: The United States and UNESCO, 1945–85*, University of Minnesota Press: Minneapolis.

Puppis, M (2009). 'Media Regulation in Small States', *The International Communication Gazette*, 71(1–2): 7–17.

Raboy, M (2007). 'Part V: Broadening media discourses. Global media policy – defining the field', *Global Media and Communication*, 3(3): 343–61.

Readers Digest (2010). *Australia's Most Trusted Professions, 2010*, accessed 10 September 2010 from http://www.readersdigest.com.au/most-trusted-professions-2010-press/article182809.html.

Reeds, N and Colbourne, F (2000), 'Fewer Gatekeepers, More Open Gates', *Strategy Magazine*, 6 November, 25.

Refugee Council of Australia (2010). 'Asking the media to correct mistakes', accessed 20 September 2010 from http://www.refugeecouncil.org.au/current/mediablunders.html.

Reimers, D (1998). *Unwelcome Strangers: American Identity and the Turn Against Immigrants*, Columbia University Press: New York.

Rennie, E (2006). *Community Media: A Global Introduction*, Rowman & Littlefield: Lanham, Maryland.

Rennie, E (2002). 'The other road to media citizenship', *Media International Australia*, 103, 7–13.

Riggins, S.H (1992). *Ethnic Minority Media: An Informational Perspective*, Sage: Newbury Park, California, London, New Delhi.

Roach, C (1987). 'The U.S. position on the New World Information and Communication Order', *Journal of Communication*, 37(4): 36–51.

Rodriguez, C (2010). 'Knowledges in dialogue: A participatory evaluation study of citizens' radio stations in Magdalena Medio, Colombia', in Rodriguez, C, Kidd, D and Stein, L (eds), *Making Our Media: Global Initiatives Toward a Democratic Public Sphere*, Hampton Press: Cresskill, New Jersey, 131–54.

Rodriguez, C (2004). 'Communication for peace: Contrasting approaches', *The Drum Beat*, 278, accessed 21 September 2010 from http://www.comminit.com/en/drum_beat_278.html.

Rodriguez, C (2003). 'The Bishop and his Star: Citizens' communication in Southern Chile', in Couldry, N and Curran, J (eds), *Contesting Media Power: Alternative Media in a Networked World*, Rowman & Littlefield: Lanham, Maryland, 177–94.

Rodriguez, C. (2002). 'Citizens' media and the voice of the angel/poet', *Media International Australia* 103: 78–87.

Rodriguez, C (2001). *Fissures in the Mediascape: An International Study of Citizen's Media*, Hampton Press: New Jersey.

Romano, A (2004). 'Journalism's role in mediating public conversation on asylum seekers and refugees in Australia', *Australian Journalism Review*, 26(2): 43–62.

Rose, M (1996). *For the Record: 160 Years of Aboriginal Print Journalism*, Allen & Unwin: Sydney.

Rosen, J (1995). *Imagining Public Journalism: An Editor and Scholar Reflect on the Birth of an Idea*, Roy W. Howard Public Lecture No. 5, School of Journalism: Indiana University.

Rosen, J (1992). 'Politics, vision and the press: Toward a public agenda for journalism', in Rosen, J and Taylor, P (eds), *The New News v. The Old News: The Press and Politics in the 1990s*, Twentieth Century Fund: New York.

Rosen, J (1991). 'Making journalism more public', *Communication*, 12: 267–84.

Rosenbloom, H (1978). *Politics and the Media*, Scribe: Melbourne.

Ross, E (1982). *Of Storm and Struggle: Pages from Labour History*, Alternative Publishing Co-operative for New Age Publishers: Sydney.

Royal Commission on Newspapers, Canada (1981). Canadian Government Publishing Centre: Hull. (Chairman: Tom Kent).

Royal Commission on the Press, Great Britain (1949). Report, HMSO Great Britain Parliament: London. (Known as 'Ross Royal Commission, 1947–49').

Royal Commission on the Press, Great Britain (1962). Report, HMSO Great Britain Parliament: London. (Known as 'Shawcross Royal Commission', 1961–62).

Royal Commission on the Press, Great Britain (1977). Final Report, HMSO Great Britain Parliament: London. (Known as 'McGregor Royal Commission', 1974–77).

Ruotolo, A.C (1988). 'Monopoly and socialization', in Picard, R, McCombs, M, Winter, J and Lacy, S (eds), *Press Concentration and Monopoly: New Perspectives on Newspaper Ownership and Operation*, Ablex: New Jersey.

Schiller, H (1989). *Culture, Inc.: The Corporate Takeover of Public Expression*, New York: Oxford University Press.

Schmuh, R and Picard, R.G (2005). 'The marketplace of ideas', in Overholser, G and Hall Jamieson, K (eds), *The Press*, Oxford University Press: Oxford, 141–55.

Schoonmaker, M.E (1987). 'Has the alternative press gone yuppie?', *Columbia Journalism Review*, 26: 60–64.

Schudson, M (1995). *The Power of News*, Harvard University Press: Massachusetts.

Schudson, M (1978). *Discovering the News: A Social History of American Newspapers*, Basic Books: New York.

Schultz, J (1994). 'The paradox of professionalism', in Schultz, J (ed), *Not Just Another Business*, Pluto Press: Monash University.

Schultz, J (1992a). 'Encouraging competition and diversity without offending the monopolists', *Media Information Australia*, 65: 53–62.

Schultz, J (1992b). 'Our Future: Media and Democracy Special Liftout', *The Journalist*, September/October: 5–8.

Schussman, A and Soule, S (2005). 'Process and protest: Accounting for individual protest participation', *Social Forces*, 84(2): 1083–1108.

Seaton, J and Curran, J (1991). *Power Without Responsibility: The Press and Broadcasting in Britain*, Routledge: London.

Seneviratne, K (ed) (2007). *Media Pluralism in Asia: The Role and Impact of Alternative Media*, Asian Media Information and Communication Centre: Singapore.

Seneviratne, K. (1993). 'Giving a voice to the voiceless: Community radio in Australia', *Media Asia*, 20(1): 66–74.

Shoemaker, P.J (1984). 'Media treatment of deviant political groups', *Journalism Quarterly*, 61: 66–75, 82.

Sim, J (1969). *The Grassroots Press: America's Community Newspapers*, Iowa State Press: Iowa.

Simons, M (2005). 'The underground news is a going concern', *Sydney Morning Herald* online, smh.com.au, 2 February 2005, accessed 9 March 2009 from http://www.smh.com.au/articles/2005/02/04/1107476806777.html.

Skinner, D, Uzelman, S, Langlois, A and Dubois, F (2010). 'IndyMedia in Canada: Experiments in Developing Global Media Commons', in Rodriguez, C, Kidd, D and Stein, L, (eds), *Making Our Media: Global Initiatives Towards a Democratic Public Sphere*, Hampton Press: Cresskill, NJ.

Sosale, S (2003). 'Envisioning a new world order through journalism: Lessons from recent history', *Journalism: Theory, Practice and Criticism*, 4(3): 377–92.

Sparks, C (1985). 'The working-class press: Radical and revolutionary alternatives', *Media, Culture & Society*, 7: 133–46.

Squires, C (2009). *African Americans and the Media*, Polity Press: Cambridge.

Squires, C (1999). *Searching Black Voices in the Black Public Sphere: An Alternative Approach to the Analysis of Public Spheres*, unpublished PhD thesis, Northwestern University: Illinois.

Staff Writers and Wires (2009). 'Thousands' of refugees queuing up, news.com.au, April 21, 2009, available at http://www.news.com.au/thousands-of-refugees-queueing-up/story-0-1225700405442. Also published in the online version of News Ltd's Adelaide Advertiser newspaper, Adelaide Now at http://www.adelaidenow.com.au/news/national/thousands-of-refugees-queueing-up/story-e6frea8c-1225700405442.

Stanfield, W.W and Lemert, J.B (1987). 'Alternative newspapers and mobilizing information', *Journalism Quarterly*, 64: 604–07.

Steel, J (2009). 'The 'radical' narrative, political though and praxis', *Media History*: 15(2): 221–37.

Stein, L (2001). 'Access television and grassroots political communication in the United States', in Downing, J, Villarreal, T, Gil, G and Stein, L, *Radical Media: Rebellious Communication and Social Movements*, 299–324, Sage: Thousand Oaks, California.

Stein, L and Sinha, S (2002). 'New global media and the role of the state', in Lievrouw, L and Livingstone, S (eds), *Handbook of New Media. Social Shaping and Concequences of ICTs*. Sage Publications: London, 415–32.

Steinmaurer, Thomas (2009). 'Diversity through delay: The Austrian case', *International Communication Gazette*, 71(1–2): 77–87.

Stovall, J.G (2005). *Journalism: Who, What, When, Where, Why and How*, Pearson: Boston.

Streeter, T (1996). *Selling the Air: A Critique of the Policy of Commercial Broadcasting in the United States*, University of Chicago Press: Chicago.

Suine, K (1987). 'The political role of mass media in Scandinavia', *Legislative Studies Quarterly*, 12(3): 395–414.

Swan, P.L and Garvey, G (1991). *News Ltd Submission to the House of Representatives Select Committee on the Print Media, supplement to Part II*.

Syvertsen, T (2003). 'Challenges to Public Television in the Era of Convergence and Commercialization', *Television & New Media*, 4(2): 155–75.

Tacchi, J and Kiran, M.S (2008). *Finding a Voice: Themes and Discussions*, UNESCO: New Delhi.

Tacchi, J (2003). 'The promise of citizen's media: Lessons from community radio in Australia and South Africa', *Economic and Political Weekly*, May 31: 2183–87.

Tacchi, J (2002). 'Transforming the mediascape in South Africa: The continuing struggle to develop community radio', *Media International Australia*, 103, 68–77.

Texas Observer (2004). *Political Intelligence*, Thursday 9 September 2004, accessed 5 July 2010 from http://www.texasobserver.org/archives/item/14349-1745-political-intelligence.

Thompson, M (1999). 'Some Issues for Community Radio at the Turn of the Century', *Media International Australia*, May: 23–31.

Thornley, P (1995). 'Debunking the "Whitlam Myth" – The Annals of Public Broadcasting Revisited', *Media International Australia*, 77 (August): 155–64.

Tomaselli, K (1991). 'The progressive press: Extending the struggle, 1980–86', in Tomaselli, K and Louw, P.E (eds), *The Alternative Press in South Africa*, Anthropos: Bellville.

Tomaselli, K and Prinsloo, J (1990). 'Video, Realism, and Class Struggle: Theoretical Lacunae and the Problem of Power', *Continuum*, 3(2): 140–59.

Toscano, J (2008). *The Anzac Myth*, Anarchist media Centre: Melbourne. Accessed 20 April 2011 at http://www.anarchistmedia.org/pdf/The-Anzac-Myth.pdf.

Trigoboff, D (2002). 'No Good News for Local News', *Broadcasting & Cable*, 18 November, 12.

Truglia, E (2009). 'Voices of dissent: Amy Goodman and independent media', *Upstream Journal*, 22(3): 6–7.

Tuchman, G (1978). *Making News: A Study in the Construction of Reality*, New York: Free Press.

Turner, I (1969). *Sydney's Burning*, Alpha Books: Sydney.

Udick, R (1993). 'The Hutchins paradox: Objectivity and diversity', *Mass Communication Review*, 20(3 & 4): 148–57.

Utne, E (1991). 'The importance of being non-political', *The Utne Reader*, 48: 2.

Van Cuilenberg, J and McQuail, D (2003). 'Media Policy Paradigm Shifts: Towards a New Communications Policy Paradigm', *European Journal of Communication*, 18(2): 181–207.

VanVuuren, K. (2002). 'Beyond the studio: A case study of community radio and social capital', *Media International Australia*, 103: 94–108.

Vick, D (2001). 'Exporting the First Amendment to cyberspace: The internet and state sovereignty', pp 3–19, in Waisbord, Silvio and Morris, Nancy (eds.) Rethinking Media Globalization and State Power. Why the State Matters. Rowman & Littlefield Publishers: Lanham.

Wahl-Jorgensen, K (2008). 'Theory review on the public sphere, deliberation, journalism and dignity: An interview with Seyla Benhabib', *Journalism Studies,* 9(6): 962–70.

Waisbord, S and Morris, N (eds), (2001). *Rethinking Media Globalization and State Power. Why the State Matters.* Rowman & Littlefield Publishers: Lanham.

Walker, R (1976). *The Newspaper Press in New South Wales, 1803–1920,* Sydney University Press: Sydney.

Walley, W (2002). 'Fox News Sweeps to TV Marketer of Year', *Advertising Age,* 4 November, 1, 22.

Walsh, R (1993). *Ferretabilia: Life and Times of Nation Review,* University of Queensland Press: Brisbane.

Waltz, M (2005). *Alternative and Activist Media,* Edinburgh University Press: Edinburgh.

Warhaft, S (2006). *Personal interview with the author,* recorded 3 August 2006.

Weaver, D, Beam, R, Brownlee, B, Voakes, P and Wilhoit, G.C (2003). *The American Journalist in the 21st Century: Key Findings,* School of Journalism, Indiana University and John S. and James L. Knight Foundation, accessed October 2004 from http://www.knightfoundation.org/research_publications/.

Weaver, D and Wilhoit, G.C (1996). *The American Journalist in the 1990s: US Newspeople at the End of an Era,* Mahwah: New Jersey.

Weaver, D and Wilhoit, G.C (1994a). 'The U.S. journalist in the 1990s and the question of quality in journalism', *International Communication Association Annual Convention,* Sydney, Australia, July 1994.

Weaver, D and Wilhoit, G.C (1994b). 'Daily newspaper journalists in the 1990s', *Newspaper Research Journal,* 15(3): 2–21.

Weaver, D and Wilhoit, G.C (1991). *The American Journalist: A Portrait of US News People and Their Work,* 2nd edition, Indiana University Press: Bloomington.

Weaver, D and Wilhoit, G.C (1986). *The American Journalist: A Portrait of US News People and their Work,* Indiana University Press: Bloomington.

Weibull, L (2003). 'The press subsidy system in Sweden: A critical approach', in Couldry, N and Curran, J (eds), *Contesting Media Power: Alternative Media in a Networked World,* Rowman & Littlefield: Lanham, Maryland.

Weibull, L and Anshelm, M (1992). 'Indications of change: Developments in the Swedish media 1980–1990', *Gazette,* 49: 41–73.

Weingarten, M (2005). *From Hipsters to Gonzo: How New Journalism Rewrote the World,* Scribe: Melbourne.

Westerstahl, J (1983). 'Objective news reporting: General premises', *Communication Research,* 10(3): 403–24.

Westin, A (2001). ' "Minutes" master misses mark', *Variety,* 16–22 April, 35.

Whitaker, B (1981). *News Limited: Why You Can't Read All About It,* London: Minority Press Group.

White, D (1950). 'The gatekeeper: A case study in the selection of news', *Journalism Quarterly,* 27(4): 383–390.

Williams, R (1978). 'The press and popular culture: An historical perspective', in Boyce, G, Curran, J and Wingate, P (eds), *Newspaper History from the Seventeenth Century to the Present Day,* Constable: London.

Williams, R (1970). 'Radical and/or respectable', in Boston, R (ed), *The Press We Deserve,* Routledge: London, 14–26.

Wolmar, C (1984). 'From PDC to XYZ', *New Statesman,* March 9, 107: 12–13.

Zelizer, B. (2005). 'Definitions of journalism', in Overholser, G and Hall Jamieson, K (eds), *The Press,* Oxford University Press: Oxford, 66–80.

Zhong, B and Newhagen, J (2009). 'How journalists think while they write: A transcultural model of news decision making', *Journal of Communication,* 59: 587–608.

Index

214

Index